'Faith and fatherland are indivisible ingredients of the conflict and have produced barbarity.' Thus Martin Dillon, acclaimed writer and political commentator, sums up the tragedy of Northern Ireland: violence in the name of religion – God and the Gun.

This book, astonishing and terrifying in its revelations, is the first of its kind to examine the role of religion in Northern Ireland by talking directly to those involved: to the churchmen and the terrorists. It asks Roman Catholic and Protestant paramilitaries how they can reconcile murder with their Christian convictions, and what the men of God should – or could – do to stop the killing.

Informed by his own experiences, Martin Dillon shows how historical injustices and religious divisions have led to the current situation. He charts the history of the paramilitary forces on both sides of the political divide as well as the wavering attitudes of religious leaders and politicians towards them. He exposes the shocking covert role of British Intelligence in the conflict. And he points the finger at those who he feels are to blame: the Church and governments who have failed their communities, allowing the men and women of violence to fill the vacuum with bigotry and bullets.

Martin Dillon won international acclaim for his non-fiction books about Ireland, notably *The Shankill Butchers*, *The Dirty War* and *The Enemy Within*. He spent eighteen years working for the BBC in Northern Ireland. As well as seven works of non-fiction, he has written a novel, two plays for television and radio and, since leaving the BBC, has written and produced documentaries for Channel Four, the BBC and RTE.

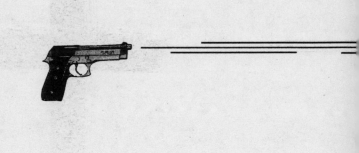

God and the Gun

THE CHURCH
AND IRISH TERRORISM

Martin Dillon

ORION

An Orion Paperback
First published in Great Britain by Orion in 1997
This paperback edition published in 1998 by
Orion Books Ltd,
Orion House, 5 Upper St Martin's Lane,
London WC2H 9EA

Copyright © Martin Dillon 1997

Second impression 1998

The right of Martin Dillon to be identified as the author
of this work has been asserted by him in accordance with
the Copyright, Designs and Patents Act 1988.

A CIP catalogue record for this book is available
from the British Library.

ISBN: 0 75281 631 4

Typeset by Deltatype Ltd, Birkenhead, Merseyside
Printed and bound in Great Britain by
Clays Ltd, St Ives plc

To my brother, Patrick, and my late brother-in-law
Dr Michael Feinberg, and his son, Samuel

Contents

Acknowledgements

During the preparation of this book many people gave me their time and insights into the complexities of the conflict in Northern Ireland. Some are named in the following chapters, while others asked me to protect their identities. Many others around my life contributed by their presence and support.

I thank Anthony Cheetham for the faith he has shown in my work from the day I arrived in his offices to discuss *The Shankill Butchers* and *The Dirty War*. My editor at Orion, Jane Wood, and Hazel Orme worked on my manuscript, giving impetus and energy to the project. Gill Hess in Ireland has been a tower of strength in times of crisis. I am always indebted to my wife, Kathy, and our children, Crawford and Nadia, who have lived with the stress of the Ireland issues and have been patient, kind and understanding at all times. Kathy has always been there in moments of crisis, and fear. My eighty-six-year-old mother-in-law, Maureen Bannon, and her sister, Meta Cassidy; my parents, Gerard and Maureen Dillon, have been a constant source of support; also my uncle, Vincent Dillon, and his wife, Maureen, who were with me when this book was completed.

My friend Tim Pat Coogan, writer and historian, has been a source of encouragement, through his words and his own writings. Professor Paul Bew at Queen's University, the historian A. T. Q. Stewart and the staff at the Linenhall Library in Belfast were ready to provide fascinating perspectives and much-needed assistance.

In the world of media, I found so many people willing to give of their time and expertise. Jim Campbell, Martin O'Hagan, Hugh Jordan and Jim McDowell of *Sunday World* provided answers to difficult questions. At the *Belfast Telegraph*, and *Sunday Life*, the editors, Ed Curran and Martin Lindsay, were always supportive when I was writing about difficult issues, believing that openness in journalism was important to a society in conflict.

There are people central to my life whose views constitute a valuable creative source. They include Dr Conor Cruise and his wife Maura O'Brien; Colin Lewis, who provided me with a bolt-hole when I was researching this book; Susan Delaney Collier, a brilliant designer and friend; my sister, Imelda Feinberg, who suffered the tragic loss of her husband, Michael, one of the world's leading radiologists; Ian Kennedy and his wife, Cecilia; Jane Lewis and her daughters, Sarah and Rachel, who suffered my presence during the research for this book; Roberta Levine and her son, Con, who both made Belfast an interesting city in difficult times (it was Con who ferried me to some of my interviews); Ursula and Brian McLaughlin; Stephen and Attracta Fay; Brian Garret and Michael Lynch at Elliott Duffy Garret; Mike and Mary Rose Cooney and their family, Aiden, Alex and Georgina, who were a constant source of love and support; Ronald and Soshana Appelton and their son, Michael; Howard Hastings and John Toner at the

Europa Hotel in Belfast; Michael Hirst, the screen-
writer, and his wife, Debbie, whose perspectives on
Ireland have been valuable; Elaine, Billy and their
children, Jack and Rosie; Alan Brebner and Martin
Anderson in London with whom late-night conversations never lacked commitment; Michael and Jackie
Finnerty; Cousins Frank and Stephen Dillon, who
turned the world upside down; Roy Garland and Gusty
Spence, who were incisive at all times, and particularly
Roy whose insights only he could have provided; Mary
Johnston, the broadcaster and journalist who makes
sense out of crisis; Jimmy Nesbitt, one of my dearest
friends whose very presence in my life has helped me
understand the precise nature of conflict; David
Malone, Susie and their family in Donaghadee; Barry
Cowan, one of the best commentators ever employed by
the BBC.

Other friends include Moore, Sandra and Siobhan
Sinnerton; Don and Rosie Anderson; Sean Rafferty at
the BBC; Ronald D. Ryan at West Kellog in Wichita. A
special tribute must go to John Bach, a brilliant
criminologist who enabled me to understand the history
of the prison system; Des O'Hagan who was willing to
open up his early life for me; Simon Bates, a special
friend, whose friendship and analysis have been always
welcome; Paddy Devlin and his wife whose hospitality
is remembered by many writers; Colin and Jane at
'Bethanie'; my cousin Philomena, her husband, Brian
O'Neill, and the twins; the writer and philosopher
François Bouan; my niece Elsa and her parents, Claude
and Marie-Claude Lambert; Hester Bantock Gordon;
David Alyward and his wife, Monique; Neil Johnston at
the *Belfast Telegraph*, who watched over my early days
with the newspaper; and Sue Corbett at *Sunday Life*;

Ian Thacker; and Northern Ireland's leading consultant surgeon, Roy Spence; Chris, Val and Kirsty Ludlow; Bob and Fiona Crookes; Fr. Pat Buckley for his frankness; Alan Williams for his legal advice; Eilis Starr from Nenagh, Co Tipperary; Joe Higgins; Kyhan Yilmaz; Anna Scragg and Peter Benjamin.

INTRODUCTION

Writing about Ireland is never easy as I have discovered over many years of producing countless articles, documentary television programmes and books dealing with the conflict. I am now aware of the difficulties inherent in talking to combatants who, after thirty years of violence, are skilled in the art of propaganda and deception. I spent two decades establishing contacts, many of whom provided me with valuable information on the understanding that they remained anonymous. They ranged from members of the intelligence agencies, to the military and the paramilitaries. The latter provided fascinating insights into the mind of a terrorist. Their reasons for talking to me ranged from self-importance to a desire to have an impact on written history. Some wished to compromise an organisation with which they had become disillusioned. When I decided to write *God and the Gun*, I believed naïvely that my task would be made easier because many of those I intended to interview were clergy on both sides of the tribal divide in Ireland. I soon discovered that it was easier to get terrorists to talk than priests and ministers. It became evident that the Churches, particularly the Roman Catholic Church in Ireland, appeared to have greater control of their members than the paramilitary bodies and the Army. The majority of those in religious life were happy to discuss dogma openly but the moment I revealed the nature of my investigations I faced a wall of silence. It was as though talking about the role of religion in terrorism confirmed its place at the centre of the conflict. Clergymen were determined to assure me that pulpits had only been used to preach the word of God.

When I requested an interview with Gerry Adams, the president of Sinn Fein, I was told to submit a list of questions that would determine whether he would meet me. For an organisation that seeks media attention and has never before put such an obstacle in my way, it was another example of how the word 'God' instils outright suspicion in paramilitary ranks.

I also met courageous people in the religious life, many of whom must remain anonymous for fear of reprisal by their superiors. They helped me to under-stand the role of religion in the conflict, the trauma faced by priests who come into close contact with terrorists, and how the word of God is damaged by unhappy alliances between religious figures and the paramilitaries.

Outside Ireland, many people see the conflict as a holy war, and with close examination of the character of the various causes, it is a view not without founda-tion. For the Protestant community, the slogan 'For God and Ulster' carries the imprimatur of religious conviction and defence of faith. Catholics tend to regard their Protestant counterparts as part of a 'godless, post-Reformation trend'. Catholicism, nationalism and republicanism are interconnected and, in essence, anti-British. The folk tradition of the gun in both communities, carries with it a moral crusade in defence of the respective traditions. Church leaders and politicians have been vocal in their condemnation of violence, but they have not sufficiently demonstrated the true nature of reconciliation, preferring to support their individual constituencies. Nowhere else in Europe has there been so much friction between Churches, such a lack of commitment to the basic Christian principle of 'love thy neighbour', and such callous disrespect for human life. It would be too easy to condemn all churchmen and religious leaders, but it is fair to say that collectively they have allowed the terrorists to fill a vacuum of despair, hatred and suspicion.

Many of those who decided to make a good confession to me recognised the role of negative religious assertions in a long war in which both communities believe that God is on their side.

Some would argue that, in a society in which the young live in ghettos and go to segregated schools, it is impossible to sever the thread of bigotry that permeates life. In 1996, the risk of civil war loomed large after events in a Protestant churchyard at Drumcree. Orangemen and loyalists demanded the right to march triumphantly through a Catholic area to assert their politics and religion. The Gods of Irish nationalism and Unionism were there – and so was the Gun. This book attempts to examine the role of religion in the conflict through the experiences of those in the religious life and within terrorism. The terms 'loyalist', 'nationalist' and 'republican' are shorthand for those who understand the conflict. To an outsider, they are best understood as

definitions of the political character of both communities. 'Loyalist' has come to signify not simply Protestants loyal to Britain but Protestants of an extreme
political variety – hence loyalist paramilitaries – though
not all loyalists use violence. 'Nationalist' could be
applied to the whole Catholic community, indicating
the shared desire for a national identity within a united
Ireland. Within nationalism is republicanism, which has
sought to employ violence to achieve Irish unity.

It is my intention to show that the British Army and
military intelligence identified the Catholic Church as an
integral part of the conflict and therefore of the enemy.
When I was researching this book, I talked to individuals on both sides whose personal stories illustrated the
connection between religious conditioning and political
violence. I realised quickly that I was dealing with a
subject that had so far been unexplored. To my
knowledge, no other writer has examined the conscience of the terrorist or the clergyman, and how
paramilitaries have reconciled killing with their religious convictions.

Many of those who spoke to me were not prepared to
talk on the record and were apprehensive about
addressing the issues. Others flatly refused to be
interviewed, fearing that their appearance in such a
book would compromise them with the organisations to
which they belonged. That was true of clergymen and
terrorists. Some were only willing to deal with the
subject in an abstract fashion, and tried to convince me
that the conflict was simply a constitutional issue in
which religion played a minor part. To help the reader
deal with the complexities of the Ireland conflict, I have
included a Chronology of Major Events, which follows
this Introduction. An Appendix of Significant Influences

contains details of relevant organisations, movements and leading figures.

I was frightened, saddened and shocked by many of the personal reflections of the people I have written about in this book. In an unholy war, the caricatures of religion starkly reflect the obscene justification of violence. In the course of my research I encountered people who claimed to be 'saved', but in many instances, they had exchanged the army of their tribe for the Army of God. I found it difficult to write this book, perhaps because it deals with a dimension of the conflict which affects all of us who live or have lived in Northern Ireland. It centres on the historical conditioning that resides within the layers of consciousness that have produced a divided society of two tribes with their respective and blunted perceptions of righteousness. It shows how we are all victims. In Northern Ireland, history and religion are more important than in any modern European country. Faith and Fatherland are indivisible ingredients of the conflict and have produced the barbarity historically associated with an unholy war.

CHRONOLOGY
OF MAJOR EVENTS

1921 King George V opens the first Northern Ireland Parliament.

1922 Northern Ireland experiences widespread sectarian violence resulting in the deaths of over two hundred people and the wounding of a thousand.

1925 The Border, shaped within the terms of the 1920 Government of Ireland Act, is confirmed by the Irish Free State and registered with the League of Nations. The two parts of the island are separate.

1931 The Irish Free State government declares the IRA an illegal body.

1949 The Free State becomes a republic and Protestants in Northern Ireland receive constitutional assurances from the British government.

1956 The IRA launches a Border campaign and internment without trial is introduced in both parts of the island.

1962 The IRA campaign is a failure and is called off. The organisation moves towards socialism and away from traditional romantic republicanism of the bomb, bullet and blood sacrifice, which had led to the 1916 Rising against British rule and the subsequent partition of the island.

1963 Terence O'Neill is the new Protestant Unionist prime minister of Northern Ireland. He faces considerable opposition within his own party and from extremists such as the Rev. Ian Paisley. They oppose his use of the word 'reform' and the first visit of an Irish government leader to Northern Ireland.

1964 There are serious disturbances in parts of Catholic West Belfast after police removed a tricolour from the offices of the IRA's political body, Sinn Fein, the 'Divis Street riots'.

1965 Elements within the Protestant community, within organisations such as the Orange Order and the ruling Unionist Party, reactivate the UVF, believing that political concessions to Catholics will lead to a diminution of Northern Ireland's position within the United Kingdom.

1966 The UVF is declared illegal after the shooting dead of a Catholic barman and the wounding of three of his friends.

1967 Catholic nationalists and republicans, including the IRA, form the Northern Ireland Civil Rights Association and demand basic civil rights, such as one man one vote. The IRA is now pursuing a socialist agenda through its Dublin leadership.

1968 Police and members of the B Specials, a State paramilitary organisation, baton civil-rights marchers in Derry. The events are seen worldwide on television screens. The Unionist government announces reforms, which are deemed inadequate. The Unionist leader, Terence O'Neill, sacks his home affairs minister, William Craig, for opposing reform.

1969 In April, Terence O'Neill resigns under pressure from within his own party and extremists such as Ian Paisley. Tension mounts with bombs at reservoirs, wrongly attributed to the IRA by the government and the police. In fact, the UVF planted the bombs to generate pressure on the State, knowing that the explosions would lead to a crackdown against nationalists.

In August, after three days of rioting, the Northern Ireland police force and the B Specials are unable to cope. British soldiers are deployed in Derry. Further troop deployments are made in Belfast. The troops are in place to protect the Catholic population from Protestant mobs as well as elements of the Northern Ireland security forces.

Traditional republicans blame the socialist leadership of the IRA in Dublin for failing to protect Catholics. They point to the refusal of the IRA's Army Council to open arms dumps when Catholic areas were attacked. Many disillusioned IRA men join vigilante organisations, which are funded and supplied by the Irish Republic government.

1970 In April the Ulster Defence Regiment, part of the British Army, comes into service to replace the discredited B Specials.

The IRA splits: traditional republicans blame its socialist trend for leading to its failure to be adequately armed. The traditionalists form the Provisionals, who have the approval of elements within the government of the Irish Republic and the Catholic Church.

In June, the British Labour government is replaced by a Conservative administration led by Edward Heath. His Northern Ireland secretary of state, Reginald Maudling, asks the Army to find a solution to the Troubles. The Army does not wish to fight a war on two fronts and conveniently defines its enemy as the Catholic population. In July, during a thirty-four-hour curfew in the Catholic Lower Falls area of Belfast, the Army is out of control, operating as though it were handling a colonial emergency such as had taken place in Cyprus. During the curfew houses are ransacked and people held in their homes, which alienates the Catholic population, and accords a major boost to recruitment for the new Provisional IRA.

The SDLP (Social Democratic Labour Party) is formed, a major change within the Catholic community.

1971 In February, the Provisionals kill the first soldier, a nineteen-year-old gunner, Robert Curtis.

In March, a Provisional IRA unit from the Ardoyne area of North Belfast abducts three young Scottish soldiers, two of them brothers. They are lured from a bar by women with promises of a party. Outside Belfast they are murdered while urinating at the side of a road.

Disillusioned with the British government's reluctance to take tough action, the Unionist prime minister, Major Chichester-Clark, resigns and is replaced by Brian Faulkner. He persuades the British government to permit him to introduce internment without trial, aimed at the Catholic population despite the presence of violent men in the Protestant community. Three hundred and fifty people are lifted in the initial internment raid, many of whom are not members of the IRA. The introduction of internment takes place against a background of poor intelligence and outdated files on both wings of the IRA, the Officials and the Provisionals. The one-sided nature of internment, and the fact that student leaders and trade unionists are among those arrested, fuels resentment among Catholics. The outdated files on the IRA mean that the new Provisional IRA leadership is not targeted. Widespread violence follows, with the emergence of the Ulster Defence Association, a paramilitary body formed from Protestant vigilante groupings.

On 4 December, the UVF kills fifteen Catholics in a bomb attack on McGurk's Bar in Belfast, but the Army blames the IRA, describing the incident as an 'own goal', implying that the IRA had a bomb in the bar that detonated prematurely. No effort is made by the security forces to investigate Protestant paramilitary involvement. The mass killing is only attributed to the UVF a decade later.

1972 On 30 January, Bloody Sunday, the British Army Parachute Regiment shoot dead thirteen innocent civilians after a civil-rights march in Derry. A fourteenth dies later.

In March, the British government reacts to international condemnation of Bloody Sunday by imposing direct rule on Northern Ireland from London. The ruling Unionist Party is left without its majority-rule government in Northern Ireland. Loyalist paramilitaries react viciously, killing innocent Catholics.

In June, after secret meetings between the Provisionals and the British government, the IRA declares a ceasefire. Secret talks take place between IRA leaders and representatives of the British government at a house in Cheyne Walk, Chelsea. Among the Provisionals present is the young Gerry Adams, released on licence from the Long Kesh internment camp. The meeting is inconclusive and coincides with tensions in Belfast and an end to the IRA ceasefire.

The IRA blames the British Army for provoking events in West Belfast, which contributed to the end of the truce, and in retaliation bombs eleven civilian targets in Belfast, killing nine innocent people. The event becomes known as Bloody Friday.

1973 Five tons of arms bound for the IRA are seized off the Irish coast.

1974 Brian Faulkner leads a new power-sharing administration of Unionists and nationalists. It is opposed by many Protestants, including loyalist paramilitaries: they see it as leading to the involvement of the Irish government in the affairs of Northern Ireland. A workers' strike follows, in which loyalist paramilitaries have a prominent role. Massive intimidation stops people going to work, and loyalists control power supplies. The British government is advised by the Army that it could not hold the line against a Protestant rebellion. Unionist members of the power-sharing government resign and it collapses. Catholic members feel betrayed by the British refusal to confront the loyalist paramilitaries.

Bombs explode in the Irish Republic, killing twenty-seven people. The Irish security forces believe that the bombs were planted by loyalists acting in collusion with elements of British military intelligence. Before the end of the year, the Provisional IRA kills twenty-four in the bombing of pubs at Guildford and Birmingham on the British mainland.

1975–6 Another 550 people are killed in continuing violence.

1977 A loyalist strike, orchestrated by Ian Paisley, fails because the British government is well prepared.

1978 The European Court of Human Rights rules that

the British Army used inhuman and degrading tactics against internees in the 1971 internment round-up. It also rules that the treatment did not amount to torture.

1979 The violence continues, and the Irish National Liberation Army kills Airey Neave, the Conservative Party's shadow secretary of state for Northern Ireland. A bomb explodes as he drives out of the House of Commons car park in London.

On 20 August the Provisionals kill eighteen soldiers at Warrenpoint and, in a separate operation, murder Earl Mountbatten of Burma.

1980 Northern Ireland's prisons, always a place of controversy, experience a fifty-three-day hunger strike by republicans, demanding the restoration of political prisoner status to IRA prisoners. An apparent concession is made that they may wear civilian clothing. When the prisoners realise that it will be issued by the authorities, they feel they have been duped. This provides the basis for a second, more serious hunger strike.

1981 On 1 March, Bobby Sands, a convicted Provisional, begins a new hunger strike. He and others make five demands: the right to wear their own clothes; to refrain from prison work; to associate freely; to have one letter, visit and parcel per week; and for lost remission time to be fully restored. On 5 May, Sands dies on the sixty-sixth day of his fast. Widespread disorder follows, and the deaths of nine more hunger strikers. Under pressure from Catholic priests and families, the republican prisoners call off the hunger strike. Three days later Margaret Thatcher's government, until then intractable on the prisoners' demands, agrees that they can wear their own clothes and that 50 per cent remission will be restored if they abide by prison rules.

In November, the Democratic Unionist Party of Ian Paisley announces the formation of a 'Third Force', and in a loyalist day of protest, 5,000 men march in a military-style parade before him.

1982 As a result of the support for republicans during the hunger strike, the Provisional IRA's political wing, Sinn Fein, emerges as an electoral force. In local elections, Sinn Fein polls 10.1 per cent of the vote.

The IRA bombing campaign continues on the British mainland, with the deaths of nine soldiers of the Household Cavalry.

A major controversy follows the deaths of six people at the hands of undercover police squads supported by military intelligence. Allegations of a police shoot-to-kill policy lead to the Stalker Inquiry.

1983 In June, Gerry Adams, president of Provisional Sinn Fein, wins the West Belfast seat in Westminster elections.

1984 Allegations of a British government shoot-to-kill policy continue. Seven tons of arms bound for the IRA from the Libyan President Colonel Gadaffy are seized from a trawler off the west coast of Ireland.

On 12 October, the IRA almost succeeds in wiping out the British cabinet in a bombing of the Grand Hotel in Brighton, where the Conservative Party is holding its annual conference.

On 14 December, the first British Army soldier is convicted of murdering a civilian while on duty. He is sentenced to life but serves only twenty-six months, and is released to rejoin the Army.

1985 The IRA kills nine policemen in a mortar attack

on Newry police station. The banning of an Orange march through the Catholic tunnel area of Portadown leads to violent confrontation between the security forces and loyalists.

The Anglo-Irish Agreement is signed between the British government, led by Margaret Thatcher, and the Irish government led by Dr Garret Fitzgerald. Unionists proclaim it a sell-out.

1986 On 3 March, a day of action by loyalists, to protest against the Anglo-Irish Agreement, leads to violence.

Weeks later, loyalists and police clash in Portadown when an attempt is made to stop Apprentice Boys marching through a Catholic area. During the violence, twenty-year-old Keith White is the first Protestant to be killed by a plastic bullet. Fifteen Catholics had already died in this way.

During the summer, more violence erupts from loyalists after the rerouting of Orange parades in Portadown.

In November, Ian Paisley, wearing a red beret, appears at a secret paramilitary-style rally in Belfast's Ulster Hall, signalling the emergence of a new paramilitary organisation, Ulster Resistance. A video of the rally is obtained by *World in Action* and shown on television.

1987 French customs seize 150 tons of weapons and explosives bound for the Provisional IRA. The seizure is made on the coaster *Exsund*, which left Libya *en route* to the west coast of Ireland. Three previous shipments had got through undetected.

On 11 November an IRA bomb explodes without warning at a Remembrance Day parade in Enniskillen, killing eleven people and injuring sixty-three.

1988 Police seize a large quantity of guns bound for loyalist paramilitaries, including Ulster Resistance. The Irish government expresses dismay at the refusal of the British attorney general, Sir Patrick Mayhew (later secretary of state for Northern Ireland) to prosecute eleven police officers named in the report resulting from the Stalker Inquiry in connection with a shoot-to-kill policy. Sir Patrick Mayhew uses national security as a reason for not proceeding against the officers.

On 6 March, under orders from the British government, the SAS shoot dead three unarmed IRA members in Gibraltar. The British government claims that the three left a bomb in Gibraltar but this is found to be untrue. At the Belfast funerals of the three, a loyalist gunman, Michael Stone, kills three mourners. His intention had been to assassinate leading Provisionals in attendance. Three days later, at the funeral of one of Stone's victims, two undercover Army soldiers are dragged from their car by mourners and beaten to death. The mob savagery is captured on television.

In the following months fifteen soldiers are murdered in attacks within Holland, Britain and Northern Ireland.

In October, the British government bans Sinn Fein from using the broadcast media.

1989 On 12 February, a Catholic solicitor, Pat Finucane, is shot dead by loyalists. There is little doubt that British military intelligence knew he had been targeted: one of their prime agents was chief of UDA intelligence, the organisation that carried out the killing.

In April, three members of Ulster Resistance are

arrested in Paris and accused of trying to exchange missile parts for weapons. Ian Paisley's Democratic Unionist Party announces that it severed its links with Ulster Resistance soon after the organisation was set up.

By the end of August, a new controversy surrounds allegations of collusion between members of the security forces and loyalist paramilitaries. Such claims had been made before but on this occasion a BBC reporter, Chris Moore, is shown security forces' documents by loyalists. An English policeman, John Stevens, is asked to investigate. His inquiry offices, within a secure building, are mysteriously fire-bombed.

In October, the IRA kills ten Royal Marines bandsmen at Deal in Kent. The London Court of Appeal overturns as unsafe the convictions of four Irishmen who had served fifteen years for the 1974 Guildford pub bombings.

1990 Undercover soldiers shoot dead three members of a criminal gang, reviving allegations of a shoot-to-kill policy. The overall death toll to this point in the Northern Ireland Troubles is 2,781.

1991 The IRA continues its campaign of bombing and killing in Britain.

In March, the 'Birmingham Six' are released after their second appeal in sixteen years. As with the Guildford Four, an example of serious miscarriage of justice has been uncovered.

Loyalist paramilitaries murder seven people in two separate attacks.

In April, British government census figures claim that Catholics represent 38.4 per cent of the Northern Ireland population. The figures are regarded as unreliable because a large number of people refused to state their religion.

In June, an Irish family, the Maguires, are cleared by the London Court of Appeal after serving sentences ranging from four to fourteen years.

During the summer months there are killings by paramilitaries on both sides.

The year is characterised by an increase in loyalist violence, which claims the lives of thirty-four Catholics.

1992 An IRA bomb kills seven Protestant workmen. Gerry Adams's reaction is that the tragedy was a horrific reminder of British policy-making in Ireland.

In March, a MORI poll on British attitudes to Northern Ireland concludes that 23 per cent of British people favour a united Ireland, 29 per cent prefer the Province to remain part of the United Kingdom and 31 per cent advocate its independence.

Violence continues on both sides of the sectarian divide, and so do confrontations over Orange marches in Catholic areas.

On 10 August, Sir Patrick Mayhew, secretary of state for Northern Ireland, announces the banning of the Ulster Defence Association (UDA), which shocks some observers because the organisation has been legal for twenty years despite its history of murder and savagery. Sir Patrick declares that he is satisfied that the UDA is actively and primarily engaged in the commission of criminal terrorist acts and merited proscription. The decision is taken against a background of increased violence by the UDA and its illegal military wing, the Ulster Freedom Fighters.

Ian Paisley claims that the ban on the UDA is a sweetener to Sinn Fein to enter political talks, and that the British government has succumbed to pressure from Dublin. A UDA official tells a journalist that, for a decade, UDA operations had been controlled by the security forces. The claim is deduced to be a reference to Brian Nelson, the UDA intelligence chief who worked for British military intelligence. He had been in a position to sanction the killing of Catholics, such as the solicitor, Pat Finucane.

August 21 marks the death of the three thousandth victim of the conflict. The figure does not include 241 people killed in the Republic of Ireland, Britain and Europe; from 1969 a staggering 558 people had been murdered in North Belfast alone.

In December, an IRA bomb devastates the centre of Manchester, injuring sixty people. In a year in which over eighty people are murdered in Northern Ireland, the UDA threatens to increase its violence to a 'ferocity never imagined'.

1993 On 11 January, Sir Patrick Mayhew says that the IRA is looking for a way out of the conflict. He does not reveal that the British government has been involved in secret talks with the organisation.

In February, the IRA continues its bombing campaign in Britain and loyalist paramilitaries continue to target and shoot Catholics.

On 20 March, a bomb at a shopping centre in Warrington, Lancashire, kills a three-year-old boy. Days later, a twelve-year-old boy dies from injuries received in the blast, in which sixty other people were hurt.

Two days later, government figures confirm the sectarian character of the Province: half the population lives in areas that are 90 per cent either Protestant or Catholic, and less than 110,000 people live in districts in which there is an equal number of people of both denominations.

On 25 March, after the deaths of five Catholics at the hands of the Ulster Freedom Fighters, the organisation publicly applauds its weekly killing rate.

On 10 April, John Hume, leader of the SDLP, and Gerry Adams, president of Provisional Sinn Fein, meet for talks.

In November, the British government deliberately leaks a document revealing secret contacts between it and the IRA. It then denies publicly that there had been any negotiation with the IRA. The British prime minister, John Major, tells the House of Commons that it would turn his stomach to talk to Gerry Adams. The leaked document is a ploy to offset any possibility of the IRA telling people that secret talks had been in progress for some time. The leak takes place at a time when the British know they cannot make progress in their secret dealings with the terrorists and when the risk of exposure is too great. It is better to use a devious mechanism whereby the matter comes into the public domain and skulduggery is used to deny that the secret talks were anything but the normal range of contacts and communiqués with the IRA, that they were part of an attempt to get the IRA off the hook. The British government produces dubious communiqués, implying that the IRA is desperate to give up violence and has approached the British government to help it achieve that goal. But the talks between the two sides had been of a serious nature. The Major government cleverly succeeds in convincing the British people that it simply responded to a cry for help from the IRA and acted with the moral objective of helping the

terrorists detach themselves from violence. While the
IRA tries to expose the lie, the British and Irish
governments prepare a peace initiative.

On 15 December, both governments announce the
Downing Street Declaration, aimed at resolving the
conflict.

1994 The Provisionals, under pressure from within
their own community and from the Irish and American governments, pretend to debate the potential
value of the Downing Street Declaration. Behind the
scenes, the IRA is told by the Irish government that
the Declaration will lead to a place for the Provisionals in any decision-making about the political future
of Northern Ireland.

Meanwhile, loyalist violence increases, with the
targeting of innocent Catholics and members of the
IRA.

In March, the IRA launches mortars at Heathrow
Airport, which appears to be the organisation's
answer to the Declaration.

Again behind the scenes, the IRA Army Council
votes not to reject the Declaration publicly.

On 31 August, the IRA announces a complete
cessation of military activities.

On 13 October, loyalist paramilitaries respond
with a similar ceasefire announcement.

1995 In the political shadows, the British and Irish
governments are at loggerheads over the British
refusal to respond positively to the IRA ceasefire. At
Westminster, the Conservative government needs the
support of Northern Ireland Unionist MPs. The
prime minister, John Major, cannot afford to alienate
them and lose their support by pandering to demands

from the IRA and the Irish government for swift progress towards inclusive talks.

In July, at Drumcree churchyard, Portadown, there is a three-day stand-off between police, Orangemen, the Unionist MP David Trimble, soon to be his party's leader, Ian Paisley and leading loyalists, over the Protestant demand to be permitted to march through the Catholic Garvaghy Road area. Paisley compares the right to march as a choice between freedom or slavery, light or darkness, and deems it a matter of life or death. The Orangemen are allowed to march through the Catholic district without their bands. In Belfast, Catholics are angered when police route an Orange march through a Catholic enclave on Belfast's Lower Ormeau Road.

1996 On 9 February, a massive IRA bomb at Canary Wharf in London signals the end of an eighteen-month IRA ceasefire. The IRA's Army Council concludes that the British government is not willing to concede any ground or permit Sinn Fein unfettered entry into peace talks. A British and Unionist insistence on IRA decommissioning is seen as one of the major stumbling blocks. The IRA points out privately that it knew that the British were happy to use that issue because they could not move the peace process forward except on a Unionist agenda.

Loyalist paramilitaries already in peace talks hold the line with their ceasefire.

In July, at Drumcree churchyard, another stand-off takes place between Orangemen, among them the Unionist Party leader, David Trimble, himself a committed Orangeman. The issue, once again, is the demand to march through the Catholic Garvaghy Road area. The British government learns that if the march is not permitted to go ahead, violence on a scale never seen in Northern Ireland will follow. Some security advisers warn that Northern Ireland could be brought to the brink of civil war by the Protestant population. Catholics in Garvaghy Road and elsewhere are astounded when Orangemen are told that they may march from the churchyard at Drumcree and through the Garvaghy Road.

Widespread nationalist violence follows, leading to the worst rioting for twenty years.

1997 In July, at Drumcree churchyard, and against the wishes of Catholics in both parts of Ireland, the Drumcree march takes its traditional route through the Catholic district. A leaked British government document confirms that the decision to permit the march had been based on security and public-order considerations. Catholics react with dismay, and widespread rioting follows. It is believed that the new British Labour government is frightened to confront the loyalists, much as its counterpart of 1974 had been.

THE MANIAC?

My passage into the world of terror within the Northern Irish Protestant community was made possible by Kenny McClinton, a latterday fundamentalist preacher, a murderer who became a celebrity. He claimed a prison-cell conversion and secured early release from a life sentence to promote a new political gospel.

Kenny McClinton admits that he once advocated beheading Catholics and impaling their heads on the railings of Woodvale Park in the Protestant Shankill area of West Belfast. McClinton told his paramilitary boss that he was 'up for it' and that it was the best means of terrorising the IRA. In the 1970s, Protestant paramilitary organisations believed that butchering innocent Catholics was an effective way of dealing with the IRA, and McClinton made his proposal when the Shankill Butchers were selecting their victims in the night-time streets of North and West Belfast. They tortured young and old alike, and slit the throats of their victims. They were convicted of nineteen murders but the real total was nearer thirty, making them the greatest mass murderers in British criminal history.

McClinton aimed to upstage them. From the early to

mid seventies, he was prepared, given the order, to kill anyone. Now, an evangelical pastor of the nineties, he says he has graduated from maniac – murderer – to follower of Jesus Christ. I knew of his reputation as a cold-blooded assassin, his close association with some of the Shankill Butchers, including their leader, Lenny Murphy, and his lasting friendship with Billy Wright, a well-known loyalist hard man, and was intrigued to meet the 'new' McClinton. We had our first discussion over lunch at his home in the autumn of 1996.

Previous research had confirmed that many imprisoned loyalists 'converted' to gain favourable treatment from the prison authorities and a reduction in their sentences, but McClinton's metamorphosis seemed to have stood the test of time.

McClinton was born in 1947. His father was alcoholic, abusive, and frequently swapped his job as a coal-delivery worker for a prison cell. McClinton's recollections of childhood are littered with 'almighty rows' between his parents and the 'abject poverty' of his surroundings: home was an ex-Army Nissen hut, with no water supply, in the Shankill district. When his parents' marriage ended, McClinton found himself in a household that seemed even poorer than those of other working-class families: 'We were,' he complained, 'lower working class.' He was still haunted by memories of shabby clothes and 'scuffed-up' shoes. He and his brother became the targets of jibes: in the school playground, other boys would surround them, chanting, 'Your old man's in gaol, your old man's in gaol.' McClinton said, 'We learned that in order to get peace, it was necessary to deal out to our tormentors a dose of instant violence. So those who were our source of torment became a source of plenty because they would

compete with each other to give us a share of their
sweets etc.'

His anger towards the State grew from his visits with
his mother to the National Assistance Board: 'I remember my mother begging bureaucrats in pin-striped suits
for some money.' The phrase 'pin-striped suits' produces an image that does not fit the reality of that period:
the civil servants who handled benefit claims were
minor functionaries. However, as I soon discovered,
McClinton could use language and imagery adroitly to
enhance his story. Notwithstanding that, he developed a
resentment towards those he believed to be persecuting
him, and an explosive hatred of authority. 'I remember
the big room with people filling out forms and they
shouted out your business: "Mrs McClinton, you say
your husband's in prison. How long has he been in
prison this time?" You're humiliated for asking for just
a few pence for your existence. There were many times
we returned penniless to that rat-infested hut.'

Although the family lived in a staunchly Protestant
enclave, Mrs McClinton, perhaps in desperation, took
the unusual step of applying for a new home in
Ballymurphy, which subsequently became a republican
stronghold. Her application was rejected, which left
McClinton believing that his family were outcasts, unfit
even for a house in a working-class Catholic estate.
Then Catholics were regarded as second-class citizens,
and that the McClintons were considered unworthy to
be among them produced an added dimension to his
resentment. 'In my mind, it made a mockery of Catholic
claims that they alone were the victims of discrimination.' He told me that in the 1970s the Protestant
working class was equally deprived but, unlike the

Catholic community, was reluctant to condemn the
State because it was 'their country'.

McClinton spoke of the traditional symbols that
divided the two communities, the wall painting of King
William of Orange on a white charger, and slogans such
as 'Kick the Pope', which seemed 'a part of life, just like
breathing'. Only retrospectively was he able to detect a
philosophy underpinning the sectarianism but in his
youth he accepted that the slogans defined him and the
rest of the Shankill community. 'We suffered under the
gentlemen farmers and the mill-owners who were
running the country at that time. Perhaps we didn't feel
things just as severely as the Catholics.'

It was in such statements that I discovered the
character of a loyalist analysis that emerged through
political re-education in loyalist circles within the
prisons: the acceptance that the Unionist ascendancy
was corrupt, that Catholics and Protestants alike suffered discrimination, with a grudging acceptance that it
had a greater impact on Catholics. In some respects,
McClinton's assertions derived from an emerging
awareness within loyalism that the Catholic community, through its demands for civil rights gained worldwide recognition of its grievances, while no one within
the working-class Protestant community had yet
attempted to highlight the plight of its people.

In the 1950s, the McClintons led a nomadic life,
moving from house to house and school to school. Life,
according to Kenny McClinton, was riddled with
violence, and three years of borstal training had no
effect on either him or his brother. 'We had chips on
both shoulders, and as soon as we saw anything that
was going to oppress us, we responded with a dose of
violence.'

In 1962, aged sixteen, McClinton left school on a
Friday afternoon and was employed as a labourer two
days later. He was determined to emulate his father,
working in a job that demanded physical strength.
However, a friend convinced him that life in the
Merchant Navy would remove him from the daily
drudgery of life in Belfast: he would see the world, have
a woman in every port.

McClinton fought with shipmates, and in bars on
shore leave. He returned home to Belfast every four
months, to a city in which, he recalled, both communities were living in harmony.

But that was a distortion of life in West Belfast in the
early to mid 1960s: in 1964, there was serious rioting in
the Catholic Lower Falls, Paisleyism was in the ascend-
ant and the Ulster Volunteer Force (UVF) was reforming. In 1966, several Catholics were shot, one
killed, in Malvern Street in the Shankill; it was also the
fiftieth anniversary of the 1916 Rising in Dublin, which
had been aimed at overthrowing British rule in Ireland,
but which culminated in partition. The Rising came to
symbolise Irish revolutionary fervour, and was cher-
ished by the IRA as a glorious episode in its history. In
1966, the anniversary commemoration ceremonies were
used by Unionist politicians to heighten Protestant
anxiety that the IRA would mark the event with a
campaign of violence. The Unionist government frequently used fear as a political weapon to keep the
communities divided, and to strengthen the Unionist
political stranglehold on the Province.

Although he was at sea for much of the time,
McClinton must have been aware of the tensions at
home. The people who could not see it were those in the
then Labour government who were content to leave

Ulster to govern itself as long as the Unionists, who
were in power as they had been for fifty years, kept the
lid on the melting pot of hatred and injustice. The
British economy and Rhodesia dominated political life
in Britain, and Northern Ireland was kept 'out of sight,
out of mind'.

When I asked McClinton if he had been aware of the
civil-rights agitation in the 1960s, he replied that it had
been hijacked by the IRA and it would have been better
if Catholics and Protestants had united in a campaign
for social justice.

But there was no unifying ingredient between the two
communities that would have permitted them to campaign together for social justice. The Protestant community did not perceive itself as a victim and regarded
Catholic demands for equality in franchise, employment
and housing as part of an IRA conspiracy to overthrow
the State – their State.

From August 1969 to the end of 1972, Northern
Ireland experienced its worst period of violence since
the 1920s. Those three years saw some of the most
grisly killings of the conflict. The lawlessness was
defined by the barricades that ringed Catholic and
Protestant ghettos. Vigilantes on both sides were
involved in an orgy of slaughter, and many innocent
people who strayed into enemy territory were abducted,
tortured and murdered.

In 1972, in response to the fall of the Stormont
Unionist government, and secret talks held between the
British government and Provisional IRA leaders, loyalist
killers went on the rampage. On 21 July, in what
became known as Bloody Friday, 26 bombs exploded in
Belfast, killing 11 people and injuring 130.

McClinton responded by joining the Ulster Defence

Regiment (UDR), a British Army regiment comprised
mainly of Protestants, of whom many were members of
loyalist terror groupings. It had been established as a
mainly part-time force in April 1970 and was intended
to replace the Ulster Special Constabulary, known as
the B Specials, historically the paramilitary arm of the
Unionist State, and anti-Catholic. They had been disbanded after the civil unrest of August 1969 when
evidence showed that they had been involved in the
burning of Catholic homes. In the early 1970s, the
British Army and the UDR leadership were happy to
accept into their ranks loyalists from within the paramilitary Ulster Defence Association (UDA) because, unlike
the IRA, it was not an illegal organisation. The
consequence was that for two decades the UDR served
as a training ground for loyalist terrorists. Weapons
disappeared from military barracks, intelligence gath-
ered at roadblocks was used for assassinations, and
members of the UVF and UDA used the cover of their
uniforms to kill innocent Catholics.

McClinton, I believe, joined the UDR for training, as
did other young men from the Shankill district.

Looking back, McClinton said, 'I left the Merchant
Navy a disillusioned man. I tried nearly everything the
world could offer and I found no satisfaction in the
stuff. I was indulging myself in drink, womanising and
the old violence.' Yet in 1972 he swapped one jungle for
another. At sea he received a total of 200 stitches for
wounds received in brawls and had hurt many people.
Most of the fights involved the use of knives and
hammers, and he carried a Stanley knife with him while
on shore leave, ready to use on anyone who crossed
him. McClinton admitted, 'I walked quite naturally into

the Troubles, prepared to do something.' It was hardly the attitude of someone disillusioned with violence.

Early on, it seems, the British Army had identified not just the IRA as the enemy but the Catholic population. On 3 July 1970 British soldiers sealed off the Catholic Lower Falls area, imposing a curfew that lasted thirty-four hours. There was looting and ransacking of homes and an overuse of military force in a densely populated urban enclave. From then, the Army concentrated its efforts on rooting out the IRA while ignoring loyalist paramilitaries, citing as a reason the fear of having two enemies and being trapped between them. The Unionist government, then still in place, exercised influence on military strategy, and in 1971, internment without trial was introduced against the Catholic population even though a tribal war was in progress.

A society at war was a dangerous place, made even more dangerous by the presence of young men like Kenny McClinton. Paramilitaries swaggered into bars, and were heroes to their communities. The more violent they were, the more infamous they became. McClinton told me he was 'goaded by frustration' because of the 'inaction' of the British government, but it is likely that in the 1970s, as the product of a deprived background and with a propensity anyway towards violence, he saw, perhaps unconsciously, the killing process as a means of raising his stature.

McClinton spent six months training with the UDR and was frustrated by the rules of engagement: 'I carried this Yellow Card which told me when and if I could shoot at these rebels. If I loosed off a round, it meant I had to fill in sixteen reports, explaining why I loosed off a round at suspected petrol bombers.'

The history of the regiment is peppered with a record

of its members charged with bombings, shootings and killings and it could hardly have been a disciplined organisation. A former officer explained to me why he left the UDR: 'I had been in the British Army proper. I couldn't believe what I was dealing with in the UDR. There were many good men in there with genuine motives, but the riff-raff were too difficult to handle. There were thefts of weapons and explosives to name some of the offences I came across. We even had to search our own men coming off duty to make sure they hadn't stolen lead from some of the installations. To quote one famous general [Wellington], "I didn't know what they did to the enemy but by God they sure frightened me." '

McClinton identified the lack of freedom of action within the UDR as the catalyst that moved him towards the UDA. I pointed out to him that the UDA did not have a glorious history, and he said 'It was a wonderful concept of the Protestant community rising up and forming a people's army to defend the community. That concept seemed good.'

Within what he described as 'good' were butchery, thuggery and murder. Some victims were in the hands of their killers for over twelve hours. Mental handicap was no defence against loyalist assassins, as twenty-three-year-old Patrick Benstead discovered: he was tortured with red-hot pokers, the soles of his feet, the palms of his hands and his back branded, then he was shot. A UDA gang raped a young Catholic mother in front of her mentally handicapped son, then shot them both, killing the boy.

McClinton said that within a year of joining the UDA, he and others recognised that people like him were not being given a real opportunity to display their skills: 'I had been in the British Army and knew my stuff, and I started training with other people and became better. There was nowhere to fight and a whole gangster element arose out of the ranks of the UDA.' He went on, 'There were many like myself who were more idealistic, who would not have touched a penny or stolen anything, even though we had a life of violence. There was a warped sense that you didn't go out stealing or taking bribes.'

Warped it was and it reminded me of Lenny Murphy's mother who said, after her son was killed by the IRA, that he 'wouldn't have hurt a fly'. He just liked killing people.

In a later conversation, McClinton told me that he had been suited to a life of terrorism because he had natural leadership qualities, and that his specialised knowledge of weapons and explosives had helped him graduate into the ranks of the Ulster Freedom Fighters (UFF), a branch of the UDA. In the UFF, the UDA leadership had an organisation that could claim responsibility for murder. It knew the UFF would soon be declared illegal, like the IRA, but its existence permitted the UDA to operate openly and its leaders to remain at large and apparently 'within the law'.

In an attempt to reinforce his claim that he was an idealist and could not remain in the gangster-run UDA, McClinton tried to convince me that the UFF was an entirely separate organisation. However, he knew that the UDA leadership controlled the UFF, much in the same way that loyalist politicians refer to IRA/Sinn Fein to indicate their indivisible character. He also knew that the head of the UDA in West Belfast, James Pratt Craig, sanctioned UFF killings. Craig, a stocky man in his early forties, had a flamboyant lifestyle, and purchased expensive clothes and jewellery. He ran protection rackets on building sites, and extorted money from shops, pubs and clubs.

His associates did not know that he kept himself out of the hands of the law by acting as a police informant, or that he protected himself from the IRA by setting up for assassination members of the UVF and some of his own colleagues. Craig betrayed the leader of the Shankill Butchers, Lenny Murphy, and the UFF supremo, John McMichael, both killers, to the Provisional IRA and eventually met his own death at the hands of the UFF.

The UFF was modelled on the IRA with a series of units or cells to make it difficult to penetrate. Its policy, as McClinton told me, was to terrorise Catholics using 'the most macabre means': Thomas Madden, an inoffensive middle-aged Catholic, was ritually carved, as a sculptor would carve a block of wood. None of the 147 stab wounds to his body was sufficient to kill him and he died slowly of strangulation, suspended from a beam by a slowly tightening noose. Madden was not interested in politics and worked as a security guard in a mill on the Crumlin Road but his journeys to work took him through borderline areas.

McClinton agreed that although the killings curtailed the social life of Catholics, they did not deter the IRA from its campaign of violence. In fact, they served only to encourage the Catholic community to look to the IRA as its protector. McClinton told me that when he left the Navy, 'I had no faith in human nature. I had been hit, stabbed. People had slashed me with stuff. I'd seen my blood running out and I'd seen just how easy it was, and I began to work the same way. Life had

brutalised me.' Throughout our discussions McClinton
tried to attribute blame for his actions to this premise.

He also told me that he was made commander of
several active service units and was personally involved
in the 'most heinous stuff'. He chose the word 'heinous'
carefully. It means abominable, wicked in the highest
degree, and could reasonably be assumed to refer to
killings of the type carried out by the Shankill Butchers
and similar loyalist gangs.

But McClinton limits his crimes to those with which
he was later charged, in particular two murders. 'On St
Patrick's Day 1977, I was ordered to assassinate
everybody in a car ... anything that moved in that car. I
took a team up to Cambrai Street off the Crumlin Road
and, as this car slowed at a ramp, I opened fire and shot
the driver dead. I then turned the gun on the other
occupant and discovered it was a nine-year-old boy.
Even in spite of my total commitment, I found I couldn't
shoot the young man.'

The driver was Daniel Carville, who died instantly,
and the child was his son.

The second murder to which McClinton admitted
occurred several months later during the abortive
Paisley-inspired workers' strike of 1977. McClinton
told me that his superiors were unhappy with the
response to the strike call and, in particular, with the
willingness of bus drivers to keep public transport on
the roads. They 'needed to be taught a lesson', and
McClinton was ordered to kill a bus driver in Protestant
West Belfast. The UDA leader, James Pratt Craig, and
his associates knew that the sectarian geography of the
city determined that their victim would be Protestant.

Harry Bradshaw stopped his bus on the Crumlin
Road to allow McClinton to get on board. McClinton

shot him in the head at point-blank range and was covered in his victim's blood. In the wake of condemnation from Protestants for the killing of one of their community, the UDA wrote a hollow letter of apology to Sheila Bradshaw, wife of the victim. They enclosed a £10 note and said that they thought her husband was a Catholic.

McClinton denied writing that letter. He told me that after those killings he felt 'lower than low' and that his reluctance to kill the boy signalled that something spiritual was manifesting itself in his life. However, there was something revisionist about this, as though he was analysing the event to fit neatly into his story of conversion. He reminded me of another loyalist terrorist who had told me that there was no greater conversion than that of a man who went to the gates of Hell and repented because the Lord was there in his soul.

McClinton described the kernel of belief that had never left him during his killing spree: 'If you come from a Protestant background, you are sent out rigidly ... at that time ... to Sunday School. At Sunday School, you are taught the basic rudiments of Protestantism, and Protestantism at that time was based on the Bible ... the basic tenets of the Bible. "I know because the Bible tells me so." [He repeated the sentence rhythmically, as he often had in childhood.] You must not do evil, you must believe in the Lord Jesus Christ and try to do the things he has taught us to do.' If that had been part of his thinking while he was a terrorist, it was not apparent. McClinton was quick to remind me on several occasions that he had sunk to subhuman depths, but qualified the statement by saying that he had not committed 'the grossest crimes'. He was sending out

confusing messages with curious linguistic distinctions:
by his own admission, he was guilty of the 'most
heinous' crimes, which he never catalogued, yet never
guilty of 'the grossest'. It seemed a contradiction that I
should address. Meanwhile, though, McClinton had
insisted that even in his terrorist career, 'the seeds of
faith were beating within him'.

'Those little lessons of my youth had stuck there.
Those people who taught me had done their work
faithfully, and well. There is a scriptural verse which
says: "Train up a child in the way he shall go and when
he is old he shall not depart from it." Proverbs 22 Verse
6. There was a spiritual side of that working through
me even at that stage.'

When I pressed him about his claim to have experienced a spiritual awakening, he responded that he was
not aware at the time that it was taking place. It was
happening at a subliminal level. His version of the
summer of 1977 is that he was constantly operating as a
terrorist, planning the assassination of leading members
of the IRA. His strategy was to construct bombs from
plastic explosives, conceal them in hollowed-out books
and mail them to his targets. The packages also showed
forwarding addresses so that if the potential victim was
not at one location, he might be found at another. He
was, McClinton alleged, determined to wipe out men,
women and children at those addresses – this, while he
was subliminally experiencing a conversion.

The stress of constructing bombs was offset by bouts
of heavy drinking. 'After the drinking, I woke up in my
girlfriend's bed. I had a dreadful hangover and was
sweating pure alcohol. I had gradually become more
disgusted with myself and the actions I had taken
against other human beings. Basically, I wanted a new

beginning to my life. I did not like the monster I had become.' It was at around this time that he proposed to his terror boss, James Pratt Craig, that they should behead Catholics and impale their heads on the railings of Woodvale Park. However, other things were happening close to McClinton: Craig was about to deliver him into the hands of the law. Craig was worried that McClinton was a loose cannon, a maniac who might bring down too much heat, and he needed favours from his police handlers because of a killing he had personally carried out. McClinton had helped him bury the body, unaware that his boss had been the hitman, and that Craig had secretly identified him as one of those who had buried the corpse. Which brings me to wonder whether Craig sacrificed McClinton because he was a low-level operator or if it was because he was such a dangerous terrorist that even his boss feared what he might get up to?

Whatever the answer, McClinton was not only oblivious to his spiritual awakening but also to the treachery of his boss.

THE ARMY OF GOD

On the morning of 27 August 1977, police surrounded a house in the Rosapenna district of North Belfast where McClinton was living with his girlfriend. It was an unusual place for him to be, sandwiched between the Catholic Cliftonville Road and Oldpark areas. He never explained to me why he was living there and not in Shankill. He was arrested and taken into police custody for interrogation. He contends that two days before his arrest he asked God to help him make a new start in life. He was, he claims, mentally and spiritually relieved to be apprehended and removed from a society to which he posed a terrible threat. He was disgusted that he was a murderer, that he created widows and orphans and had sunk to 'such terrible depths'. He was not, in his words, an armchair general like others in the UDA. He had been prepared to kill for an objective. However, I found no evidence in the transcript of his interrogation by the police to substantiate his claims that he wanted to unburden himself or rid himself of his commitment to terror. Indeed, he said of it, 'During my interrogation, I covered up for other people. If I was going down, I was going down alone. I was taking it full on the chin.' He seemed, even now, to revel in his then reputation as a hard man, someone even the police interrogators could not break, and told me that he withstood the efforts of his interrogators for a week, never flinching under their questioning.

He admitted the killings of Carville and Bradshaw and was remanded in custody to Crumlin Road prison and, there, his propensity for physical violence took his life into a different phase: 'No one could tame me. I had the tiger by the tail.' He retracted the admissions he had made to the police and decided to plead not guilty at his trial. In this light, McClinton's unconscious 'spiritual awakening' and desire for a new start appear hollow.

He undertook a leading role within the loyalist prison structure and ordered prisoners to strip naked when they appeared in court as a means of displaying contempt for the system. The judiciary, he claimed, was incarcerating freedom fighters.

In 1978, in prison, he wrote a poem. Here are some stanzas from 'A Patriot's Reward':

> My country has abandoned me,
> Tho' grizzly deeds I've done
> For Ulster, so she might be free,
> From Bomb and rebel's gun.
>
> To keep the link with Britain's shores
> I volunteered to fight.
> I gave my very best and more
> In battles day and night.
>
> Anti-terror was my game,
> Eye for eye my pledge;
> Vengeance for our dead and lame;
> By gun or knife's-honed edge

> Now Britain has imprisoned me,
> A champion of her cause!
> And gives me weeks of solitary,
> Like gifts from Santa Claus!

The clear message of the poem was that McClinton, like many imprisoned loyalists, couldn't understand why he was there. If he had thought he was killing people for Britain, it had been a shock to find himself in the same place as the IRA, and 'A Patriot's Reward' shows the anger of an embittered man. He introduced the IRA tactic of the hunger strike, which he alone undertook and which lasted twenty-four days. He gained a stone in weight. The prison authorities were naturally puzzled and found the episode comical: they had not known that two of the Shankill Butchers, 'Basher' Bates and Willie Moore, were secretly supplying McClinton with food.

His violent behaviour in prison landed him in solitary confinement for varying periods of time and the governor finally sent him to the H-blocks in the Maze prison, believing that he could be tamed in a facility that held the most hardened terrorists on both sides.

In the H-blocks, he became known as 'the man in Cell 15' and prison officers referred to him as 'that maniac'. In the autumn of 1978, he refused to wear a prison uniform and paraded up and down the Block in a blanket. His behaviour mimicked the Provisional IRA inmates, who not only refused to wear prison clothes but also smeared their cells with excreta. McClinton told me that, like them, he had no desire to be classed as a common criminal. 'Two prison officers came along and told me to put on the prison garb. I told them, "If you think you and yer mate can make me wear that,

let's go." They'd seen it all before. They'd been calling
me "that maniac McClinton" because I was knocking
them around like ninepins.' His language reminded me
of the Popeye cartoons, except that this man was a
killer. 'I had complete and utter violence ... no compromise. I wouldn't take orders from any of them unless
they asked nicely and gave me full respect as a person. If
they tried to treat me like an underling, or a prisoner, all
they got was their noses broken or put down on the
ground.'

He carved himself a reputation as a hard, uncompromising, unpredictable individual, with extremely
violent tendencies. His reward was to become
commander of the loyalist prisoners in the H-blocks;
frequently in solitary, he was allowed only a half-hour
each morning to slop out his cell and wash naked at a
basin. During this period he wrote another poem,
'Ulster's Forgotten Army':

'Get up you tramps,' we hear them scream,
'Get those bed-packs made!'
With their hats pulled down across their eyes
Like guardsmen on parade.

We have no answer to these quips,
We've nothing left to say!
You see, we're the forgotten men
Of the loyal UDA.

Forgotten by our comrades true;
Forgotten by our mates;
Forgotten by the backroom boys
Who hand out release dates.

Forgotten by the politicians –
Violence they abhor.

These very men
Whose 'call to arms'
Started this bloody war.

'Take up the gun,'
We heard them cry,
'Shoot to kill,' they said.
At night when we faced Ulster's foes
They were safely tucked in bed.

'No surrender,' was the call.
'Not an inch,' they cried.
And many men took up the gun,
And many others died.

'Kill to stay British,' they pleaded hard.
'To Britain you must be true.'
Yet, most of the stick I'm gettin' here,
Is coming from some English screw.

It was a stark and accurate analysis of loyalist prisoners'
thought, and McClinton was not far off the mark in
referring to a 'shoot-to-kill' policy. In the early 1970s,
William Craig, the former Northern Ireland home
affairs minister and a leading Unionist, told loyalist
paramilitaries that the enemy should be liquidated (see
p. 286).

In February 1979, McClinton appeared before Justice
Turlough O'Donnell and contested the prosecution case
against him, claiming that the statements he had made
to police had been given under duress. He believed that
he could successfully defend his position. Nothing in his
behaviour suggested that, if he was freed, he would not
have returned to terrorism. He said to me, 'I appeared
before Justice O'Donnell, and to this day nothing has
been proved against me.'

I was astonished that he should say this: he had
admitted to me that he had been involved in the
murders with which he had been charged. Indeed, the
evidence against him had been based on the statements
he had made to police but I could not understand why,
in 1996, he should still air this boast. Perhaps even now,
and despite his religious calling, McClinton likes to
portray himself as the hard man who never cracked
under interrogation, who was so professional as a
terrorist that the authorities could pin nothing on him.
But it is a strange light in which to view an evangelical
pastor.

Justice O'Donnell, sitting alone in accordance with
the rules of the Diplock courts established to deal with
terrorist crimes, found McClinton guilty. Describing
him as a cold-blooded assassin, he handed down life
imprisonment, recommending that he serve no less than
twenty years.

When the reality of life in the H-blocks finally sank
into McClinton, he directed his thoughts elsewhere. He
says he had believed that Christianity was for sissies,
homosexuals and wimps until the arrival in the prison
of an Anglican priest, David Jardine, who held half-day
current-affairs discussions with loyalist prisoners.
McClinton initially saw this as temporary escape from
the boredom of prison life, but then Jardine announced
that he was planning a poetry anthology entitled *In Jail
with Jesus*. He asked the prisoners if they wished to
contribute, promising that anyone who joined the
project would be provided with a pen and notepad. 'I
was after the pen and notepad ... it was for nothing. I
began to write poetry and he printed fourteen of my
poems.'

McClinton contends that writing for Jardine was

therapeutic and not the result of a genuine interest in things spiritual – he knew prisoners who became Christians for two weeks and went back to their old habits. His violent behaviour continued, and the periods spend in solitary confinement with an old edition of the King James Bible. 'Faith cometh by hearing, and hearing by the word of God, but I had no theology at that time – just, "Jesus loves me this I know, because the Bible tells me so." I began reading the Bible at Genesis and enjoyed all the Old Testament stories of intrigue. I had nothing but an empty cell and the Bible. Nothing was allowed in or out. I enjoyed the stories of political intrigues, whoring and all that. I only had a basic education but I understood all that.'

He was entitled to a monthly visit from a relative or family friend, but prison procedures made the end of visits a humiliating experience. Each prisoner was ordered to strip and squat over a mirror to allow officers to determine if he was concealing something in his anus. The Provisionals, in particular, were adept at smuggling messages by that method concealed in tampons. At one stage, female visitors to the Maze were also subjected to strip searches. McClinton told me he refused to be searched and, on several occasions, it took five prison officers to subdue him and return him to his cell. When the prison regime reversed the procedure, introducing it at the start of each visit, non-consenting prisoners like McClinton were unable to see friends and relatives. He told me that his refusal led to longer periods of solitary confinement, and his fellow inmates took bets on whether he would kill a prison officer or be killed by prison staff. His rage against the prison regime finally boiled over on the night of 7 April 1979. 'Two young loyalist prisoners were abused by the prison staff for refusing to accept the prison search and their visits were cancelled. In each cell on the block we had punched a hole in the wall to communicate with each other. I told the guys in the next cell that when the door of my cell opened, I was getting stuck into the prison officers. I reckoned the abuse had to be high-lighted. The two young prisoners were only seventeen years old and were brutalised and degraded. As soon as my cell door opened, I hit a prison officer and knocked him down. Five others fought with me and got me back into my cell and wanted me to run the gauntlet between two lines of officers with batons and boots. The first man who took a swing at me was a big brute of a man. As soon as he swung at me, I got him by the ears, hit him with my head and pulled him down. I was talking to him while the other officers were like a rugby scrum, beating and thumping at me with their batons and their boots. And I said to him, "I don't care what they're doing to me, I've got you." He squealed. The maniac had him, and the maniac didn't care if he lived or died. The commitment frightened the life out of that brute of a man.'

In the months following that incident, McClinton told me, he was in a tug of war between Satan and the Holy Spirit. He read the New Testament and identified a passage that promised he would be cleansed if he called on Christ and subjected himself to Him. He was convinced that Christ through the Cross would suffer in his place. He would be saved, granted eternal life and his 'black sins' would be forgiven, but he was not prepared to tell his fellow inmates that he was ready to repent. 'I still had the tiger by the tail. My reputation inside would have been in tatters. I was still a military commander. I had to hide my Bible reading.'

He was terrified that anyone should see him praying on his knees in his cell: it would have convinced other loyalists that the system had tamed him. That period he defines as a time of 'split personality'. He privately sought salvation while publicly he 'strutted his stuff', threatening prison officers. (His reputation as a maniac, the uncompromising rebel, remains a central feature of his story: without it the 'miraculous' nature of his conversion, and the testimony he now gives to audiences in the United States, Britain and Ireland, would be less credible to those to whom he preaches.)

It was, in his words, a time of an internal war, and a developing belief that Christ could love 'black hell-deserving murderers'. He dreaded Judgement Day, knowing what awaited him if he did not commit himself fully to Christ and walk in the Light. On the evening of 12 August 1979, he fell on his knees in his cell, cried and told God he believed in Him. 'I told him I was not an educated man but that I believed if I called on Him, I could be saved. I told him I was taking Him at His word. I said, "I'm trusting you. This is a big thing for me. Please, Lord, save me, forgive me my black murderous sins and the misery I have caused others but, particularly, the misery I have caused you and your Son." '

Shortly before that night an event had occurred outside the prison which might perhaps explain McClinton's emotionalism. A leading member of the Orange Order had demanded the death penalty for all terrorists, and his words had sent shock waves through the loyalist H-blocks. McClinton admits that he was shocked: it was inconceivable that someone from the major institution in his tradition should recommend capital punishment for Ulster patriots of the UDA and UVF. He had been placed in the same category as IRA captives, whom he regarded as the enemies of Ulster. The people he had believed he was defending now wanted him hanged, which presented McClinton with a stark choice: his own tribe had rejected him so where could he turn? The answer undoubtedly lay in another army, the Army of God, an even more powerful force than the UDA. The internal war that raged within him had been won by a new conviction, that the only way to escape the darkness engulfing him was through Salvation. Minutes after the 'spiritual' experience in his cell, McClinton got off his knees and decided to go public about his experience: 'I said to myself, "God's either a liar or true to his word. He will save me or not. I came down on his side. He gave me the faith to trust in Him. I wasn't really taking a chance. I had nothing to lose.' With a blanket wrapped round him, he walked to the cell door. The inmates had a rule that required anyone who wished to air their views or read a poem to announce his purpose by shouting from the cell door. Other prisoners in the block would hear him and decide whether or not they would allow him to speak. McClinton declared that he wanted a 'meeting', which meant that everyone approached their cell doors to hear what he had to say and offer their opinions. Prisoners often used meetings to deliver a verbal broadside at the prison authorities as a means of boosting morale on the block. 'I began, "Men, tonight I want to tell you that I have taken the most serious step of my life. I have committed my life to the Lord Jesus Christ. From this day forth, I renounce violence and the paramilitary way. I cease to be UFF military commander and only want to be a mere volunteer in the Army of the Living Christ. I wanted you guys who have been suffering with me all this time to be the first ones to know that." '

McClinton cleverly chose words that would lessen the shock many men must have felt at what he had said: he remained a volunteer in the ranks of an army, but an

army responsible to a higher authority. The new army
was similar in structure to the UDA: it had volunteers,
and everyone in the UDA, IRA or UVF was a volunteer
irrespective of rank.

One prisoner asked, 'What the fuck is that maniac
McClinton at now?' His question was directed at James
'Tonto' Watt, his cell-mate. Watt, a UVF bomber,
became a born-again preacher in 1995.

The public declaration had its downside, though, and
McClinton became the butt of jokes and ridicule from
inmates and prison officers alike. Young prisoners who
had previously feared him enjoyed goading him, knowing that any violent reaction would be a betrayal of his
claimed conversion. McClinton began to educate himself: he took O-levels in English language and literature,
and eventually an Open University degree in criminol-
ogy and social science. He also undertook a correspondence course with the Emmaus Bible School in Liverpool,
studied theology and started to convert fellow inmates.
His enthusiasm and commitment drew twenty-four
prisoners into his circle, among them Robert 'Basher'
Bates of the Shankill Butchers. Of that number eight fell
by the wayside.

Bates was a big catch. He was a notorious killer who
had pleaded guilty to ten murders, and may have
committed others with which he was never charged. His
trial judge described his crimes as so cruel and revolting
that they were beyond human comprehension. He told
Bates that he saw no reason, apart from terminal illness,
why he should ever be released. Less than twenty years
after he was sentenced, Bates was walking the streets of
Belfast.

McClinton maintains that he was ruthlessly tested in
his new life as a born-again Christian. 'If I had

performed miracles, there would still have been sceptics. Even after thirteen years of commitment, a prison governor told me I was only doing it to get time off my sentence. During football, young men would kick the backs of my legs – people who would previously have been frightened to be in a cell with me. Even some of my writings for my O-levels disappeared in the prison system. It was the old enemies getting their revenge.'

I was unable to verify with the IRA McClinton's claim that he called Martin Meehan, the Ardoyne Provisional, into his cell and apologised for having tried to assassinate him with a letter bomb. 'Meehan forgave me when I told him I had changed my life and regretted the attempt on his life.'

The alleged episode occurred in 1983 when McClinton knew he was under a death threat from the Provisionals. It would be conjecture to suggest that the meeting with Meehan was designed to avert it, but it remains a possibility: at that time the prison authorities were attempting to integrate those prisoners who were perceived to have detached themselves from their paramilitary associates. Segregation allowed paramilitaries to run the H-blocks with their own command structures, but the atmosphere in the prison was dangerous. Ten IRA hunger strikers had died in 1981: they had campaigned for special status as political prisoners and, like the loyalists, were opposed to the government's policy of treating them as ordinary criminals. Neither loyalists nor republicans wanted integration, knowing that it would lead to violence, a diminution of their self-styled paramilitary status, and would symbolise a victory for the prison authorities.

A previous attempt to introduce integration had led to loyalists wrecking their H-blocks but the government

had instructed the prison to try again. A unique
opportunity presented itself in the form of the Christian
Fellowship group established under McClinton's auspices. Inmates who subscribed to his born-again doctrine
lived in one block, agreeing that they would respect
each other and peacefully co-exist. But no one, including prison officers, believed that integration would lead
to anything but chaos.

McClinton was told that on a given day he would be
in the workshop with republicans. He could not
complain to the prison's loyalist command because his
religious group was creating a wing of loyalists and, if it
worked, republicans, who wished to be free of paramilitary control. A mixed wing would receive preferential
treatment from the prison authorities. Both loyalist and
republican paramilitaries saw the dangers in this: if
integration could work in one wing of the prison, it
would reinforce the argument for total integration of
the prison population, which was exactly what the
British government wanted. Officials at the Northern
Ireland Office were determined to make the Maze a
normal prison instead of one in which the paramilitary
bodies controlled their own blocks. However, someone
within the prison system, or at a political level, was
either naïve or wanted to scupper the integration
process: 'I was ordered to go to Compound 22 to work
with forty militant republicans. I told the prison
authorities that I would not be alone, the Lord would be
with me. I said that I was a prisoner and it was my duty
to respect the prison authorities.'

When he arrived, he was directed to 'a tea hut', a
holding area adjacent to the workshop. The republicans, all Provisionals, surrounded him threateningly,
and asked why he had chosen to be in their company.

He replied that he was a prisoner serving a life sentence. 'They knew my reputation, that I didn't fear them and that accorded me a particular status.' He made clear his reluctance to be with them, and said that he was only following orders from the prison governor. He told them about his conversion, and also said that as they were in the majority he was entitled to equality and respect as a minority figure. Throughout the Troubles 'equality' and 'respect' had been the demands of the Catholic population. He also revealed that he intended to use the salary he earned in the workshop to support a starving child in India. Nevertheless in the weeks following his plea for peaceful co-existence, he was ostracised by his republican workmates. On 24 March 1983, he was summoned to a meeting with a senior prison officer and told that his life was in danger. The prison governor had information that he was to be killed in the workshop by the Provisionals to prevent further integration. McClinton claims that the prison officer told him that he would be protected by prison staff.

One aspect of McClinton's account of this incident puzzles me and I have been unable to verify it. Why would a senior prison official make a prisoner aware that his life was in danger when he knew that if McClinton was killed the system would be liable for his death? McClinton had no wish to be sacrificed in the cause of integration, regardless of his religious beliefs – to this day he is understandably careful about his personal security. And why then did McClinton agree to return to the workshop? He says that it would have been against his Christian principles to refuse to do so, but it is perhaps more likely that, having established himself as a man who feared no one, who believed he was walking with a Higher Authority, he believed he could 'brave it out', that the danger was overestimated or that God would protect him.

'At ten o'clock one morning, I walked into the hut and immediately sensed danger. Steam from a small boiler used for making tea was rising to the ceiling. There was so much steam that condensation was forming on the ceiling. Believing the prison officers were behind me, I sat down, lifted a cup of tea and looked around me. Some of the republicans were armed with hammers, others with lengths of wood. I looked round and my protectors weren't there. As I reached into my pocket for a copy of the New Testament, a bucket of boiling water was poured over me from behind. It stripped the skin from my neck and back. I was beaten with a hammer and lengths of wood. I lifted one of them up by the ankles and threw him over my damaged back then ran at the rest of them, bowling them over. I ran out of that tea hut. When the boiling water was poured over me, I never felt a thing ... absolutely nothing. I knew I had been roasted. There was a large bubble of skin on the side of my face. I knew I was badly injured but I was not in pain.'

According to McClinton, five minutes after the attack he knelt down in front of twenty prison officers and prayed that God would forgive his attackers and help them to be saved. His failure to experience pain during the attack was a classic symptom of trauma though he preferred to think of it as miraculous, a word he used to describe his conversion.

What is not in doubt, and is very much to McClinton's credit, is that during the remainder of the 1980s, he gained an honours degree, expanded his Christian Fellowship, and provided inmates with legal advice.

'Raise me up some brothers in the Lord,' he prayed, and others followed his example and were saved.

Most of those who joined him were lifers, and orthodox prison chaplains were sceptical about McClinton's Fellowship, believing it a tactic to impress the Life Review Board, which examined requests for early release, and accused him of using his Fellowship to distance them from the flock.

In 1993, after sixteen years in prison, McClinton walked back into society proclaiming his conversion. He was baptised a pastor in an evangelical mission based in Texas and founded by one of the Watergate burglars. Irish society was still at war, and he blamed the continued bitterness of both communities on a 'weak-willed' British government. He quickly became a celebrity, with newspaper headlines proclaiming his conversion: 'Killer Turns Pastor' and 'A Battered Bible Led to Conversion'. His former prison governor, Bob Gibson, told journalists that McClinton had been one of the worst prisoners to enter gaol and one of the best to leave it. One of McClinton's achievements that attracted attention was the setting up of 'Higher Force Challenge', a project to present youth with alternatives to violence which also sought to encourage a dialogue between young Catholics and Protestants. No one doubted McClinton's commitment to it and the involvement of ex-loyalist prisoners in making it work.

However, he was unable to leave behind his commitment to a form of politics that placed him firmly in the camp of leading loyalists. In 1995 and 1996, events at Drumcree churchyard in Portadown presented him with a real challenge, which I believe he failed.

Drumcree was the traditional gathering place for Orangemen who walked through Portadown. Until the

beginning of the present conflict in 1969, Orangemen
were permitted to march wherever they wished. During
fifty years of Unionist rule, Catholics were forbidden to
express their cultural roots by flying an Irish tricolour
or to object to Orange marches, an expression of the
triumphalism of the Protestant community over the
Catholics. During the present conflict, traditional
Orange parades had produced civil unrest and a
deepening gulf of sectarian conflict.

In 1995 the Garvaghy Road district became a
flashpoint even though it was not a traditional Orange
route. It was a newly built Catholic estate but Orangemen considered it the best way to reach their traditional
route.

The Royal Ulster Constabulary was instructed to
prevent the Orangemen marching along Garvaghy
Road. After three days of clashes between Orangemen,
loyalists and the police, it was agreed that a contingent
of Orangemen might parade along the Garvaghy Road
but without bands or banners.

Later that summer, the RUC were strongly criticised
when they re-routed an Orange parade past the Catholic Lower Ormeau Road. The Irish government made a
protest to Westminster, and the scene was set for a more
dangerous confrontation in Portadown in July 1996. In
the context of the then ongoing peace-process negotiations, Catholics expected the authorities to take a stand
against the insistence of Orangemen to parade through
Catholic districts. But Orangemen maintained that they
were entitled to march wherever they liked.

Catholics argued that surely Orangemen should not
march where their presence would give offence: was it
not more positive in terms of community relations to
march in predominantly Protestant neighbourhoods?

Orangemen were not unaware of the conflict between
the two traditions, and the dangers of marches that
might be construed as triumphalist. In 1996 David
Trimble, leader of the Unionist Party, was in Drumcree
churchyard sporting his Orange sash. Alongside him,
and on television screens throughout the world, was the
shaven-headed figure of paramilitary Billy Wright, a
native of Portadown.

In a stand-off with police that lasted days, threats
were made behind the scenes by dangerous men, who
warned the RUC and the British government that if the
march was not permitted along the Catholic Garvaghy
Road before the morning of 12 July, there would be
bloodshed on an unprecedented scale: a hundred thousand Protestants would descend on Drumcree. There
were also warnings that loyalist elements were prepared
to take the Province to the brink of civil war.

However, the British government was not prepared to
use the Army against the Orangemen. In 1996 John
Major, prime minister in a weak government, could not
risk alienating Unionist MPs' support for his government. The RUC had been in the front line to prevent the
Orange march, but was told that, despite the opposition
of Catholic residents, a contingent of Orangemen would
be permitted, once again, to march along the Garvaghy
Road without bands or banners. Many senior RUC
figures, including the Chief Constable Sir Hugh Annes-
ley, were dismayed at this but when the decision was
made public policemen had to face the most serious
unrest in Catholic areas for a decade. The Catholic
hierarchy and the Dublin government were united in
their condemnation of Major for backing off the issue.

The events at Drumcree illustrated the historical and

religious divisions between the two communities, widened the sectarian rift, and epitomised the dispute over territory, which had led so often to tribal confrontation. They also demonstrated the need to resolve the parades issue, which threw into sharp relief the spectre of future conflict. Sanity, reason, understanding, compromise, and tolerance had been absent at Drumcree. In terms of faith, the two communities were addressing a different God and Christian principles were not in evidence.

When I talked to Kenny McClinton about Drumcree, I wanted to discover if his conversion had led him towards tolerance or understanding. He referred me to a poem he had written about Drumcree in 1995 as an expression of how he still felt in 1996, which may offer some insight into the mind of a man who professes love of Christ and, therefore, love of his fellow man.

THE SIEGE OF DRUMCREE

There are stirring tales told
Of strong hearts, brave and bold;
Of the Orange and Blue;
And King William so true –
How our forefather fought to be free.

But a latterday cry
Is now filling the sky,
Throughout city and town one can see
A new spirit abroad,
Giving glory to God –
It's Drumcree, Drumcree, Drumcree!

On the ninth of July
In the year 'ninety-five,
To a churchyard near proud Portadown;
A traditional march

Of the old Orange sash,
To its church made green nationalists frown.

Then Sinn Fein, backed by Rome,
Rudely blocked the route home,
In rebellious, illegal intent.
Orange culture was banned,
At Garvaghy's demand
While the laws of the land were all bent!

Like storm troopers in dress,
Policemen turned to oppress
Peaceful marchers who'd just been at prayer.
Christian men looked quite dazed,
When police batons were raised,
Like an unspoken threat in the air.

RUC, RUC,
Oh, your shame at Drumcree!
As political puppets employed!
By oppressing your own,
Like a dog with a bone –
With your own heritage you have toyed.

What e'er will you say
To your children one day,
When they ask, 'Daddy, why are we slaves?'
While in Ulster's fair land
Chains bound the Red Hand
That protected faith from Papal knaves!

Then in Old Portadown
Rallied men of renown,
To support the old sash at Drumcree.
Led by bold Billy Wright,
'Twas a heart-warming sight
As they challenged the crass RUC.

Police resources were drained
As, by dozens they came,
To confront Billy's brave gallant group.
In a bid to contain
The protest at Corcraine,
Policemen rushed to the town and were duped.*

RUC, RUC,
Lines were stretched at Drumcree
Till in chaos, they buckled and broke –
And big Paisley broke through,
With the Orange and Blue –
Ulster hearts shall not ever stay yoked.

Down Garvaghy Road they came,
Putting Jesuits to shame,
Yet devoid of the old Orange flute!
Till, from up the town, near
Came 'The Sash' loud and clear;
Played by Protestant men of repute.

The images of bitterness and the language of tribalism
are starkly evident. The references to 'Papal knaves' and
Jesuits, and the identification of Catholics with a threat
to the Protestant faith were the old rallying cries of
loyalist bigots. The poem shows that McClinton's Army
of God was imbued with a rhetoric which strongly
resembles that of the paramilitary organisation he left.

McClinton has become a leading figure in the Ulster
Independence Movement, and has issued papers on the
nature of citizenship, the need for a tougher line against
what he has dubbed 'Fenian rebels' and the right of

* A reference to a tactic to draw policemen from Drumcree by creating a
false situation elsewhere.

loyalists to bear arms if the British government failed to put down the nationalist rebellion. In the autumn of 1996 he presented me with a political tract he had written. It read:

> These rebels, encouraged by British Government neutrality, are seeking to wreck the Protestant Orange culture by violently disrupting lawful Protestant marches. They detest the Protestant Bible-based faith.

McClinton was defining a religious war very much in hardline loyalist terms, using language that reinforced the tribalism, division, fear and superstition which have led so many young men into a life of violence.

In one document on citizenship, he showed no recognition that two cultures existed in Northern Ireland and that their separateness in peaceful co-existence could produce a cross-fertilisation which would lead to a society of peace and equality. His advice to his followers was that Catholics should only be entitled to citizenship in his Ulster if they gave due respect to the Union Jack and 'time-honoured traditions'.

'Whose traditions?' I wondered.

The answer appeared to be Protestant traditions. Concepts such as 'compassion', 'understanding', 'love of one's neighbour' did not spring from the pages of his tracts.

I had been intrigued by a remark McClinton had made to me, that during his imprisonment he had received regular visits from detectives seeking to clear their files of outstanding crimes. He told me that he had admitted to a score of other crimes that did not surface at his trial and which the prosecution had agreed to wipe 'off the books' because he was serving a life sentence. 'They got no information from me except the fact that I did X, Y, Z. I was not going to be a Judas Iscariot because he is the most despised person in the scriptures. I still had that high moral code that I would not be an informer, ever.'

Pastor McClinton, the Christian, was comparing the betrayal of Jesus Christ with that of terrorists, possibly murderers. And the 'high moral code' related to a life McClinton had forsaken, yet he talked about it as though it was still part of his philosophy of life. It reminded me of that apparent contradiction between McClinton's acknowledgement that he had committed the 'most heinous' crimes but never 'the grossest'.

He went on: 'I received word from the Crown Prosecution Service that my back trail was cleared and no other charges could be brought against me. I didn't understand that at the time God was leading me to make these confessions ... things I was never suspected of. All the skeletons were pulled out of the cupboard, looked at and treated. It cleared the police books.'

McClinton was told by the detectives that if he admitted any crimes he had committed, no charges would be preferred on his release from prison. So self-interest may have had more to do with his confession than God. And who can say that it was a full confession? Perhaps he mentioned only the crimes of which he believed there might be evidence lying in the shadows, and he compromised no one else.

I decided to talk to a detective who had been central to police investigations of that period, and asked him to look at the files on McClinton's 1977 interrogation. I received the following information.

'During his interrogation he was sullen and uncommunicative. Late on the second day, he admitted the murders of the bus driver and Carville. When describing the shooting of Bradshaw, the bus driver, he referred us to a famous piece of news footage taken during the Vietnam war. It showed a South Vietnamese officer shooting a member of the Vietcong through the head. We all remembered it and how graphic it was as blood spurted into the air. McClinton told us that was just what it was like ... he saw it all in slow motion.'

I returned to McClinton's version of the interrogation, in which he had portrayed himself as the hardened terrorist who had held out for a week, and only unburdened himself then in response to God's answer to his prayers. I put that to the detective.

'If McClinton is telling you that he told us nothing for one week because he was taking it on the chin, he is lying through his teeth, and the record confirms that. In the Bradshaw killing he acted alone so there was no accomplice to protect. As for the Carville murder, we had already convicted his accomplice, "Hacksaw" McCaw. He wasn't protecting him. The guy was in prison. He's been feeding you a line to depict himself as the tough guy who wouldn't inform on his buddies ... Bullshit.'

So why had McClinton failed to mention his accomplice in the Carville shooting? It was in the court record, and surely he knew I would discover that. Like McClinton, McCaw pleaded not guilty to Carville's murder, but was declared guilty and sentenced to life imprisonment. He reappeared in court at McClinton's trial, determined to take the rap for the Carville killing. As a witness for the defence, he told Mr Justice O'Donnell that he, not McClinton, had fired the fatal bullets into Carville. His presence in the court and his dishonesty showed the extent to which McClinton was

prepared to go to escape justice: this was a killer who
wanted to get back on to the streets and it did not sit
well with his statements to me that he was glad God
had taken him out of circulation and that he was
prepared to face up to his crimes. It was clear that the
reason he had never mentioned to me McCaw's role in
the killing or in the trial was that it did not fit with his
self-drawn profile of a man who had faced up to his
crimes.

When I told a policeman who had been present at
McClinton's interrogation of McClinton's having
'taken a team' to kill Carville and how he had not been
able to bring himself to kill the boy, I was told: 'When
terrorists talk about a team, they're usually referring to
a unit of anything from three or four men. The Carville
killing was a two-man job and it didn't take much
planning. They knew that any car emerging from Flax
Street would be driven by a Catholic because it was
coming from the Catholic Ardoyne. Cambrai Street was
a through route for many people travelling to Catholic
West Belfast. Sam "Hacksaw" McCaw was the look-
out in another car. McClinton was standing in Cambrai
Street near a road ramp that slowed cars. When
Hacksaw saw a car leave Flax Street, he knew they had
a potential target. He followed the car and flashed his
lights to let McClinton know that the car in front
contained a Catholic. McClinton ran forward and shot
the driver at point-blank range. It happened so quickly
that he didn't have time to make any decision about the
kid. If he's telling you that he pondered on whether he
should shoot the kid, that's contrary to the evidence. It
was a crude sectarian killing.'

Neither did McClinton resolve satisfactorily his role
as a terrorist between 1972 and 1977. The crimes

attributed to him had been perpetrated in 1977, which left a considerable period during which it is likely that he was not inactive. The police interrogator provided one explanation. 'Until we arrested him, he was unknown to us. We reached the conclusion that until the killings in 1977, he was a loner, a drop-out. There was no evidence of him frequenting bars or illegal drinking dens in the Shankill. When we arrested him he was living in Rosapenna, a mixed neighbourhood between Cliftonville and Oldpark.'

I suggested that the absence of his name in police files was insufficient proof to claim that he had not been a seasoned killer before 1977.

'Yes, but there is something of which you may not be aware,' the policeman responded. 'McClinton was handed to us on a plate. If McClinton had been involved in other crimes, we would have been told.'

(The informant to whom the policeman referred was, of course, James 'Pratt' Craig.)

'Why,' I asked, 'did your informant not tell you about eighteen other serious crimes McClinton admitted to while in prison which were wiped off the books?'

The policeman looked puzzled. 'If anything was wiped off the books it related to minor offences such as burglaries.'

I had anticipated that. Unknown to him, I had gained access to a 1983 Crown Prosecution file, which confirmed that McClinton had confessed to eighteen other offences and they had been struck from his record. The matter was not for public consumption and the offences could not have been described as 'minor'. Eight related to sending bombs through the post, another was classed as attempted murder. One of the explosives offences contained details about the interception in a postal depot of a bomb addressed to Martin Meehan, the Provisional to whom McClinton had said he had apologised. Other crimes included an explosion at Mackie's engineering firm, and a bomb placed outside a bar. The file also contained details of an attempted murder of a Catholic, who was not injured, and who refused to make a complaint. Other offences included hijackings and the burning of public transport.

Attached to the Crown Prosecution file was a note from the detectives who had talked to McClinton in prison. It advised that McClinton's involvement in the crimes was never fully explored and his admissions of guilt contained inconsistencies only to be expected years after the events had taken place. But McClinton's 1983 revelations referred only to other crimes committed in 1977. There was nothing about his whereabouts or activities between 1972 and 1977. The file appeared to confirm his claim that he was an active terrorist in 1977, and contradicted the police interrogator's view that he was a loner, guilty of two murders and of assisting in the burial of a murder victim.

Yet the file pointed to a discrepancy in McClinton's account of the bombs he had made before he was arrested. He had told me they were constructed from plastic explosives – and as he was an expert, from his UDR training, he would have known what he was talking about. Police forensic staff had examined one bomb, a device intercepted in a post office. The parcel was labelled with the name of a bogus publishing company, and contained a hollowed-out book, as McClinton had described to me. The forensic analysis confirmed that the bomb was constructed from two sticks of Penobel, an ICI commercial explosive used for mining and made of nitro-glycerine and otherwise

known as gelignite. No one with any experience in
bomb-making would confuse nitro-glycerine sticks and
plastic and, in fact, the IRA were the only grouping to
have access to plastic explosives such as Semtex. In
1977, the UVF bomb expert James 'Tonto' Watt was in
gaol, and his speciality had been to use gelignite in metal
pipes – which became known as pipe bombs – or to
construct devices from metal beer kegs. 'Tonto' Watt
was arrested in the same month as McClinton and given
nine separate life sentences.

I wondered if it was possible that McClinton had
agreed to have someone else's offences struck from the
books. My police source told me, 'McClinton told you
he was in the UDR. Well, there's no record of that.
However, I'd have to say that could be explained by the
fact that people joined, attended one or two sessions
and never returned. Their names were struck from the
files. A lot of UDR files of that period have been
destroyed. As far as the 1983 business is concerned
McClinton offered to admit to eighteen crimes which
could never be tagged to him. In doing so he demanded
a deal and was also showing what a good boy he was to
the authorities. Don't think for a single minute that the
McClinton we knew didn't plan to get himself early
release. Inside, there are guys who'll also take the rap
for somebody else. Who is to say he made bombs? He
was in prison with guys who discuss their whole history
– in writing you call it plagiarism. Once the crimes he
admitted to were out of the way, nobody could be
charged with them. The matter was handled by the DPP
[Director of Public Prosecutions] and not by the RUC.'

Despite Kenny McClinton's past, I found him a charming, thoughtful, personable individual, and the steel

bars on his front door testified to fear of assassination
by republicans. The 'born-again' Kenny McClinton is
preferable to the murderer but he has not rid himself of
the sectarian values that have caused so much death and
destruction on both sides. His God is not a God of
tolerance, compassion and understanding. And after
nineteen years, Sheila Bradshaw still weeps for the loss
of her husband who was killed for doing his job, for
providing a public service in difficult circumstances.

When this book was being written, Robert 'Basher'
Bates was shot dead in the Shankill, where he had killed
some of his victims in the 1970s. He was dispatched
with the ferocity that had characterised his life as a
terrorist: several bullets were fired into him at close
range. Within hours of the killing the IRA was accused
of his murder, and loyalist commentators warned that
their ceasefire was in danger of collapsing. Within
twenty-four hours the RUC pointed out that it had an
open mind about the killing and believed that republicans had not been involved. The IRA and INLA denied
shooting Bates. A police source told me that detectives
believed it had been a revenge killing by a Protestant.
Bates had been a leading member of the Shankill
Butchers, and their orgy of killing also included Protestant victims. Some were murdered in feuds between the
Butchers and another UVF gang who threatened the
supremacy of the Butchers in the Shankill area. In the
wake of Bates's murder, much was made of his
conversion, and little of his history as a vicious killer.
While it was right to applaud his conversion, perhaps
media representatives should also have reflected on the
nature of his crimes and the plight of the families of his
victims.

WALKING WITH CHRIST?

Many of the paramilitaries I met, loyalist and republican, were intelligent, well educated, and thoughtful. To anyone who did not know of their role as killers they would have appeared normal people with normal preoccupations, problems and ambitions. However, their obsessiveness, single-mindedness, lack of moral fibre and genuine compassion for their fellow man sets them apart from the rest of society.

What constitutes a terrorist? What are the elements in society and within the individual that provide the dynamics for violence and place human life at risk?

In the autumn of 1996, I was driven to Portadown to meet Billy Wright, a loyalist paramilitary whose youthful features, shaven head and tattoos had dominated television screens throughout the world during that summer. With the Unionist leader, David Trimble, he had faced the barbed wire of a police cordon that ringed the edge of Drumcree churchyard to prevent Orangemen marching through a nearby Catholic district. Trimble was condemned by nationalist politicians and church leaders for being seen with a notorious loyalist such as Billy Wright, but he was just one of many who recognised that Wright was pivotal to events.

Wright's story epitomises the character of politics, terrorism and religious fundamentalism in his tribe and presents interesting parallels with his enemy, the IRA. Born in Wolverhampton in 1960, Wright spent the first four years of his life in England. His parents were from the Northern Ireland Presbyterian tradition and went to England to escape discrimination from fellow Protestants. Their problems had begun when Billy Wright's grandfather stood as an Independent Unionist candidate and defeated the local Unionist MP. That was in the 1950s, when no one within the Protestant community would have dared confront the monolith of the Unionist Party. Wright told me his grandfather believed that the Unionist Party was rotten to the core and that he disagreed with discrimination policies aimed at Catholics. The family was well known in the Northern Ireland political arena: Wright's great-grandfather had once been Royal Commissioner.

After four years in England, Wright's parents believed they were free to return to Ulster, bought two shops and settled into a peaceful life. They lived in the mainly Protestant village of Mount Norris in South Armagh near the Border. Wright remembered considerable interaction with Catholics in the nearby village of Whitecross. He said that the Protestant tradition of Sunday closing forced him to visit a shop in Whitecross, and that he often played Gaelic football there. He claimed that Catholics sometimes attended dances in the Orange Hall in his village. He painted a rosy portrait of his youth and it is possible that when he was a child there was more contact at that level between the two communities.

However, during the 1960s, the tense atmosphere in the Province, the civil-rights marches, sectarian clashes and finally, in August 1969, the bloodshed and arrival of British troops, dominated conversation in Wright's household, and his role models were the men in balaclavas manning barricades or parading under the banners of paramilitary bodies such as the UVF and the UDA. His route to membership of the UVF was similar to that of a young republican entering the IRA. He 'offered himself' to the Young Citizens Volunteer Force, a youth wing of the UVF, active in 1974–5. A police constable told a court in February 1975 that the YCVF was set up with the sole purpose of killing Catholics and was heavily involved in petrol-bombing Catholic homes. It was controlled by the UVF and, in structure, resembled the IRA's youth wing, Fianna Eireann. Wright said that after he applied for membership, he was required to wait six weeks while the UVF examined his family background.

At the initiation ceremony he was not pressured to join, was offered the opportunity to reverse his decision, but agreed to take an oath on a Bible with the Ulster Constitution flag held above him. He admits that part of the attraction was the glamour surrounding the UVF in his community and he was impressed by 'ordinary working-class men' who were heroes. Like his IRA counterparts, he was quickly trained for terrorism: 'There were training sessions and volunteers in Mid-Ulster where I lived. We were taken away and trained in the use of weapons and explosives. We were taught that the emotional fear within the human being emanates from the stomach, and one can actually feel fear. However, if one sits and says, "I'm frightened", and then tackles that consciously, quite rapidly you can overcome your fear ... the fear of death or whatever. I firmly believe I'm immune ... it doesn't affect me.' I

knew Billy Wright's reputation and that, coupled with
the quiet, assured, deliberate way in which he talked,
left me in no doubt that he spoke the truth.

He told me that the deaths of leading UVF members
Horace Boyle and Wesley Sommerville had propelled
him into terrorism. As Wright's role models, it is
important to understand the character of the two dead
men and what they represented which so influenced the
fifteen-year-old boy.

In the early hours of 31 July 1975 Boyle and
Sommerville led a UVF unit to the main Belfast–Dublin
road at a point between the towns of Banbridge and
Loughbrickland. They were not only terrorists: like
many other loyalist paramilitaries in the 1970s and
1980s, they were also part-time members of the UDR.
On that fateful night, the UVF unit was dressed in UDR
uniforms and their objective was to set up a roadblock –
a common UDR strategy at that time, intended to
monitor the movements of terrorist suspects. That
night, the intention of the UVF unit was to stop a van
containing musicians bound for Dublin, and conceal a
bomb in it so that it would explode in the Irish Republic
several hours later. The musicians were members of the
Miami Showband, one of Ireland's best-known bands
with a string of best-selling albums. That night they
were playing a gig in the mainly Protestant town of
Banbridge. Like musicians the world over, they had no
interest in politics and were prepared to travel anywhere
in the troubled Province irrespective of the religious
character of an audience.

The band's minibus was flagged down by the bogus
UDR patrol, and the musicians were lined up against
the side of the vehicle. As Boyle and Sommerville
attempted to lay the bomb, it exploded killing both of

them. One of the musicians, Des McAlea, later testified that before the explosion Boyle, who was the terrorist leader, had been angry with his men because two joked with the musicians about the success of that night's gig. The musicians were told to place their hands over their heads when they were first taken from the vehicle and made to face a ditch. Stephen Travers, a guitarist, who had joined the band six weeks earlier, heard the explosion, felt a searing heat and was flung into the ditch. There was machine-gun fire and someone said, 'C'mon, those bastards are dead. I got them with dumdums.' Indeed, Travers had been hit by several bullets, one of which had been a dum that exploded inside him, but he and McAlea, the band's saxophonist, survived. With Boyle and Sommerville dead, the other UVF gunmen shot the musicians, killing three. The band's lead singer, Francis 'Fran' O'Toole, was struck by twenty bullets, and forensic evidence confirmed that he had been shot as he lay on the ground, face upwards. He was a handsome, talented young man with a huge female following.

Police found the bodies of Boyle and Sommerville a short distance from the van, each blown in two. Nearby lay an arm with the tattooed inscription 'UVF Portadown'.

The UVF issued a statement claiming that the bomb had already been on the minibus and that its unit was acting as a defensive patrol. The lie was intended to offset the public condemnation that the UVF knew would follow the bungled operation: had the bomb exploded while the band was either on the road to Dublin or in the Irish capital, the UVF would have been able to claim that the band had been carrying explosives, but police files on Sommerville confirmed that he

was suspected of a vicious attack on a Catholic housing
estate the previous year.

Six terrorists were in the UVF unit that night, of
whom two died, two were brought months later to
justice, and two were never caught. It was a hideous
crime and its effects were felt sharply by young people
and musicians, who realised then that no one was safe.
It was 'the day the music died'. Nevertheless, the deaths
of two of the murderers by their own hands had
provided the impetus for Billy Wright's entry into the
UVF. Any terrorist in death provokes a form of hero-
worship in those young men susceptible to the distorted
allure of violence in protection of their own community
and its prejudices.

However, when Wright joined in 1975, it was being
led by men who were trying to change its political
direction. Like the Provisionals, they favoured the twin-
track approach of politics and violence and politically
there were interesting developments. In 1974, the UVF
created the Volunteer Political Party, whose chairman,
Ken Gibson, contested the West Belfast seat in a
Westminster general election, but polled only 2,690
votes. The VPP supported the link with Britain and
warned that a united Ireland or an independent Ulster,
favoured by some loyalists, would result in higher taxes
and swingeing cuts in social-security benefits. The
reason for the change in character of the UVF was a
developing prison culture and the influence of Gusty
Spence, the UVF icon imprisoned for life in 1966 for
killing Catholic barman Peter Ward. Like IRA men of
the 1950s, in prison Spence's political views took a
leftward shift, as a consequence of self-education,
exposure to political works and dialogue with republican socialist prisoners. When young UVF men arrived in

the Long Kesh internment camp in the early 1970s, they
came under the political influence of Spence, then the
UVF brigade commander. He stressed the importance of
developing a socialist policy, and on their release, his
political converts imposed his thoughts on the Belfast
leadership. However, socialist concepts did not sit easily
with loyalism, and in 1975, the brigade staff of the UVF
was overthrown and the organisation returned to its
former ultra-right-wing convictions. (Ironically, one of
those who led the 1975 coup returned to UVF politics in
the 1990s, was prominent in the peace process and,
according to Wright, 'embraced the godless socialism'
he had rejected twenty years earlier.)

Wright's paramilitary career was short-lived, and in
1977, aged seventeen, he was arrested and charged with
possessing weapons and hijacking a van. He received a
six-year prison term and was released on parole in
1980. Within months, he was rearrested, on the
evidence of UVF supergrass Clifford McKeown,
charged with murder and held in custody. At that time,
the authorities used the remand process to take dangerous paramilitaries out of circulation. Frequently, people
were charged with offences that were dropped after
several years but the strategy enabled the security forces
to deprive terrorist organisations of some of their best
operators. While Wright was awaiting trial, he began to
read the Bible: 'After serving four years of the six-year
sentence, I was out only a couple of months when I was
lifted and charged with murder, attempted murder, five
conspiracies to murder and possession of explosives. In
my cell I started t' study Christianity, more out of
boredom. However, that deep respect for God and for
Christ was always there. I studied it but I made no

commitment to it. The charges against me were dropped, I was released in 1982 and rearrested months later
charged with possession of weapons with intent. My co-
accused told me in prison that there had been an
ambush by the SAS and they believed that I was present
at the place of the ambush and there was over four
hundred rounds fired. He said that the British Army had
been trying t' murder me. An active service unit of the
Ulster Volunteer Force had been apprehended while
picking up an arms dump. The SAS opened up, firing
over four hundred rounds. One volunteer escaped and I
was accused of being that volunteer. I was arrested in
Portadown, spent fourteen months in custody and was
found not guilty. My co-accused said that at the time of
the ambush, the SAS soldiers were heard to say: "That's
that bastard, Wright." They were coming up and just
riddling the hedges. The Army later stated that they
believed I was that person. During all my periods in
gaol, my time was spent studying for O-levels and A-
levels and reading. I always felt I didn't want t' waste
my time and I started t' study the scriptures and seek
explanations and answers I needed to the direction of
my life. I made no commitment to Christianity. I
wanted to avoid that because I'd heard so many times of
people that would have made a commitment and the
perception was that these people wanted a reduced
sentence. I felt I couldn't do that.'

Several months after his release in 1983, he decided
that it was possible to 'live quietly through Christ', and
chose to do so, knowing that he would be morally
obliged to abandon terrorism. He was apprehensive
about undertaking a lifestyle that would require a
rigorous commitment to Christian principles, and a way
of life alien to him, but to his surprise, he experienced

little difficulty in putting aside a life of violence –
though politics was something he felt he could not
escape. 'Such was the depth of my belief,' he said, 'a
belief in my country and the people, I found it very
difficult to disassociate myself from my emotional
feelings towards Northern Ireland and its people. That
was later to be my downfall in walking with Christ.'

The 'downfall' came after he had spent eighteen
months preaching the gospel and, to the astonishment
of his enemies, appearing publicly on religious platforms, seemingly unconcerned about the threats to his
life from republicans. The catalyst that returned him to
a paramilitary lifestyle was the Anglo-Irish Agreement
of November 1985, made between the Dublin and
London governments. It was the most far-reaching
political arrangement between them for sixty years and
sought to create closer co-operation between the two
governments in finding a solution to the problems of
Northern Ireland. A radical dimension was the setting
up of a joint ministerial body with a secretariat, based
at Maryfield on the outskirts of Belfast, given responsibility to monitor issues central to the concerns of
nationalists. Unionists saw the role of the Irish Republic
as a betrayal, and the beginning of a policy that would
lead to a united Ireland.

The overwhelming majority of Protestants were
opposed to the Agreement, and young men like Billy
Wright regarded it as a call to arms. In describing his
feelings at that time, he compared himself to an 'ex-
alcoholic trying to live in a bar'.

'I was emotionally torn in two. The British government betrayed our people, and our community had been
rewarded with an act of treachery. I was gutted. It
created bitterness in my heart and I knew that was a

contradiction in relation to trying to live the Christian life.'

However, I wondered if the Anglo-Irish Agreement merely provided an excuse for someone who could not live with constitutional politics to turn to violence. His reply confirmed my doubt.

'I had never seen the benefit of constitutional politics from within Unionism. I'd always realised that Irish nationalist politics were aggressive, and through that process gained ground, and if I was to be involved in politics, in a sense it would be from a paramilitary prospectus. There's absolutely no way one could walk with Christ and align oneself to paramilitary activity.'

I was struck by Wright's directness, his reluctance to shirk difficult questions, the answers to which defined him as a paramilitary. He is still, in any case, a member of the UVF.

In the mid to late 1980s, his home in Portadown was constantly raided by police and the Army. He was questioned about killings in Mid-Ulster, and was a target of IRA and INLA (Irish National Liberation Army, see pp. 280–1) assassins. He was forced to close a grocery shop he owned in Portadown and the *Sunday World* newspaper nicknamed him 'King Rat'. He said that that label, the threats to his life and the police raids on his home resulted in the breakup of his marriage, though he remains friendly with his ex-wife, whom he described as a good Christian. He alleged that he was told by the late Westminster MP Harold McCusker that the security forces had him on a target list in 1982 during the period when the RUC is supposed to have had the shoot-to-kill policy, which resulted in the deaths of a number of IRA activists. He talked openly about his views on politics and God, but was not prepared to provide details about his paramilitary career since 1986.

I was intrigued by his references to God, the way in which he defined his views on politics, terrorism and religion in his community, and his perception of his enemy. It was the first time I had encountered such a lucid explanation. Here is a transcript of parts of my interview with him.

Q. Is this a religious war?

A. I certainly believe religion is part of the equation. I don't think you can leave religion out of it.

Q. How would you define the religious dimension to the conflict?

A. I firmly believe that if you are born into the Protestant faith, and you practise that faith, you will stand by the State and obey the laws of the State. If you're brought up in the Catholic faith, you'll lean towards Irish nationalism even though that will contravene some of the teachings of the scriptures by going against the State. You can't leave faith out of the equation.

Q. The slogan which is constantly an element of the Protestant tradition is 'For God and Ulster'. What do you take that to mean?

A. You've got to go back to 1912 when we opposed Home Rule for Ireland. There was a religious explosion within the Protestant faith in Ireland. People were saved in their hundreds and their thousands and the political situation at that time of the Home Rule Bill was very tense. Protestants in those days – and indeed today – felt that their very existence was under threat and if they were to take up arms to defend their homeland, they felt they were defending their faith also. They felt that the Roman Catholic Church or its people would take over Ireland in its totality, that the faith of the Protestant people would no longer exist. It's about a defence of the faith, the culture and the politics.

Q. Are you saying there is moral justification for the use of violence?

A. In our own faith we were brought up to believe there was war in heaven and that where our being is to be eroded, or where truth, which is salvation through the Cross, should be denied, we believe that we have the right to fight, to defend and to die for what we believe is Truth. Should that Truth disappear, then in our opinion, it will lead to the losing of the souls of our people and other people.

Q. Are you arguing that terrorism is justified?

A. There's no doubt that within every terrorist, he justifies it morally within his own mind. He would probably feel that he is the victim. He would justify it from that point of view. I've seen an erosion of the Protestant way of life in Northern Ireland. We do feel that we have nowhere else to go. We do feel that the uniqueness within us as human beings is being attacked. We see the ecumenical movement, we see it in the parades issue, we see by and large the British government shifting its position. We feel – in every avenue of our life, in what makes a Unionist what he is – all the strands are being attacked and eroded. We feel that uniqueness within us will no longer exist within the next generation or next two generations.

Q. How far would events have to slide before Northern Ireland was engulfed in civil war?

A. The Protestant community breaks distinctively into

two: there are those who would align themselves to Protestant fundamentalism and they are potent, but when it comes to violence, you will not see those people become involved in violence unless they believe the British government is no longer their government. Should they set up a provisional government and that provisional government declares the right to fight, then I have absolutely no doubt those people will go to war. I see that happening if a united Ireland became inevitable against the wishes of the people. Within the secondary category – the ordinary Protestant, not the saved or fundamentalist type – I see no difficulty coming to terms with violence, with armed struggle to defend the homeland. Those type of people don't struggle with the use of violence. Within the Protestant community, the justification for the use of war rests on the shoulders of the Dublin government and the IRA.

Q. Does that also apply to the present leadership of the UVF and its political arm, the Progressive Unionist Party, which is involved in the peace process? They issued a *fatwa* against you last autumn and it was only lifted after the intervention of Unionist politicians.

A. I wouldn't define them as loyalists. They may have emanated from within loyalism but they are no longer loyalists. They are in a prominent political position within the movement and are controlling it. They see socialism as being able to interact with Irish nationalism and that's the way to pacify nationalists and I think they're wrong in that.

Q. Are you implying that they are taking God out of the equation?

A. Absolutely. My understanding is that some of them are atheists. It defies logic as to how they were able to take over the movement. I would say they are a tiny, tiny minority.

Q. Could we return to this question of the moral justification of violence? You said you couldn't walk with Christ and be a paramilitary. If that is so, how can you seek to offer a moral justification for terrorism?

A. Well, first of all paramilitary activity is illegal and against the State. Then it's against the scriptures. One couldn't combine the two but if one steps outside and declares one's interest in humanity and society, as far as humans go, I still believe there is a moral justification for a struggle from within Unionism to defend what is theirs.

Q. There are variables in there which I need to grasp. I am confused about your need to walk away from Christ, particularly when you seem to believe that violence is morally compatible with scriptural teaching.

A. Such was the depth of my feeling about our own people and Northern Ireland that I was prepared, in a sense, to lose the faith and perhaps my soul for what I believed in. It's hard to understand that a person can love their country and their people so much that whatever happens to them individually, it doesn't really matter.

Q. When you talk about losing your soul, you are implying that your actions as a paramilitary are against the laws of God and your soul is consequently endangered.

A. The scriptures teach us that anyone who doesn't fully commit themselves to Christ, that their soul is lost. Having learned that, and then to walk in the opposite direction, it holds very serious consequences for any human being. If you are committed to Christ you will seek the greater goal and not be a paramilitary, and the greater goal will be to work actively for the glory of God.

Q. Are you saying that people within the paramilitaries are godless?

A. I would have to say that's correct.

Q. You understand that when I use the term godless, I am not saying they are satanic?

A. Yes. I would have to say they are godless. I would define such people more as loyalists than as Protestants.

Q. Help me understand that distinction.

A. It has been my experience that very few from within the Protestant paramilitaries practise the faith and have little knowledge of it.

Q. Yet they will defend God and Ulster.

A. There are two types of Protestant. There are those even within the Orange Institution, which defines itself in two ways. There are those who hold fervently to the faith, faith would be of paramount importance, more important than the land, and then there would be those for whom the land holds pre-eminence. I would say loyalists would care more about their country and their people than their God, than their faith. I think we're seeing that in the leadership of the Progressive Unionist Party.

Q. How do you feel about the way you are portrayed, with the label 'King Rat' and the death threat from the UVF leadership? [The leading paramilitary organisation regarded Wright as a threat because he was voicing violent sentiments while they were engaged with the peace process. They saw him as an inflammatory ingredient which could create imbalance in their own ranks, with some of their own followers drawn to his fiery politics.]

A.   I've learned to cope with that. I'm not a politician. I've been thrust into the limelight by the actions of others. I come from a community which has suffered greatly, not just at the hands of the IRA but at the hands of the sovereign government. Being a Unionist and a Protestant in Northern Ireland is to live a life of uncertainty. I don't seek power or fame. I seek peace but it must be on democratic terms. I want my children and other people's children to know where they are going to be in the future.

Q.   You lead a life under threat. It is said you constantly move house. How do you cope with that?

A.   Contrary to what the *Sunday World* says, I don't move house. My life has been under threat since I was twenty years of age.

Q.   As I understand it, your life has been under threat from the IRA, INLA and elements within the UVF. Should British intelligence be included in that list?

A.   Absolutely ... British intelligence. I'm immune to fear.

Q.   When you joined the UVF, and in the intervening period, loyalist paramilitaries have in the majority of cases killed and tortured innocent Catholics. Why was there such a policy?

A.   There is no doubt that the mindset within the working-class Protestant community was that the trouble was coming from Catholics and, initially, you were fighting the hidden army, who were the

IRA. What did they look like? Had they three arms
and four legs? There's absolutely no doubt that the
venom that followed from within Unionism was
taken out on ordinary Roman Catholic people. It
was only towards the end of the war [here he
appears to suggest that the war ended with the
loyalist ceasefire, yet there were examples of loyalist violence from the start of that ceasefire in 1995
into 1997] when by and large the UVF were
identifying their targets and attacking the Republican movement. Before that, loyalist violence was
sectarian. But then again, the Protestant community felt the Catholic community could not be
trusted and any member of it was the enemy.

Q. Was there a loyalist paramilitary policy in the
seventies of terrorising the Catholic community to
get them to give up the IRA or reject them?

A. The decisions that were taken at the highest level in
relation to activity in those days would, I imagine,
have been to create internal pressure in the Catholic community, bringing home to them what was
being done in their name to the Protestant community but it didn't work.

Q. Could I ask you to address the issue of Orange
parades? People in Britain think the whole thing is
crazy.

A. What people have to understand in relation to
Orangeism is the depth at which it goes into our
community. You have to understand that for a
parade, any parade, to take place, that if you go
into that community you will find that every week
for perhaps six or seven months there will be band
practice and that will be the focal point for perhaps
fifty men, meetings, perhaps a pint of beer after the

meetings. A large section of communal life is
directed towards that and manifests itself in
parades.

I asked him to consider the attitude of Catholics, who
believed that Orange parades were offensive, an example of Protestant triumphalism. I suggested that it was
undemocratic to march through Catholic neighbourhoods simply because it was a tradition permitted by
successive Unionist governments because Catholics
were not allowed to object. Perhaps Protestants should
parade in their own districts and not where their
presence was considered a threat to civil order. When
Orange bands played songs that attacked Catholic
beliefs, it was hardly the basis for good community
relations. But Wright preferred to talk about the history
of the July parades in Portadown and, particularly, the
events of the summer of 1986, following the signing of
the Anglo-Irish Agreement. He pointed out validly that
the British government that year, under pressure from
Dublin, had decided to prevent an Orange parade from
passing through the Catholic Obin Street area. The
RUC were in the front line when rioting broke out, and
it was then that Billy Wright had forsaken his preaching
for paramilitarism.

A.   The Protestants of County Armagh, the Protestants
     of Portadown have overcome so much … There's
     so much depth to their suffering that they'll never
     give up. You can go back to 1641. Of all the issues
     which typify us, of all the issues within the
     Northern Irish sphere, the parades issue is the most
     important. It is the faith combined with the culture.
     There was a hidden agenda and it's not surprising

that ten years later, after the confrontation in
1986, that Drumcree in Portadown became such a
major event. Had that parade not gone through, I
can assure you that Orangemen, ordinary Protestants, would have died at Drumcree. In my belief
they would have turned out a hundred thousand
men and the chief constable of the RUC knew that.
The leadership of the loyalists [a clear reference to
the political leadership of the UVF and UDA] were
so out of step because they'd left the faith.

Q. Are you saying that the leadership of the UVF, the
political leadership, were not willing to take on the
Drumcree issue?

A. That's correct. They had set aside the faith because
of their socialist philosophy. They had set aside the
culture and if you take out of the equation the faith
and culture and hold only to politics, then you are
no longer a loyalist.

Q. People will look at the Progressive Unionist Party,
which is involved in the peace process, and in the
Stormont Forum, and say that that is a major part
of the UVF political thinking.

A. Most of the significant loyalists of Northern Ireland have distanced themselves from the beliefs of
the PUP. There is a self-belief on the Shankill Road
in Belfast that they should dominate Northern
Ireland. I think it's fair to say from the last two
years that the heartland of Ulster, the land of
resistance, is Mid-Ulster and Portadown, not the
Shankill Road. Shankill dominance ... those days
are over.

Q. Is there room for compromise in Northern Ireland?

A. I feel there is a decision which has been taken that
the Irish culture will dominate, that Orangeism is

not a culture, it is wrong, it is ugly. It is not wrong to seek peace, at some point in the future to compromise. One thing I studied was the history of Protestantism in Europe, and you will find that where the Protestants feel victimised to the point that their life is being eroded, whether it was in France or Spain, there is an explosion of violence. If this continues and the people are disregarded then you will not have peace in Northern Ireland or in Ireland and irrespective of what the Provisionals will do you will not have peace.

Q. Has a life as an activist detached you from normality?

A. I am conscious of the fact that people even from within our own community are wary, wouldn't see you as completely normal.

Q. Are they frightened of you or is it simply that they do not understand you?

A. I don't believe anyone in my own community or in this locality is frightened of me, and I say that because I walk among the people. At the end of the day there is a belief within our community that had it not been for people like myself and others, the IRA would have butchered us and the British government would have given us away long ago.

Q. Do you understand the perception of you within the Catholic community?

A. Oh, yes. Hatred, absolute hatred ... a bitterness. Let me say I have Roman Catholic friends and Roman Catholic members of my family. I have a sister married to a Catholic from Tipperary and they live in New York. I have another sister married to a Catholic who became a Christian missionary. I have no difficulty with them. I

probably feel inferior before them ... they're so full
of love and understanding. I know it must be so
hard for them to warm to me and I'm conscious of
that.

Billy Wright agreed that the prison culture had been
an important factor in defining the objectives of loyalism and its proximity to a developing fundamentalism.
In the autumn of 1996, the major rift between loyalist
paramilitaries like Billy Wright who were allied to
fundamentalist beliefs, and the political leadership of
the UVF, had led to the death threat issued against
Wright, but he was not an isolated activist, and his
views were not those of an isolated fanatic: in rural
areas there was considerable support for him. Many
rural terrorists resented being controlled by the city
cells: countryside operatives were often more active
than their urban counterparts and felt that they were
due more praise for their efforts from the leadership.
Also, in regions like Co. Armagh, which is close to the
Border, loyalists were more extreme because they felt
under greater threat from those who opposed them.
Within the Mid-Ulster ranks of the UDA, there was a
faction who supported Wright's contention that the
peace process was doomed and that violence was the
only way forward.

At the start of 1997 political expectations were at an
all-time low: the IRA campaign was continuing, Sinn
Fein was excluded from the peace-process talks, and the
nationalist SDLP was doubtful about the success of the
talks without the Provisionals. The British government
was determined to keep the loyalists on board the peace
'train', fearing that if they went back to conflict,
violence would escalate to the levels of the 1970s.

Billy Wright's claim that the loyalist political leadership was out of step with the paramilitaries was justified when the UVF was forced to withdraw its death threat against him: it had been made clear to the UVF leadership, both military and political, that a move against Wright would split the UDA and UVF and lead to a bloodbath, perhaps a coup in which the leadership of both organisations were overthrown. Wright was articulating views similar to those that had resulted in the overthrow of the 1975 UVF leadership, which was then pursuing a conciliatory agenda, and in 1996 the leadership's tone was again moderate.

For men like Wright the peace talks represented a betrayal. Loyalism has always manifested that inwardly volatile character, and the spread of a fundamentalist policy is deemed by some to be dangerous to loyalist unity and the continuance of the UVF and UDA in a peace process. The loyalism of Wright is linked to the phenomenon of prison conversion, and many paramilitaries turned preachers believe he is a hero. Wright regards Ian Paisley (see pp. 290–7) as one of the great defenders of the loyalist tradition, and in the autumn of 1996, the presence of the Rev. William McCrea MP on a platform with Wright confirmed the closeness between Paisley's Democratic Unionist Party and Wright's brand of politics. McCrea was at a rally in Portadown to offer support to Wright, condemning the death threat against him. The reaction from nationalists was immediate and severe, pointing out that Paisley's party was irresponsible to ally itself with a controversial figure like Wright.

David Trimble attracted similar condemnation in the summer of 1995, not only from nationalist politicians

but from the Catholic Church and the Dublin government. What no one appeared to understand was what I
term the Apprentice Boys' myth: that a Unionist leader
walks away from orthodoxy and grass-roots opinion at
his peril. In 1689 the Protestants of Londonderry were
betrayed by their own community leaders, who opened
the city's gates to James II's forces. Before the city could
be sacked, however, the Apprentice Boys closed them.
The event has reverberated throughout the history of
Unionism. In the 1960s when the Unionist prime
minister Terence O'Neill suggested that moderate
reforms might be introduced to deal with the plight of
Catholics, he was a 'Lundy', a traitor, the type of man
who would have opened the gates of Derry to the
invaders. O'Neill's departure from the orthodoxy of the
period, which was enshrined in the ethos of a Protestant
parliament for a Protestant people, was regarded as an
act of treachery. He was moving against the tide of
grass-roots Unionism and this caused his downfall.
Brian Faulkner made the same mistake in accepting a
Council of Ireland in the Sunningdale arrangements,
which led to the power-sharing executive of 1974, and
ultimately to *his* downfall. Trimble is an astute lawyer
and student of history: he is steeped in the Apprentice
Boys' myth, and his accession to the throne of Unionism
was achieved through his commitment to Orangeism.
When the Orange Order was confronted with a decision
to ban the Drumcree march through a Catholic district,
Trimble was there wearing his sash. Some would say it
was political opportunism on his part but I would argue
that it was a matter of political survival.

Unfortunately, the balancing act he chose to play
carries with it the risk that in defining himself as the
saviour or, as he might put it, the peacemaker at

Drumcree, he took on a mantle that will never be easy
to wear: Wright was there alongside him, and it is
Wright who forecasts that loyalism will one day replace
Unionism.

I asked Wright about the future of politics in the
Protestant community, and he began by identifying the
new political dimension emanating from the prison
culture.

'By and large working-class people entered the gaols
because they believed they had fought for their country.
They went in there, studied and many of them found
God. When they left, those that found God had all the
ingredients from within a Unionist family to forward
themselves, and present themselves to the community,
i.e., they had the credibility of being loyalists and having
suffered without reward on behalf of the people and the
country. That sacrifice and involvement gives credence
to the person. The moral standard that's needed within
Unionism is demanded by the people because we have
come from a class-type society and most nationalists
haven't. If that godliness and respect is there, then that
links the loyalist with the Protestant and the person
becomes presentable.'

Wright, and many like him, are tired of the kind of
politicians who have represented the Protestant Union-
ist community. He describes them as self-seekers and
part of the old-boy network; men who only joined the
Orange Order to enable them to win electoral seats.
Nationalist politicians, he says, were the envy of the
Protestant working class because they were concerned
only with political ideals and objectives. The late John
McMichael, a leader of the paramilitary wing of the
UDA, once told me he detested Unionist politicians:
'They like using the loyalist paramilitaries as the big

stick but they don't want us in politics. They want to monopolise the political scene in our community. That's always been the way. We had the big landowners, the landed gentry like Terence O'Neill and Chichester-Clark, and they wore their sashes in Orange parades once a year but they never really cared about the working-class Protestants for the rest of the year.'

Wright's description of Unionist politicians as men in politics for a career contrasted sharply with the language he used to describe middle-aged men who were beginning to develop a political strategy in working-class areas: 'These are men who suffered the ignominy and shame of imprisonment, gave up years of their life without benefit, and the community can see that they are not interested in politics for personal gain. They educated themselves in gaol. Our people always want to look upwards – they look to the Orange Order to guide and unite them and they look to the Church to lead them and to Christ to save them. If you get those things in a human being you get all the strands of Unionism and of the Unionist family being able to put their trust in that person.'

Q. If there is such an explosion of fundamental belief and the born-again movement coming into the political arena, what effect will that have?

A. There is no doubt that official Unionism, that dead, dull, sour type of politics, must change rapidly. People see hope in something that's new. The people representing loyalist politics from within the UVF will not last. They've left aside the faith. The membership of the Force who voted for them in the local elections didn't know their policies. The vote was for the badge of the movement.

Towards the end of my visit to Billy Wright's Portadown home, where he lives with his girlfriend, we
talked about the difference between IRA and loyalist
activists. He said, 'I don't wish to sound sectarian, I
don't mean to be sectarian. In the past Protestants made
bad terrorists, and they made bad terrorists because
simply by being brought up in the Protestant faith, and
in the knowledge of Jesus Christ, of Heaven and Hell,
with Heaven and Hell clearly defined and Judgement
clearly defined, if that's in your conscience, no matter
what ideology, political ideology, you instil within
yourself, it is very difficult to come t' terms with acts of
violence which you believe subconsciously will lead you
to lose your soul and what we found was that
Protestants reacted to the IRA, to their violence, to a
political situation. They acted emotionally, they committed acts of terrorism or whatever, and when the
emotions died down and they were challenged for those
acts, they normally confessed. It wasn't that they were
weaker human beings than nationalists, or less committed to what they believed in. It was that spiritually they
were challenged far greater by their faith than the
Roman Catholic or Irish nationalists.'

From the early 1970s until the late 1980s, the nature
of loyalist violence was reflex, the only definable target
any Catholic who was in the wrong place at the wrong
time. Since there was no definable enemy, and no clear
ideological objective, it was inevitable that when they
had time for reflection, particularly in custody, many
loyalist killers confessed. Others turned to God within
the isolation of their prison cells. The same did not
apply to the IRA, although they had also been tutored
in the concepts of heaven, hell and judgement. They had
a history of prison culture, a romantic ideology, the

availability of absolution in the confessional, and a belief that violence was morally justified because they were victims fighting oppressors.

In the late 1980s and early 1990s there was a perceptible change in the choice of loyalist targets: victims were to be members of Sinn Fein or Sinn Fein workers. This was, to a degree, motivated by the fact that Provisionals were now prominent public figures sitting in local council chambers. The IRA was no longer 'hidden': loyalist hit squads had the faces and names of members of the republican movement, some of whom had served prison sentences for terrorist offences. Loyalist terror became more efficient, which, to a large extent, can be attributed to the involvement of British military intelligence, one of whose leading agents was Brian Nelson, chief of intelligence within the Ulster Freedom Fighters. Nelson held computer files on known republicans, and his military intelligence handlers constantly supplied him with updates on their movements.

My final exchanges with Billy Wright took us back to the dilemma of 'walking with Christ' and being a terrorist.

Q. You have told me that you cannot walk with God and fulfil the obligations required of a paramilitary.

A. You can't glorify God and seek to glorify Ulster because the challenges which are needed are paramilitary. That's a contradiction to the life God would want you to lead. If you were to get yourself involved in paramilitary activity in its present form, or the form in which it manifested itself during the Troubles, then I don't think you could walk with God. I don't believe you can involve yourself in loyalist activity such as shootings, bombings and so on. You are breaking the law of the land.

Q. You've said you are at risk of losing your soul, and yet subliminally I hear this voice saying to me: 'I'll be okay. At some time in the future, I'll repent and things will be all right.'

A. There's always the hope that in some way, some-day – and there are precedents within scripture – your hope would be that God would draw you back to him. All those who have the knowledge of Christ would seek to walk with him again. People would say, 'Billy Wright, that's impossible,' but nothing's impossible if you have faith in God. I would hope that he would allow me to come back. I'm not walking with God.

Q. The conclusion some people would draw is that you are walking with the Devil.

A. Without getting into doctrine, without getting too deep, it is possible to have walked with God and to fall away and still belong to God.

Q. Surely what you're saying is that now I'm walking with the Devil, and at some point in the future God will let me return.

A. Well, you're certainly not working for the glory of God and wasting your years.

Q. Why do you shirk from the concept of walking with the Devil?

A. There are places in scripture where humanity fails God and goes its own way but, nevertheless, God would describe it as an unruly child but that child's still a part of the family of God.

Q. Do you have regrets, sadness about what you have done?

A. I've been involved in a war and, like any other

person, I would love to have lived at a time when there was no war.

Q. Have you ever prayed for people who have been killed?

A. I don't believe in praying for the dead. If you're asking me if I have sympathy, understanding and care for my enemies, the answer is most definitely yes. I understand the IRA and the young men who are in it. I grew up with Irish nationalists and I understand they are no different as human beings from myself or you. There's an ideal within their head, however an ideal is made up, whether it's from the experiences of life or whether it's a chemical, that ideal is the only thing which defines them from myself. They feel the same, they look the same. At the end of the day, I often sit and wonder if they sit down and say to themselves, 'Why not get on with life?' The greatest friend I ever had in life was Jesus Christ and I remember, before I walked with God, asking an old man what the experience was like. He told me it was like emptying a bottle of whisky down your neck. The way you feel the effects of the whisky is the way you feel salvation, and I suppose that sounds strange but it's the truth. I'm in a position now where by and large ... to call me back to God it would take God to change the circumstances. I'm very conscious that it would be very difficult for people to accept that there was godliness within me.

Q. They might say, 'That guy walks with the Devil.'

A. I can understand that.

Q. Would you not like to return your life to 1983

when you began preaching?

A. Of course I would. On the night I committed
    myself to Christ, until then, the Provisionals in
    Mid-Ulster were cracking up looking for me. I used
    to lie in bed with a hammer beside the bed and I
    was told by one of my advisers that the SAS were
    to shoot me. I had letters from the MP Harold
    McCusker in which he warned that I was to be the
    first victim of the shoot-to-kill policy. So I had the
    Provos and the security forces after me and I felt
    that at any moment I would be murdered. And yet
    I committed myself to Christ and, instantaneously,
    the fear was gone, the hammer was gone. I got up
    the next morning and I had a boldness about me. I
    was able to tell people. I wasn't embarrassed about
    it. Protestants will always accept it because they
    know it is real. They have seen it – they've seen the
    wino coming out of the gutter. It was lovely but
    that seed of politics was within me. I stood with my
    wife on the streets of Portadown in 1986 and I
    watched young Keith White being killed. I was feet
    from him. He was a young member of the YCV
    [Young Citizens Volunteers]. It was the RUC who
    killed him with a plastic bullet. In one estate alone,
    a hundred and ten people were hit with plastic
    bullets. That was it. I stood on the streets of
    Portadown and watched the law of the land, which
    claimed to be above the people, killing, beating,
    sexually molesting, urinating over churches. At the
    same time the Provisional IRA had taken out six
    leading loyalists I had known in Belfast. The
    bitterness that was going on inside me told me I
    could not walk with God.

When he received the death threat from the UVF in Belfast, he judged it to be God's providence.

'I always said, "The arm of flesh will fail you," and sometimes, sitting alone, I have said, "You were forewarned. You left God for an objective. You were at the top of the tree of what you believed in and then it turned on you." Many a time, I said to myself, "Well, this is God saying, 'You obtained what you left Me for and now it's turned on you.' It was all for nothing in a sense." Now that is personal.'

Billy Wright's name strikes fear into the Catholic community, and it is easy to understand why after an examination of his brand of fundamentalism and paramilitarism. Throughout our discussions he was charming, yet I could not help sensing a dark side to his character. I was reminded of a childhood fear of shadows on a bedroom wall, and he lives in the shadows. Wright uses God as the ultimate defence. He knows he is acting against the commandments he quotes, but hopes there will be time for redemption. Lenny Murphy, leader of the Shankill Butchers, also had a background that shaped him for killing. Murphy was a psychopathic personality who killed Catholics to disprove a myth in his community that he was a Catholic by virtue of his name. He was what one leading loyalist called a 'super Prod'. To demonstrate his credentials as a true loyalist, he felt he had to be more bitterly sectarian than others and a more ruthless killing machine. Within Wright, I detected the 'super Prod' mindset. His family had been forced to leave Northern Ireland because his grandfather was viewed as soft on Catholics. What better way to erase that history than to be a super-loyalist, an icon in his own

community of Portadown and Mid-Ulster, an uncompromising figure who knows how to merge all the
elements required of a true loyalist: faith, fatherland
and family.

While I was writing this book, Billy Wright was
convicted of intimidating a female who was a potential
witness of a crime. He received an eight-year prison
sentence. A few months later, rumours circulated that
he was back on the 'salvation trail'. One source told me
that he had begun to restrict the circulation of pornog-
raphy among loyalist prisoners.

After this book was published Billy Wright was murdered by members of the Republican INLA within the
Maze Prison.

THE BATTLE FOR SOULS

The process of prison conversion is an exclusively loyalist phenomenon and cannot be considered without reference to motive. The system of periodic reviews of life sentences has meant that some prisoners, particularly 'lifers', have claimed religious conversion in an attempt to impress a review panel. Prisoners on remand for serious terrorist offences have also used conversion as a means to persuade the judge at their trial that they are set on a different lifestyle. Prison chaplains, however, seem to have played no part in the conversion phenomenon.

John Bach, a highly experienced criminologist who has worked for twenty years within the Northern Ireland prison service as a Church of Ireland chaplain and chairman of the Board of Visitors, accepts that the Victorian era is the starting point from which the conversion process should be examined. In the late nineteenth century, the moral and welfare aspects of prison life were overseen by chaplains, who enjoyed an exceptionally high standing in the world of prison administration. On every prison estate, the governor occupied the largest house, and his neighbour, the chaplain, enjoyed residential facilities that were only marginally inferior.

At that time, it was widely held that exposing prisoners to religious teaching would have a reforming effect, and they spent long periods in reflective confinement, with the Bible as their only reading material, and the chaplain as chief visitor. Churchmen saw prisons almost as laboratories in which the conversion process could be truly tested. John Bach explained to me his view of the underlying rationale. 'It was believed that only the Christian gospel could lead to a truly radical inner transformation, all else was mere tinkering with the symptoms. It was the philosophy of Mark 2, 22: "No one else puts new wines into old wine skins; if he does, the new wine will burst the skins." Therefore, it was concluded that reform was no reform at all if it did not address the deepest soul of man.'

The appeal to depth was textually supported in John 3 where Jesus advises Nicodemus of his need to be 'born again'.

So why, in past decades, was there a gradual, and clearly defined, erosion in the role of prison chaplain? It may be that many people entering prison had few religious convictions, their lack of belief a product of the neighbourhoods in which they lived. John Bach suggests also that lack of faith among prisoners could no longer be cited as the sole difference between the offender and his law-abiding neighbour: unbelief might be part of a prisoner's problem but not all of it.

Growing secularisation in the outside world also put the traditional and pivotal role of the chaplains under the microscope, and some chaplains had misgivings about what they saw as the emotional blackmail of traditional conversion methods, which led them to direct more of their energy towards resolving inmates' immediate social problems. The result was a blurring of the distinction between the old chaplain and the new welfare officer.

There was also genuine concern that the 'born-again' motif of John 3 might, if not properly understood, have a negative effect, which led to the dismissal of all who could not name the date and hour of their 'second birth': Kenny McClinton, for example, was able to give the hour and date of his cell conversion. This alarmed many with a lifelong loyalty to Christ and the Church, who could only speak of growing in faith. Even a literal interpretation of 'born again' implies a new life that moves from infancy, through adolescence, to adulthood. Scriptural texts about this maturation process abound, but many who claim conversion suggest that they experienced an instantaneous transformation into theological cognoscenti. Roman Catholic and High Anglican chaplains link being 'born again' with baptism and insist that Christian living is a response to a gift freely conferred at the font: they have become the target of fundamentalist abuse. John Bach argues that however much the born-again motif may be over-simplified and misunderstood, the rich Christian tradition of inner transformation remains: 'Without that inner transformation, Christianity would be much impoverished. The gospel message of the undeserved but real love of God is, of necessity, highly emotional but any lasting transformation must involve more than sentiment. Unless the emotive message of divine love engages the reason and will-power of the hearer, it will be of little effect.'

What is never in dispute is that a prison cell is an unusual if not a dangerous place to experience a religious conversion: solitariness and self-pity may combine to create an atmosphere in which a highly emotional message can have real, albeit superficial, appeal. Many prison conversions have lasted only a short time. John Bach says that cell conversion, and promotion of the experience, should be treated with caution: 'Every prisoner has the right to be protected from the cheap emotionalism which so easily flourishes in conditions of confinement. Good prison chaplains know this well. Their role is to elicit mature moral and religious choices and without facing the damaging charge of brainwashing or of using undue emotional pressure.'

In the context of his warnings, it is no surprise that some of the chief advocates of being 'born again' are not chaplains. The Prison Fellowship, to which McClinton belongs, is one such grouping. It is part of an international evangelical mission associated with Watergate veteran and ex-prisoner Charles Coulson. Prison chaplains vary considerably in their response to it. There is nothing to prevent individual prisoners requesting visits from the organisation although many chaplains would argue that it should not be given open access to prisons. The Prison Act provides special privileges for chaplains, some of whom believe that the Prison Fellowship could undermine their work. And, after all, the arrival of a new group of proselytisers was never going to be whole-heartedly welcomed by those who had always held centre stage in the faith business. In England, the marginalising effect of secularisation on the prison chaplaincy was accompanied by another development: the growing numbers of prisoners who adhered to a religion other than Christianity. The

Church of England, which once dominated the religious scene, is now just one player among many.

John Bach believes that the undoubted right of prisoners to receive spiritual succour should be balanced by the reasonable fear that, as the history of Northern Ireland shows, different religions provoke more enmity than good. Nonetheless, he puts forward a solution that could be applied in England and Northern Ireland: 'One way is to differentiate between chaplains formally appointed by the Home Office, and visiting ministers licensed to visit any prisoner requesting a religious visit. In Northern Ireland, the latter, more modest status once applied to ministers of Ian Paisley's Free Presbyterian Church. Ulster's mainstream chaplains, appointees of the Northern Ireland Office, were happy to have it that way. They feared that any upgrading of Paisley's men to full chaplains would undermine the co-operative ministry already in place. In particular, they feared that their informal no-poaching agreement would never be endorsed by Paisleyites.'

The no-poaching agreement related to the Protestant chaplains who knew from experience that, in the outside world, Paisley's Church was taking members of their own flocks on a large scale and bringing with it a brand of sectarianism dangerous to society. With the arrival in prison of the Fellowship, which is closely linked to the Free Presbyterian Church, a battle for souls began between the born-again preachers and the mainstream Protestant chaplains. The Northern Ireland Office upgraded Paisley's Free Presbyterians to full chaplaincy, and a significant number of new 'consumers', although not Free Presbyterian when sentenced, became Paisley converts while in prison.

One reasonable explanation for this lay in the dual

role of Ian Paisley, Moderator of the Free Presbyterian Church. As a preacher, politician and man given to paramilitary displays, his brand of religion appeared as attractive to terrorists as it had in the 1960s when the UVF was reactivated: one of the promises given in the then UVF oath was to accept the teachings of the Rev. Ian Paisley, and, understandably, it was feared that transfers to his Church related more to politics than to religion. Also the transfers occurred when politico-religious segregation was a live issue in the Maze prison.

McClinton's 'mixed wing' was in reality the Fellowship wing, and received visits from part-time Free Presbyterian chaplains. At one stage, the Rev. William McCrea – who in 1996 appeared on a platform to support Billy Wright – conducted a week-long 'mission' there. Afterwards his congregation asked to be housed together to facilitate their meetings. It was not an unreasonable request but the prison authorities and the Northern Ireland Office feared it would foster political segregation when the government was promoting a policy of integration. John Bach says, 'The sectarian segregation of the working-class population makes it difficult to forbid similar segregation in prisons, but government policy while allowing governors freedom to segregate prisoners where it is deemed desirable, has absolutely ruled out any supposed right of a prisoner to determine in whose company he will serve his sentence.'

The prison authorities have never encouraged prisoners to change their recorded denomination. However, within the Maze prison certain chaplains have been readier than others to offer cigarettes to prisoners to gain their participation in religious meetings. It was evidence of such inducements that led to the requirement that the Board of Visitors should scrutinise requests to transfer from one religious denomination to another 'to assure itself, as far as possible, that the request is genuine'. The Board has *never* sat as a theological tribunal, merely as a body charged with satisfying itself as to 'honourable intentions'; nor has it ever denied an application to join Paisley's Church.

Chaplains with long experience of prison ministry are aware of the mixed motives and emotional vulnerability of prisoners, particularly lifers. Perhaps by their policy of restraint in not using Old Testament rhetoric, they left a vacuum that was filled by the Free Presbyterians and the Fellowship who, uncontaminated by theological sophistication, provided a Christian choice to scores of loyalist prisoners. Time will test the outlook, disposition and vision of the converts, but if Kenny McClinton's poem 'The Siege of Drumcree' is an example of the revivalist view, the future looks bleak.

Conversion, though, has certainly led to a reduction in the sentences handed down to dangerous men, perhaps at risk to society: the system aims to reward prisoners who appear to detach themselves from paramilitary control. Government policy also dictates that the prison terrorist population should be reduced: this reflects the demand of the communities to have their respective prisoners released and is also believed to be effective in eroding the power of paramilitaries – prison has been as important a training ground for terrorists as either Antrim or Donegal. Nonetheless the concept of retribution, as understood in the rest of the United Kingdom, has been sacrificed on the altar of political expediency – bargaining behind the scenes with terrorists. When I asked why 'Basher' Bates, the multiple murderer of the Shankill Butchers' gang, had been released I was told that the Northern Ireland Office did not comment on individual cases. I was not surprised: most of the Shankill Butchers, and other men on both sides who have committed mass murder, have been quietly released. Of Bates' release, Kenny McClinton said: 'Bobby baptised me in a bath tub in H-block 8 in 1980. I got out of the tub and baptised another prisoner. There were just three of us Christians at that time in the H-blocks. Christianity is not easy in prison and especially for Bobby because people tried to test his faith. But Christ worked a remarkable transformation in Bobby. He has proved himself a sincere and dedicated Christian who has come through right to the end.'

The IRA, with a long history of prison culture, always knew why they were in prison: they perceived themselves as freedom fighters, martyrs for a cause, and they did not present renewed religious conviction as a testimony to change or as a ploy for early release. Many were indeed pious, and their adoption of the hunger strike strategy, with its overtones of the cult of the martyr, reinforced the connection between faith and violence. In 1981, Bobby Sands died on the sixty-sixth day of his hunger strike. Sands' history outside prison mirrored that of many young men caught up in the conflict. He was born in 1945, and at the beginning of the present Troubles, his family had moved to a housing estate at Rathcoole outside Belfast. In the midst of sectarian strife in 1972, the family home was set alight by loyalists and Sands moved to the outskirts of West Belfast. A year later, he was imprisoned for possessing weapons and released in 1976. Within a short time he was back in prison after being caught in a car with guns. He claimed afterwards that he had been interrogated and subjected to ill-treatment by police before he was found guilty of arms possession and sentenced to fourteen years' imprisonment. In the Maze he was regarded as a devout and committed member of the IRA, whose prison leadership saw in him the commitment to lead a hunger strike. They knew from their own history that only those with unswerving loyalty to the republican cause could see it through to the death. In April 1981, Sands was elected MP for Fermanagh/South Tyrone at Westminster.

Father Denis Faul, who regularly said Mass in the Maze prison, knew Sands and the other hunger strikers. 'They were very determined young Irishmen and I think they felt they were representing their people inside and outside the prison. They came from a very oppressed class of people who had suffered ferocious discrimination, and the burning out in the Falls Road in August '69 was a very big thing with them ... That whole business which was linked to the Orange Order and the bonfires ... that kind of Ku Klux Klan stuff. They felt that their people were basically defenceless and they had to do something about it. They were a lot different from the types in the Provos now. They felt they must make this sacrifice for their people. There was internment first of all, ill-treatment, torture, sensory deprivation techniques at Ballykelly and Palace Barracks, then Castlereagh and that didn't end until '79. They felt they were representing their people against all of that, and they were representing the prisoners. The prison officers were giving them a rough time, the government started this silly business of criminalising them and trying to force them to wear prison clothes, and they wouldn't wear the clothes. Then after two years of that, and there was interference with their visitors, with their letters, they went on the dirty protest, which was a terrible thing, and finally they went on the hunger strike. Being

in the prison at that time, being in the cells and saying
Mass for these men, it was a tremendous challenge to
me as a Christian minister, as a priest. I really felt these
men were beating us at our own game. Quite fantastic.
You see, we had been at the seminary in Maynooth. It
reminded me of Maynooth. You did seven years there
and you worshipped the Cross as your symbol, a
crucified criminal, which Jesus was to the Roman and
Jewish world at the time, and a tremendous martyrdom
and passion of Jesus, and then the passions of the
martyrs and this was the whole thing. Also in the fifties
when I was in Maynooth we were inspired by the
persecution of the Church in Eastern Europe ... Poland,
Romania, right across to China and Korea where there
were deaths of a lot of Irish missionary priests. We
never actually imitated them. We were at Maynooth
and we came out into a very safe, comfortable, very
Catholic country, and we saw these men acting out
before our very eyes the scene that was really our scene,
the scene of total ascetic denial, these quasi-naked men
hardly getting anything to eat, deprived of all help.
During the naked and dirty protests, they had no
wireless, no pens, no pencils, nothing to write on. It was
really an awful scene. As priests we go on retreat every
year for about a week and I must say I find it dreadfully
boring to be deprived of normal comforts for a week ...
the wireless, television, newspapers. I said, "How do
these fellas do it?" They were ordinary working-class
men, they were men without what you would call the
imagination of literature. There were two of them in
each cell, and it was a tremendous challenge to the
Church, to us. Here were these men doing for a
temporal cause, a doubtful, disputable temporal cause
in many ways ... they were making the very sacrifices

that Jesus had done, and that Catholic priests and Catholic people were called upon to do. They were doing it ... and there was a religious motif in it ... they were doing it for their people.'

A week before the hunger strike began, Sands asked for a meeting with Father Faul who warned him that the hunger strike of the previous year had caused great distress in the Catholic community and had been a failure. He warned Sands that a hunger strike might once again collapse, and it would cause mayhem in the community. Sands looked carefully at him and replied: 'Greater love than this no man hath, than a man who lays down his life for his friends.'

'It really stunned me and I said, "Bobby, there's no argument with that." I felt he had a good religious motive as well as another motivation. He said there was ill-treatment going on and he would stop it and he did. In a way he would rank as the number-one prison reformer of the twentieth century. All the paramilitary prisoners, including the loyalists, have been running round the prison for the last fifteen years dressed in their own garments because of Sands.'

It is evident that Denis Faul admired the steadfastness of Sands and the nine others who followed him to their death, and that Sands recognised this. Perhaps he saw the priest as the symbolic presence of Mother Church, and at that time, Denis Faul agrees, the Provisionals saw themselves as the defenders of the Catholic Church. In the early 1970s Faul had known the devout Billy McKee, one of the founders of the Provisional IRA. He had met McKee in Long Kesh internment camp and attributed the then religious zeal of the Provisionals to a Dublin leadership that mirrored itself on Padraig

Pearse, who had been a devout Catholic and one of the
central figures of the 1916 Rising.

In 1981, the Catholic Church opposed the hunger
strike but would not define the actions of the hunger
strikers as suicide, which is, to Catholics, a mortal sin.
The Church in Ireland was appalled when Cardinal
Basil Hume paid a visit to the Province and, on his
return to London, said that Sands was committing
suicide. Denis Faul says, 'There was fierce strong
feelings among the priests about Cardinal Hume's
comments. In a sense it was none of his business, and
secondly, theologically, we thought he was wrong.
Theologically we can justify the hunger strikes but you
have to be an Irishman to do it. I noticed in various
theological articles and journals in German and Spanish
about the hunger strike. They nearly all just said it was
suicide.'

The theological argument presented to seminarians at
Maynooth was that if there was a grave violation of
natural human rights which a government ignored, a
person was entitled to fast, not with the intention of
committing suicide but with the intention of fasting to
bring attention to the grievance. The late Professor John
McCarthy of Maynooth once gave Denis Faul a simple
metaphor to justify the tactic of hunger strike: 'He said
that if you were driving a big lorry down a road and a
little child was lying on the road, a person at the side of
the road might realise that the lorry driver will not see
the little child but he will the adult. If the adult runs to
save the child, he might lose his life, or the lorry driver
might see the danger, stop and remedy the situation.
The hunger strike was to draw the attention of the
government to grave, grave grievances ... ill-treatment,
criminalisation. You would have to live in the prison

world to know it. I said to Bobby, "What about your family, your relations?" He couldn't see that. He's been interned and then imprisoned. They felt the British government was picking on them in response to Unionist pressure.'

Father Faul took a strong stand against the hunger strike and was branded a traitor. At the time he talked to Brendan McFarlane, the Provisionals' leader in the Maze, to try to bring about an end to the deaths. He was beginning to feel that Cardinal Hume's assessment of the situation had not been misplaced. He says, 'I give the Provos full marks. They could pick their leaders excellently. I wish the Vatican could pick its bishops as well as the Provos could pick out these fellas. They seemed to see the true qualities of leadership in Sands and McFarlane ... excellent leaders. They had all the qualities of leaders. I said to McFarlane at a certain stage after three or four had died, "The motivation doesn't seem to me to be about drawing the attention of the British public to the situation by fasting. It seems to me to be about drawing attention to death and big funerals. This thing is no longer a valid public political protest. It's becoming suicide." '

Faul's central argument was that after four had died, the strikers had won the right to wear their own clothes and that it was time to negotiate. He pointed to the moral right of strikers to go for the 'big push' and, once concessions had been granted, to negotiate on other demands. Faul was worried that in the prison the IRA had thirty or forty men willing to die. The enormity of what faced him was the then essentially Catholic dimension of the Provos. The cult of the martyr was present in a real and almost virulent form.

During the hunger strike the power of the Church

waned and, in terms of the Provos, its influence
declined: Sands and his fellow hunger strikers were
adamant that no one could speak for them. The British
government would have to negotiate directly with Sands
and the others.

Eventually, in response to the mother of one of the
hunger strikers, Faul called a meeting of the families and
convinced them to put pressure on the Provisionals to
call it off: 'We went to see [Gerry] Adams and told him
to go in and tell them to call it off. Adams said he
wasn't IRA and we told him he could contact them. We
knew he wore all the hats. The next day he rang me at
the Cardinal's house and said he wanted to bring in
Owen Carron [a Republican, and former election agent
for Bobby Sands]. My heart sank. I knew it was going
political. With a by-election coming up for Bobby
Sands' seat in Fermanagh/South Tyrone, I knew they
were not coming off their hunger strike. I knew others
would die and, in fact, Mickey Devine died on the day
of the by-election, which Carron won. Adams, at the
time we asked him to go in and end it, went in but no
matter what he says, he didn't do the job ... He didn't
do it right. He messed it all up. Eventually the prisoners'
families took them off one by one.'

The battle between Faul and the Provisionals was
bitter. Every time the priest met a hunger striker to
persuade him to cease, members of Sinn Fein were
present who read letters of support from relatives. Faul
reckons that many of those letters were forgeries
'written somewhere on the Falls Road'.

The Church also failed in its attempts to turn people
away from violence. Father Faul talked about the
emotionalism that followed each hunger striker's death.
'The Brits didn't understand. A friend of mine said to a

British minister, "Why don't you go to a hunger striker's wake?" There was the whole community, lined up outside a house, and the hunger striker emaciated in the coffin and fellas standing round with the balaclavas. Talk about a recruiting job, it was perfect. The whole community were going to these wakes and they were recruiting wholesale. The British and Britain being a completely pagan country, they couldn't understand that the Irish always win by sacrifice. It's the history of our people. They didn't understand you could win by dying. We understand that you *can* win by dying. We can understand it perfectly. Pearse understood that and the hunger strikers understood that.'

If one accepts his thesis about sacrifice, and there is no reason to doubt that it exists within the IRA psyche, it offers a salient explanation for the lack of religious conversion within the history of IRA prison culture: the IRA conditions its members to recognise that whatever they do, whatever time they have to spend in prison, they are making a sacrifice and, in the context of Catholicism, there appears to be no need for them morally to question their actions. When placed against the loyalist experience of religious conversion, the Provisionals of the 1980s and 1990s are either unconcerned about God or believe that faith is a private matter and that there is no conflict of interest between faith and terrorism.

The hunger strike strategy was one to which loyalists could never give themselves with any certainty of seeing it through. A former loyalist prisoner said, 'We admired the hunger strikers. If you're in prison you see it differently. Their struggle in some ways was also ours but we didn't have the people with that kind of commitment. We had loads of guys who were happy talking to God but nobody wanted to be that close to him.'

I asked Denis Faul why he thought loyalists were incapable of sustaining a hunger strike. He pointed out that he could only speak speculatively, but said, 'Their religion hasn't the capacity to welcome death. They have a horror of death, which the Catholics haven't. Death is the end of everything for them whereas for us it is maybe only the beginning. The fact is that death could be used as a sacrifice whereas all the Orange struggle and the Protestant struggle is for the past. The Vietcong had no bother beating the Americans because they were fighting for the future. They didn't mind being killed. It was for the future of their people. The IRA are the same. They are fighting for the future and the Protestants are fighting for the past. It's the battle of the Boyne of 1690 so they have nothing to fight for. In prison they go through conversion and it doesn't happen to the republicans. To put it crudely, it is the terrible preaching of hell-fire. We have confession, the opportunity of forgiveness, of the sacrament which they don't have. It's a lonely thing to be a murderer if you're a Protestant. Is that a horrible thing to say? He hasn't got the resources to get rid of his guilt and know that his repentance has been accepted. He's kind of alone and therefore the nearest thing they can get to is conversion because it fits in with John the Baptist and Jesus in the Bible.' However, Faul believes the conversion phenomenon has been a positive development and that it corresponds to a degree with confession.

After lengthy theological debate, the Church has directed a campaign against the Provisional IRA and their philosophy of a just war. For some time, it has been worried that the Provisionals have put across the message that as the conflict is a war, killing is justified and there is no need to confess it. The Church, though, makes strenuous efforts to persuade youth that it is wholly wrong to kill anyone. Father Faul says that Provisional 'back-up people' – those who handle strategy and propaganda – have tried to counter the Church, anxious that its position would create an inevitable guilt complex among terrorists if they accepted what it was saying. Father Faul believes that the Provisionals won this battle when the Sinn Fein leadership of Gerry Adams, Martin McGuinness and Danny Morrison took over the reins of power in the late 1980s, during a general falling-off in church attendances in republican districts. That was a consequence of years of lawlessness but society's social and sexual mores had changed dramatically, leaving the relevance of the Church in question. The decline was heightened by resentment against Bishop Cahal Daly, later Cardinal. The IRA felt that he had criticised them while ignoring the excesses of the police, the Army and the policies of the British government. Father Faul said, 'Some of the bishops hadn't learned that you can't condemn one side only. You have to condemn all violence. In the seventies and to some extent, the eighties, they kind of accepted people like myself and Father Raymond Murray because we condemned all murders whereas the bishops were rather one-sided for a while.'

Denis Faul is one of the few priests not frightened to attack the Catholic hierarchy for 'not getting it right': 'They improved in the early eighties but Bishop Philbin [Down and Conor diocese, early 1970s] just didn't understand the suffering of his own people. Cahal Daly succeeded him and was ferociously against the IRA and Sinn Fein without balancing it up. In the nineties he came to Armagh as cardinal and changed his mind to some extent because all his best parishioners here were members of Sinn Fein. He took a more balanced view.'

Faul believes that Catholics are morally bound to reject the IRA and is unsure whether that should include Sinn Fein. As for Protestants, they must reject Paisley, and the Unionist leader David Trimble. He uses the phrase 'mortal sin' to define the way in which the IRA terrifies Protestants, and employs mass intimidation against Catholics: 'They're scaring the life out of Catholics who join the police or don't nod the head at Sinn Fein. They have taken over businesses and farms. People just walk away, go into their own homes and close the doors. The same is happening on the Protestant side. The Catholic Church can't do a lot. The Church has no army, no vigilante force. I know of examples where the Provos took over social events and community halls in Fermanagh/South Tyrone. People just disappear. The Provos will learn there is only a limited time span to that sort of oppression. People are not stupid.'

THE LAST CONFESSION

The most harrowing role of a priest is to perform the Last Rites for a dying person, and watch life ebb away. During the course of conflict in Ireland, priests have often been at the scene of tragedies, ministering to the injured and dying. Everyone remembers the television images of Father Edward Daly waving a handkerchief as one of the Bloody Sunday victims was being carried across a Derry street as paratroopers continued to fire into the Bogside. His was a brave, selfless act, performed in the midst of danger, yet other events in priestly life have been more shocking and have never made the headlines. Priests have been summoned to a lonely hillside or a derelict house to hear the last confession of someone condemned to die by the IRA. The reason why this has remained a guarded secret is because of the dilemmas it presents for the Catholic Church in Ireland, and the risks it poses for individual priests, should they break an imposed silence. Few priests are prepared to discuss that side of the conflict, first because what passes between priest and penitent in the confessional must be kept secret, and second, they know that even priests are not immune to bullets. Some in the Catholic Church feel that if a priest who had been

in such a situation were to compromise the execu-
tioners, the IRA would no longer allow their victims a
last confession.

Two priests spoke to me about their experiences in
this shadowy world of religion and violence, and their
experiences highlighted the acute problems facing all
those summoned to perform the Last Rites or hear a
final confession. To protect them, and at their request, I
will refer to them as Father Pat and Father Jim. They
did not, at any time during their discussions with me,
violate the secrecy of the confessional, or act in any way
to compromise their priestly vows.

Father Pat is a sprightly curate in his early seventies
with a disarming smile, and sharp features creased with
lines that convey a troubled soul. The weekly queue
outside his confessional implies that he is popular with
sinners, and understanding of sin. He is a priest of the
old school, who believes that the faithful need the
sacraments of confession and the Eucharist to keep
them on the straight and narrow. He has watched what
he describes as the 'modern disease' of occasional visits
to church and a commitment to materialism, and he has
also observed that young people have lost respect for all
authority, and are easily trapped in a spiral of violence.

'The paramilitaries control the kids in this area,' he
declared. 'The paramilitaries have usurped God. They
declare that they've the power of life and death. How
can someone like me tell them that this is a falsehood?
In reality, it is hard to argue otherwise. People have
stormed out of the church during some of my sermons
when I condemned the IRA. What sort of message does
that send out to the young?'

Father Pat's face was drawn in anguish when he
described what he called the 'crude justification' of

violence. 'Seemingly intelligent people have said to me
that war can be just. They don't see the real destructive
character of violence and how it dehumanises everyone.
How they can see God in that is beyond me. They trot
out these old clichés about fighting injustice, and I tell
them you can do that effectively without killing the
innocent. I ask them why they abdicate responsibility
for intellect, and why they cannot see that the voice of
reason has a more plaintive and persuasive sound than
that of anger.'

As he talked, he drew heavily on his pipe. 'You see, I
am not blind to the power of the IRA argument,
particularly when delivered in a moral and political
vacuum. Attitudes to religion are changing while society
itself is not moving on politically. Put the decline in
moral standards against the decline in political standards, and you've a dangerous cocktail. I condemn all
violence from wherever it arises. When the British
government acts in a fashion which implies there is a
dirty war and killing is justifiable, my crusade is weak.
That's been one of the problems throughout the conflict
... neither the paramilitaries nor the military hold the
high moral ground. When agencies of the State act in a
fashion which flouts the basic principles of justice, the
chasm opens wider. Sometimes I feel torn between two
warring factions – the IRA and elements of the State
who act like paramilitaries. And, there's that old gut
tribal instinct that draws you towards the republican
argument and the history of injustice under British rule.
God, you have to get hold of that one, like the dentist,
and tear it out before the rest becomes infected.' He
paused. Then he said, 'IRA men go to confession, you
know.'

I nodded as he looked at me, expecting disbelief. 'Of

course, I cannot reveal anything that has happened in the confessional, but can you imagine what is in my head?'

I remained silent, knowing that it was not a question to which he required an answer.

'The minds of people prepared to kill and justify it to themselves are tortured minds, almost detached from the soul. I don't mean the soul is not there, but the connection is damaged. I alone can't repair it. I can only restate the Christian message about love, forgiveness and the sin of killing. The leaders of society must embrace those principles so that society's own damaged soul can be repaired and gradually the souls of the tortured minds.'

Again he paused, then began quietly, almost whispering, to address the main subject of my interview. 'I was sitting in here late one evening … just reading … and the doorbell rang. I hadn't scheduled any appointments though I always allowed for the fact that there might be an emergency. I opened the front door and there was a young man there with the collar of his coat pulled up in an attempt to hide his face. He was about eighteen. He was clearly agitated, if not embarrassed. I said, "Come in, Michael," because it was cold outside, and I was wearing my pyjamas, slippers and an old pullover. As soon as I mentioned his name he backed away. "It's nothin' t' do with me, Father," he told me. "You're wanted." '

Father Pat was handed a piece of paper containing an address.

'Instinctively, I knew this wasn't a normal request and I mentally prepared myself for the worst. I knew Michael was in the Provisionals, so maybe one of their people was injured. As I walked towards the particular street, I tried to convince myself that it was simply a request for a chat. Sometimes the IRA leaders in the area would talk to me if there was need for a mediator with the security forces.'

Father Pat's journey on foot took him to a street in which he knew all the inhabitants.

'There were no street-lamps working, and as I approached the corner, another person known to me as a member of the IRA, stopped me. He grabbed my arm and led me to a house which was at that time uninhabited.'

As Father Pat entered the house, he was bundled into the hallway and the door was slammed shut.

'I was confronted by a masked man armed with a pistol. I'd seen people on the streets with guns but when one is being pointed at you in a confined space, it reminds you of your mortality. "You've a job here to do, Father, and be quick about it," he said and pointed to the top of the staircase where another masked man was positioned. I knew the voice behind the balaclava. When you've sat behind that confessional screen for so many years, you develop an innate recognition of voices. I stared into his eyes and he pushed me towards the stairs. "What do you mean by a job?" I asked. "You'll find out," he replied. He laughed and told me it was my kind of job – "It's your kind of business," he told me.'

Father Pat was escorted into a dingy bathroom where a middle-aged man was tied to a chair with two armed and masked men on either side of him.

'One of them said, "He wants to make his confession." There was something sick about the way they addressed me. One of them said, "He's already made one to us and this is his last. You've got five minutes,

Father. Don't try to be heroic or we'll kill both of you. Just get on with it." '

Father Pat's eyes narrowed in anguish. He got up and paced the room, wringing his hands and marshalling the courage to describe the episode.

'It's hard,' he said sitting down, his eyes lowered. 'I froze when the bathroom door closed. I was suddenly dealing with evil and not just talking about it. The man in the chair was one of my parishioners. I remember looking at the bath filled with water wondering what they had done to him. He was stripped to a pair of wet underpants. His hair and body were wet so they'd obviously been holding him under the water. Looking back I observed so many things in a matter of seconds or perhaps I now just imagine that was so. Perhaps, because I have gone over it so many times in my head, I know so much that I didn't know then. He was badly bruised and his eyes were so swollen he could hardly see me. My first thought was whether I could get him out of there when the bathroom door opened. "Remember, Father," one of the gunmen told me, "any funny business and you're both for it. Anyway, there's somebody out the back even if you could get him out the window." '

The window, as Father Pat discovered, opened at the top but not enough to allow a grown person to get through it. The victim was incapable of walking.

'I put my arm around him,' said Father Pat. 'It seemed the only loving thing I could do. His lips were swollen and I heard him murmur, "Please help me, Father." '

Father Pat's eyes filled with tears as he recalled that plea, and he couldn't go on for some minutes. I sat in silence waiting for him to compose himself.

'No one can know how I felt. There were two victims in that room, and one was about to die. I whispered in his ear that God was with him. It was as if I was saying something I knew was not true at a time when all he wanted was God to set him free. I asked him if he wanted me to hear his confession and he replied that he did. The thing that struck me most was that the sacrament of confession seemed to have the effect of transforming that room. "I'm going to die. Isn't that right, Father?" I could only put my arm round him. He knew the inevitability of it and God was with him … of that I'm convinced. I wasn't so sure that God was with me. I felt so helpless. Leaving that room was a nightmare I have to live with.'

On his way out of the house, Father Pat pleaded with the terrorist whose voice he had recognised. 'This is against the law of God,' Father Pat told him.

'You look after the law of God,' replied the terrorist, 'and we'll look after our business.'

I asked Father Pat if that same terrorist had ever returned to the confessional.

'It's not a question I wish to answer.'

'Why?'

'Because there are certain things only I can deal with,' he replied. 'However, I can say, and this has nothing to do with the confessional, I believe in my heart that the IRA killed an innocent man.'

I asked Father Pat whether it was the duty of the priest to report his suspicions about the identity of the killers, and if a priest should answer a call to such a hideous event.

'For a priest, the confessional is not just that box in the Church. It extends into all aspects of life. In a

conflict like this, a priest cannot be the judge, jury or
law-enforcer. Those roles would make everyone feel
that a priestly confidence was worthless. I can comfort
the dying, I can offer God's absolution, and I can
confront violence with Christianity, but the moment I
step outside of that framework, my role as a priest
becomes compromised. Some of your readers will say
that is a cop-out, and I would understand such a
reaction. What is the alternative?'

I asked him whether excommunication was a real
alternative. 'The old chestnut! That's an outdated
practice. Even Rome considers it that. It would have no
effect on people who are convinced that what they are
doing is right. It couldn't effectively be administered and
to apply it in Ireland would mean having to apply it
throughout the world. That would bring the Church
firmly into the political arena and where would it stop?
The Church knows there are conflicts in parts of the
world where the use of violence is not easy to condemn.
It's Protestants who keep referring to excommunication
as though the Church could easily resort to that kind of
tactic. From my knowledge it was used in the distant
past against people guilty of promoting heresies. The
Church can only condemn the use of violence, not
banish those who advocate or use it.'

I referred him to the Church's Code of Canon Law
issued by the Vatican in 1983, and in particular Canon
1397 dealing with offences against human life and
liberty, which states:

> One who commits murder, or who by force, or by fraud
> abducts, imprisons, mutilates or gravely wounds a person,
> is to be punished, according to the gravity of the offence
> with the deprivations and provisions mentioned in Can.

1336. In the case of murder of one of those persons mentioned in Can. 1370, the offender is punished with the penalties there prescribed.

Father Pat pointed out that Canon 1336 dealt with people in religious life and that the penalties included transfer to another office, dismissal from the clerical state or the removal of privileges. These, he said, were expiatory and could affect the offender for a determinate or indeterminate period and were additional to any penalties the law of a country chose to impose.

He smiled at my reference to Canon 1370, went to a bookcase and read the following text from Canon 1370: 'A person who uses physical force against the Roman Pontiff incurs a *latae sententiae* excommunication. If the offender is a cleric, another penalty, not excluding dismissal from the clerical state, may be added according to the gravity of the crime.' In the same Canon less rigorous punishments were imposed on anyone who struck a bishop.

I wondered if, in theory, people committing murder effectively excommunicated themselves until such times as they renounced the use of violence.

Father Pat considered. 'Hmm ... yes, that could well be the case. For example, if someone came to confession, told me they were guilty of murder for political objectives and made it clear that they were likely to do it again, I would refuse them absolution and point out that they were in a state of sin and could not receive the sacraments. That would be a form of excommunication.'

I suggested that if the Church pointed out that those in the IRA who were promoting, planning or guilty of murder were, by their own actions, excommunicated,

many people might be deterred from involvement in
terrorism.

'No. Categorically, no. Firstly people don't come into
confession and say, "I've just killed a soldier, I would
like absolution and I'm likely to kill again." If someone
asks for absolution for such a grave offence, the person
is clearly sorry for what they've done and they have the
right to absolution. It's not for the priest to interrogate
the person to try and discover if they're likely or intent
on committing the crime again. The priest will point out
that it is one of the most serious sins in the eyes of God
and by doing so is telling the person that God will not
tolerate murder. By and large, I doubt if many priests
find themselves with people confessing to murder or
perhaps even making a confession if they are in an
organisation which promotes violence. There are a lot
of people out there who'll one day need the confessional. Perhaps when it's all over, there'll be a lot of
hard thinking by some. My advice is "Don't assume
that you'll have the time to repent." The Church is clear
on murder and anyone guilty of it who's been brought
up a Catholic should be in no doubt about that.'

As I left Father Pat I was in no doubt that his was a
tortured soul. Perhaps, if one uses his imagery, the
connection between his mind and soul was also frayed
and might never be repaired. In his own words, he was
'the living victim'.

As I walked to my car, I reflected on one of the many
unanswered questions of our discussion. 'Father, was
that the only time you were faced with that problem?' I
had asked.

While Father Pat represented the old school of clergy,
Father Jim was part of a contemporary priesthood
dealing with paramilitaries, many of whom were of his

generation and had experienced conflict for the first time in their late teens. At one time, his parish was in a rural area where the IRA had a strong core of activists who were responsible for a large number of military and police casualties. When I met him he was working in an urban environment, was frustrated by the failure of politicians to find a resolve to the conflict and was finding it difficult to encourage young people to reject the politics of violence.

'We are all to blame for what's been going on here ... and I don't exclude the Church,' he told me. 'But the real finger of blame should be squarely aimed at the politicians. Their job is to talk and compromise, and all I can see is that each side wants peace on its terms. In that environment there is little hope. People talk of ceasefires, but the bitterness in this society's going to take more than a generation to eradicate and it would be nice to say we can start in earnest before the end of this decade. I see little chance of that!'

Unlike Father Pat, his manner was busy, sharp and direct. He was a no-nonsense individual, with a clear awareness of the political framework within which he operated.

'You ask if the Churches have failed in Ireland,' he said. 'Don't presume to think they've failed everybody. There are more good people out there than we think. The problem is, they are powerless and leaderless. The Churches in Northern Ireland have found it difficult to step out of their tribal roots. Each flock is bound to its particular Church, not simply by religious doctrine but by social, political and historical factors. I'm not gonna beat about the bush and pretend to you that the Catholic Church has played a blinder, or for that matter any of the Protestant Churches, or that Paisley's brand of Christianity is anything other than a destructive influence. The fact is that none of us grasped the nettle at the outset, or had the vision to see that each community and its Church was travelling down separate roads.'

Unlike Father Pat, anger was implicit in his demeanour and language. I asked if he was hurt by a personal sense of failure and his expression showed that he considered my question inappropriate.

'That's the problem with the media and with writers. Who should we blame? Who should carry the can for the failure? I say everybody on this island, and successive British governments who prefer expediency to serious policy-making.' He went on, more gently, 'I'm sorry if I sound angry. It's simply that I get frustrated so often because no one listens. They're all trapped in their respective prejudices. Recently I spoke to a member of the Provisional IRA who works for Sinn Fein, and all I got was the predictable rhetoric about prejudice, intolerance, injustice, the moral right of those waging the armed struggle and the intransigence of the Brits. He reminded me of other guys who went through that republican education process in the Maze prison. He had all the answers and none of the questions. I asked him where was the morality in killing innocent people or waging a campaign of violence which the majority of people in Ireland reject. His response was that innocent people get killed in war. "Tell that to the innocent people who died," I told him. He didn't understand the word "majority", and trotted out the typical IRA thesis that it was not a majority who led the 1916 Rising. I told him not to draw crude historical parallels at which he turned on his heel, reminding me that the Church should keep its nose out of politics. The Provos, I should have told him, wanted the Church in politics and on their side.'

Much of Father Jim's anger was directed at the IRA, its recruitment of young men in his parish, and the fact that some of them 'went to an early death' while others languished in prison. 'The gun has its own cult,' he told me. 'It's glamorous. It has power and so does the uniform of the balaclava and the combat jacket. Hollywood knows that and all you have to do is look at the successful films – they're all about gratuitous violence. That's what we feed our children, and when it's on the streets, they relate to it in the same way as the films. I know young men who would have said hello to me in the street, but when I approached them on a roadblock, they told me to F— off. Put them in a uniform, give them a gun and they are transformed. Do that throughout this society and you have people who are beyond reason. The paramilitaries are a separate tribe with their own rules. Oh, yes, they think they've God on their side. I've seen them in church. I've given some of them communion and I have to steel myself to ignore what I'm feeling. I'm like any other normal human being watching the destruction of innocent life ... I'm bloody angry. In some ways, I'm lucky. I can immerse myself in the Christian message and find the reasons why I should forgive them. Sometimes even that isn't enough to eradicate what's inside me.'

As he talked, I was drawn to the differences between him and the older Father Pat. He spoke about everything in a personal way, leaving the abstract to find itself.

'What would you have been if not a priest?' I asked, wondering if a career in politics might best have suited his directness.

He paused momentarily, and smiled. 'Do I get the impression,' he asked, 'that you think I am not the priestly type?'

'No, not at all. It's not for me to judge.'

'Well, I suppose I could have been a teacher. The fact is I am a priest and that's what I'll remain. People think priests should manifest a saintliness and talk only about the Christian message, whereas I think we're just as flawed as everyone else. Our job is to be shepherds who sometimes must confront those people who are threatening the flock.'

I asked him to define those whom he regarded as the enemy of his flock.

'Those who threaten its spiritual and social well-being.'

I replied that his reply was abstract and asked him to be more specific.

'You want me to name the guilty men …. the guilty parties?' He laughed.

That was exactly what I wanted.

'Let's start with governments, then politicians and the paramilitaries on both sides. That's the rogues' gallery, though not necessarily in order of threat. The immediate threat is the gun. If we don't remove this cult of violence, nothing else will change. The paramilitaries will say that government has guns. My response is that people can change government policies without the gun. Look at the Martin Luther King legacy. For their part, governments and politicians must learn to find mechanisms for dialogue and compromises which don't ultimately threaten the flock while making room for the men of violence to re-enter the fold. We all have our respective roles in that process … even a priest.'

'Is it possible,' I asked, 'that you have been damaged

by your personal experiences of conflict and, as a consequence, you can only be a victim and not a motivator?'

He ran his fingers through his hair. 'If you mean by victim, have I suffered, the answer is ... not as much as others, and my suffering is an internalised thing. It resurfaces when I least expect it. Victim! I don't think that can be adequately applied to me.'

Over the years, in writing about terrorism and interviewing people who promoted it or suffered from it, I have learned much about the stress that conflict imposes on those within it. Father Jim reminded me of people living in ghetto areas in the 1970s: they were tense, quick to take offence and emotionally volatile. Our conversation constantly changed shape at his instigation, and I began to feel that he was reluctant to talk to me about the subject I had told him I wished to discuss, or that he felt emotionally unable to deal with it. I decided to adopt the direct approach.

'Let's talk about the dilemmas facing a priest summoned to an IRA execution,' I said.

There was a stunned silence.

'Fine, but understand that in telling you about this, I expect you to be honest when you write about our meeting.'

It was an assurance I had already given to Father Pat and I willingly extended it to him.

Suddenly, nervousness crept into his voice. 'You realise this is not a matter any priest likes to talk about. The Church would see it as a betrayal.'

I asked him what he meant by 'betrayal'.

'It's difficult to explain. The Church knows that these things take place. It doesn't relish the prospect of a public debate about it. It's too easily sensationalised. It impinges on the concept of confession and secrecy. It's hard to get by that one. There's a feeling in some circles that the less said about it, the better. It's a duty some of us have had to fulfil. Just remember, there were many occasions when people were denied the assistance of a priest. Think of the scores of Catholics tortured by loyalist paramilitaries. If they had sent for me, I would have gone and my response would have been the same.'

Father Jim described how late one night, he answered a knock at the door to find armed men in balaclavas staring at him. 'You're coming with us,' they told him. Like Father Pat, he was not told why he was being removed from his house or where he was going. 'At first I thought they were a loyalist murder squad, but that was quickly dispelled when one of them said, "We're members of the Irish Republican Army." They like giving themselves their full title. They hate the term Provos or Provisionals.' He was led to a car in which the back seat had been removed, blindfolded and told to lie face down. 'We don't want t' compromise y', Father,' one said. 'It's better you don't know where we're goin'. That's the orders.'

As Father Jim told his story, anguish was etched on his face, again like Father Pat. It was obvious he could not shut out painful and hideous memories.

'I knew in my heart what they were about,' he said angrily. 'One part of me was saying that I was glad to be there, another part of me was filled with anger. It wasn't simply the cavalier way they were treating the whole matter, but the fact that nominally these men were Catholics and they were treating a priest like an undertaker.'

He was led into a farmhouse and the blindfold was pulled from his face. 'Nowadays the only word I can find to describe it was surreal. Nothing in the priest-hood prepares you for it. In the kitchen was a young man being held down in a chair. His hair was caked in blood and I couldn't see his face. He was dressed in underpants, and his socks, shoes and shirt were scattered about the room. In all, there were four masked men in the room, two of them armed and all of them wearing balaclavas. One who appeared to be the leader motioned me to a corner of the room. I was about to confront him when he said, "Shut up and listen. He's a tout and we're gonna nut him. Now we've been kind enough to get you here so do the business." He waved the others from the room and told me I would not be interrupted while I heard the victim's confession. "We don't always do this," he told me, meaning that this was some sort of concession. "The Brits could be lookin' for him and we're pressed for time, so make it quick." There are times in your life when you say, "If I was there, I would ..." There are also times in your life when you are emotionally naked, when all those principles you believe you stand for cannot be realised. I ... I will never be able to fully express how inadequate I felt as the gunmen left the room and I looked at the pitiful figure in front of me. He couldn't lift his head for the pain. Some of the bruises looked like cigarette burns.'

The victim's hands were not tied, and when the priest approached him he remained with his head bowed.

'I knelt down and raised his head. The only tears there were mine ... He couldn't cry or speak ... It was as if he was frozen with fear or accepted that his life was over. Christ, what can anybody do in those circumstances? I wanted to cry out to Heaven for mercy. This was not me there, not the priest from the pulpit confronting

violence. I was suddenly a part of it. That young man
never spoke. His silence said it all. He'd made his peace
with God. He didn't really need me. When I got up to
go, he squeezed my hand. I didn't know how to reply
and I regret that ... Christ knows, I regret that. My
arrogance was always to believe I could confront men of
violence, reason with them. I was naïve and arrogant
and that handshake proved it. I said nothing as I left
that place. It wasn't just the shock of the experience ... I
didn't know how to respond ... I felt helpless and
useless.'

Father Jim's anger had gone and he buried his head in
his hands.

'Now I know,' he said, looking piercingly at me, 'that
it was important I was there. God was there in the
serenity of that handshake. Someday some of those men
who were there that night will also know that.'

I asked Father Jim if he believed the victim was guilty
of the crime alleged by the IRA.

He stared angrily at me. 'Nothing justifies the horror
I saw.'

Father Jim never learned the identity of the victim and
believes he was secretly buried. 'On the return journey, I
heard one of the men in the car say that a grave had
been dug.'

I told him that many people would argue that priests
who knew the identity of killers were morally bound to
provide the authorities with information.

'That brings us into a theological debate about the
role of a priest in conflict,' he replied angrily.

Like Father Pat, he felt that his priestly duty, no
matter how difficult, was to minister to his flock. I
pointed out that he had defined one of his roles as
protector of his flock.

'Spiritually ... yes. I cannot be the policeman. We all have different roles.'

I suggested that in helping the police he might prevent the same people killing other members of his congregation.

'There are two issues here. One is that I am taking the confessional to someone. To play the role of the policeman would potentially lead to a situation in which other poor unfortunates are denied a priest. Then there is the society divided as it is. If I play the policeman in my community, I put all priests at risk, I alienate myself and make it impossible to function. That's a harsh reality but it is the reality. There's no way round it.'

He was reverting to rhetoric to obscure an obvious sense of failure. He had faced a dilemma that few people experience, and to which he had no conclusive answer.

Like his colleague, Father Pat, he never referred the matter to the Church hierarchy, explaining, 'It's a personal matter, not even one which fellow priests discuss. You ask priests does this happen and the majority will say, no, it doesn't. They've never experienced it. It's not the kind of issue the hierarchy would wish to discuss privately or publicly. It's a matter of individual conscience, and the rules about the confessional are strictly laid down in canon law.'

In Book Four of the Canon Law text, priests are bound by the rules to hear the confession of anyone who is 'in danger of death' and using knowledge that constitutes breaking the seal of the confessional is one of the most serious crimes they can commit.

Father Jim also made the point that the nature of the confession he described appeared to cover the events of that evening, providing a cloak of secrecy to the gunmen present. He refused to explain that concept, leaving me to conclude that during his confession the victim may have forgiven his captors, leaving the priest with an intriguing dilemma. Though this is conjecture, in those circumstances, the priest might have felt that the confessional seal also encompassed his knowledge of what had happened in that farmhouse.

Father Pat and Father Jim supported the orthodox acceptance of the inviolable character of the 'sacramental seal'. My assessment of both men was that they were genuinely Christian, living in a society to which they were deeply committed. It would be much too simplistic to suggest that they could or should have acted differently when faced with terrible circumstances. They fulfilled, according to canon law, the requirements of the priestly life, they faced danger and, as they admitted, they live with the horror of what they witnessed, compounded by subsequent feelings of inadequacy. Anyone doubting their integrity should ask the question: 'What would I have done in a similar situation?'

But the concept of the tortured soul is not exclusive to priests: in the world of conflict, some paramilitaries believe that they, too, are in danger of losing the link to God.

A MAVERICK PRIEST?

'Close the curtains, have a brandy, a good wank and forget about what's out there!' That was the advice Father Pat Buckley received from a fellow cleric after he arrived as a newly ordained curate in West Belfast.

Buckley said that when he first walked around the Lower Falls 'it was like walking on the moon'. It was 1978, two years after his ordination, his first time in Northern Ireland, and he asked himself, 'What the hell am I doing here?'

Born in the Republic of Ireland, his knowledge of the Troubles had been derived from television news footage and newspaper headlines. No one had prepared him for his posting and there was no system of advice within the Church for naïve young men like him. He was assigned to St Peter's, whose twin spires dominated the Lower Falls area of the city and the nearby Divis Flats, which saw regular conflict. The crude advice he received was not from his fellow curates in St Peter's but from another priest in the city who felt that a quiet life was preferable to any involvement with the community.

Pat Buckley is a controversial priest who was in constant conflict with cardinals, bishops and fellow clergy over issues ranging from celibacy to mixed marriages to the role of the Church in a society in conflict. He is a weekly columnist for the *News of the World* and an outspoken commentator on religious and political affairs. Within the echelons of the Catholic Church, he is ridiculed because he broke with tradition, ignored the code of silence, an unwritten rule of the Church that priests did not criticise publicly either each other or Church institutions, and freely engaged in public debate. The Pat Buckley in whom I was interested was the priest who found himself dealing with the IRA, and was frequently at odds with fellow curates because of his unorthodox approach.

He was twenty-six when he was sent to Belfast and quickly discovered that priests were pro-republican, neutral or anti-IRA. When he arrived in the Divis area, 'fresh from the Republic', he did not have a 'political thought in his body'. The environment quickly changed him. 'I was becoming more and more nationalist or republican. If you feel for people, if you're working with them every day, hearing their woes, you begin to get sucked into where they're at. It was quite natural for that to happen in that situation.'

His response was not part of a rational thought process, rather a gut reaction to events. His emotions and feelings were determined by incidents such as a soldier jabbing a rifle butt into the ribs of a youth from the local social club. Buckley did not assume, as the nationalist thesis would have it, that this was how the British Army treated all youth. He simply saw 'wee Johnny' being given a 'hammering by a soldier from Manchester'. As he watched that episode he did not ask himself how he would have felt if 'wee Johnny' had been running down the street with an AK47 assault rifle. There were many paradoxes and variables in that political situation which, at that time, he did not understand or always detect. But Buckley was not without courage and he confronted the soldier. He quickly discovered that 'other soldiers' could be much more dangerous.

It was months into his ministry when the fresh-faced curate discovered that the Provisionals were encouraging young people to riot in order to lure British Army patrols into the narrow side streets. He approached prominent republicans, and tried to remonstrate with them, pointing out that they were placing young lives in jeopardy. He was told to 'take himself off' and did so only to return with a camera minus a film. He pretended to photograph the ringleaders and continued to do so in other riots.

He believed that his clerical collar protected him from the IRA, but then realised that anyone who confronted them became a target for violence. Late one evening as he walked round the perimeter of the church, three IRA men shoved him against the railings and pushed a Walther pistol into his mouth. One told him that he would be leaving the area in a 'wooden overcoat' if he continued to 'shoot off' his mouth. Of that episode, he says it made him wonder about his role as a priest and what it constituted. He had not anticipated the IRA reaction, believing that he defended republicans when they were unfairly harassed which should have guaranteed him protection, but he said, 'As a priest, I could not stand by and let them use kids as cannon fodder.'

He convinced himself that the IRA threat had been simply a threat, basing his assumption on his knowledge of the Falls area in which women and priests were the two groupings capable of confronting the IRA and living to tell the tale. Women were the mothers or sisters

of IRA men, and the killing of a 'man of God' would
lead to a propaganda backlash throughout Catholic
Ireland. So why were there not more priests on the
streets confronting the men of violence? Were they
frightened of the bullet, of stepping outside their tribe,
or did they not wish to be portrayed as political?
Buckley's frank reply astounded me.

'I'm gonna tell you something. When a priest took me
aside in another part of the city and gave me that advice
about closing the curtains, having a brandy and a wank,
he looked out of a window and said, "Look! This place
is hopeless. The people are hopeless. They're as thick
here as bottled pig-shit. You'll be wasting your time
getting involved with them." '

Buckley realised that many priests regarded the events
on the streets as a 'distasteful business' and closed the
curtains. They had no wish to get involved in a situation
that carried with it risks to life and limb, or to confront
what Buckley describes as the moral dilemmas and 'the
big hassles'. He did not need to be told that the IRA,
and not the Catholic Church, exercised the greatest
power. The Provisionals had power over life and death
and could grant concessions. It was their ability to grant
a concession to a priest, such as sparing a life, that made
their authority more potent than that of the Church.
They used that power to draw priests into their sphere
of influence, demonstrating that their superiority could
not be ignored.

'One of our kids in the youth club committed a semi-
rape and the local Provos decided they were going to
"nut him" ... give him one in the head. I had to go to a
guy in the area who was senior in the Provos and I got
the sentence commuted. Instead of a "nut job", they
picked him up and for four hours the following

Saturday night six Provos paraded him round social clubs. He was put on a stage and, during a break in music, he had to admit what he had done, that he was a rapist. He had to give his name and address and it was a question of total humiliation. To me it was the only way I could prevent that kid being shot. If you like, I was going to the Provos who were the forces of law and order in the community. I did it for a higher order to save the kid's life.'

The episode convinced Pat Buckley that he was shepherd and the IRA were 'masters of the flock'. They were, he says, into power and control and they proved it to him by demonstrating that, when he needed their help, they could be magnanimous. They convinced the community that they were the rightful people to control crime, that they were the appointed police force. It was a claim recognised not only by people living in West Belfast but also by the Church.

Buckley was quick to point out that before the onset of the present Troubles the Catholic Church and the RUC were the two organisations representing authority in Catholic districts. When Catholic neighbourhoods became no-go zones for the RUC after the burnings of August 1969, the policing vacuum was filled by the IRA. The conclusion Buckley reached as he settled into his post was that the Church had lost credibility. The erosion of its power he attributed to its failure adequately to represent its flock during years of discrimination. The Provisionals had stepped into that breach too and captured the hearts and minds of Catholic nationalists. Buckley is not alone in alleging that, during fifty years of Unionist rule, the Catholic Church in Ireland did not effectively confront State mismanagement or social injustice. Like Father Denis Faul, he

singles out for criticism Bishop Philbin of the Down and
Conor diocese. 'If Philbin had led two hundred thousand people up the Falls Road demanding civil rights,
the Provos might not have been necessary. People power
elsewhere in the world has demonstrated that. If the
Church had had the prophetic insight to see that, and
had taken peaceful action ... They should have led but
all they did was rub their hands, condemn atrocities at
funerals and never take a positive role.'

During the 1960s Cardinal Conway, the Roman
Catholic Primate of All-Ireland, warned his bishops that
they should heed the events of the 1920s and be careful
not to say or do anything that would return Northern
Irish society to sectarian war. But he failed to move the
Church towards a more central role in the political
development of the nationalist community, leaving a
vacuum for men with long-term political objectives and
a philosophy rooted in historical violence. From the
confines of his palace Bishop Philbin watched the
Provisional IRA emerge as events in Belfast in August
1969 moved its society ever deeper into conflict.

Pat Buckley's dealings with the IRA were not confined to concessions or street confrontations but also to
the confessional. It was in the context of confessional
secrecy, the 'seal' demanded by canon law, that he faced
one of the most difficult decisions of his life. One
evening, an IRA officer stepped into a confession box in
St Peter's and began to unburden himself to Buckley. He
said he had just left a meeting of senior IRA figures who
were planning the assassination of a Unionist MP. For
two hours Pat Buckley pleaded with the man to give
him permission to warn the politician of the plot.
Finally the man agreed and Buckley left the confessional

and phoned the police with details of the IRA plan, which was foiled.

I asked Father Buckley what he would have done if the penitent had not given him permission to use the information.

'I would have done it anyway! The MP did not go to the site where a sniper was lying in wait. I managed to do that without compromising the confessional!'

I pointed out that if he had breached the canon law seal to protect the MP's life, it would have led to his dismissal from the priesthood and excommunication.

'I wouldn't have told anyone who the guy was who had been in the confessional. I just couldn't have sat around for days knowing it was going to happen and then watched the television news of the assassination. I know I would have been automatically excommunicated. I believe the whole ethic of human life takes precedence over canon law. I was able to maintain the anonymity of the person in confession and save the other guy. I think morally that's what I had to do.'

His willingness to break with canon law would be regarded by many reasonable people as the moral choice of a brave man, but would not be condoned by his Church. The rule would have been upheld that the penitent, if he had refused permission for the information to be used and also since he was not to be the killer, was entitled to the seal of confession. The episode clearly illustrated the kind of dilemma faced by a young priest who had been given no guidance on how to deal with such a situation. The Troubles were already ten years old and no one in the Church hierarchy had recognised the dangers faced by a recently ordained curate.

Buckley learned that he had to make his own

decisions and choices. He heard the confession of a paedophile, who admitted to abusing children in the neighbourhood of St Peter's. Again, he convinced the penitent to permit him to break the confessional seal and he agreed. Buckley went to the parents of the abused children and warned them of the dangers. He said that, again, he felt so strongly that he would have acted without the paedophile's permission.

I told Buckley of my conversations with Father Pat and Father Jim, of how they had been traumatised, their feelings of vulnerability and their belief that the confessional seal appeared to extend to the whole episode. At first, his reaction to their experiences appeared naïve, although the more he talked about how he would have behaved in their place, the more I sensed that he would have acted differently.

'I haven't been quite in that situation. I know I'd be shitting myself but I know I couldn't live with myself if I didn't do my utmost to get that guy out of there.'

'Even if that cost you your life?'

'Yes! To the point of threatening them, exposing them, I would do it!'

'Isn't that easy to say?' I replied. 'If someone puts a gun to your head, bundles you into a car and says, "You do your business, and let us do ours," what choice would you really make in those circumstances?'

'I would attach myself to the victim. They would have to pistol-whip me, kill me, to get me away from him.'

Pat Buckley studiously avoided confrontation with the Church hierarchy until an event brought him to the attention of his bishop, Cahal Daly, later the Primate of All-Ireland. It blighted their dealings for years and illustrated the genuine instincts of the young priest.

It began with the arrest of a republican in the town of

Larne on the Co. Antrim coastline. The suspect, to whom I shall refer as Mr A, was brought to the Castlereagh interrogation centre in Belfast, and his wife, a Protestant girl, heavily pregnant, was also arrested and taken there. Mr A saw his wife being paraded in front of a glass panel and was told that if he did not become a Special Branch informer, she would be charged with murder. He refused to co-operate and his wife was released, but his interrogation continued. Two days later, Mr A's wife was about to be rearrested and taken back to the police centre.

Buckley says that a source told him that the police were again going to parade her in front of her husband. His interrogators wanted either a confession or his agreement to become an informer within the IRA. The source, whom Buckley refused to name, asked him to spirit Mr A's wife to a safe haven in the Irish Republic. It did not occur to Buckley that he was perhaps being used by the IRA. He says he believed that Mr A's wife was an innocent person and that the stress of her rearrest might damage her unborn child. For him, it was a humanitarian act that he would have performed for anyone, irrespective of their religion or politics. He drove her secretly to a prearranged destination in the Irish Republic while newspapers speculated about her disappearance.

'As I was driving back through Northern Ireland, I was under immense pressure and fear. I was stopped by police patrols several times and shown photographs and asked if I knew her whereabouts. Later I saw the *Belfast Telegraph* and a headline that "Fiona A" was kidnapped.'

When he thought his ordeal was over, he was shocked to receive a telephone call from a Catholic

prison chaplain. He said it was important that Buckley
drove to Downpatrick for a secret rendezvous.

'I drove down and there were flashing lights and all
that stuff. I got into his car and he said to me that I had
come to the attention of the RUC. They knew I had
made the trip to the Republic and they were coming to
arrest me for kidnapping. "What I would advise you to
do," he said, "is go home, put a pair of pyjamas and a
toothbrush into a bag because they are coming for
you." I replied that was fine but maybe we should tell
the Bishop, Cahal Daly. He said, "You're right, we
should." Daly wasn't in his palace but in his sister's
house, in Rosetta, so we went up there to see him. I told
him what had happened and he nearly swallowed his
false teeth.'

Buckley alleged that Bishop Daly said, ' "What you
did was right. You did it for the right reasons. You did
nothing wrong. I would have done that but you know
what this crowd is like in Northern Ireland. They could
make a meal out of this and I'd be worried for the good
name of the Church in Northern Ireland. Would you let
me sort it out at a very high level?" and he indicated it
would be with Hermon, the RUC chief constable. I said,
"You do what you want and I'll go home anyway and
pack my toothbrush and leave it up to you." So,
nothing happened, and about a week later I got a letter
from Daly, which said that he had sorted the matter out
and there would be nothing more about it if I was
prepared to give the police my full co-operation. I wrote
back to him and said, "Do you not think there are
enough informers in Ireland without the priests starting?" That was the beginning of my problems with Daly
and nobody knows that.'

Several issues emerged from that episode, one being

that while Pat Buckley may have believed that he was acting in a humanitarian fashion he was unaware of the complexities of politics and policing. An astute observer would conclude that he was a young priest who did not fully understand the possible outcome of his actions: he had risked being charged with abduction or even obstructing the course of justice. His description of his meeting with the Bishop indicated a divergence of opinion and a failure to recognise that the Bishop was trying to protect him. But Buckley was worried that in co-operating with the police he would be giving himself to something that might lead to him being compromised. There was no guarantee that they would not have put him under pressure. The outcome was that the matter was buried and the RUC made no effort to compromise him, which illustrates the power of the Church in certain situations. Bishop Daly probably recognised that if it had become known that Buckley had been involved in spiriting someone across the Border, his actions would result in other priests being branded republican sympathisers and placed on loyalist target lists. What did not come to light was that, years later, when Buckley took the Church, in the person of his bishop, to an industrial tribunal alleging wrongful dismissal, Bishop Daly's letter to him was introduced as evidence. The section of it that suggested he co-operate with the police was not read out in court on the instructions of the president of the tribunal.

The priest Buckley replaced at St Peter's, Alex Darragh, was pro-republican and Buckley says that he learned Darragh had been prepared to hold guns for the IRA. He compares Darragh's attitude with that of other priests who emerged from a republican tradition. 'He was a Catholic from Carnlough near the arch-loyalist borough of Larne. Those types of Catholic were from communities who felt they were second-class citizens, discriminated against. That kind of justified the whole republican thing to them. They would have felt that by helping "the boys", by minding the guns, or covering up, they would have been helping the cause.'

Buckley said that many priests subscribed to the thesis that the IRA was fighting a just war against an eight-hundred-year-old oppressor. He added that some clergy felt that the death of a British soldier, though sad and regrettable, was morally justifiable. 'It's all tied in with the Church's belief that God is a Catholic and Protestants are heretics. God is on their side. The IRA also has this thing. I knew active-service Provos who went to daily Mass and communion, did their novenas, went home, put on balaclavas and went out with the gun. In their pockets they would have had their prayer to St Joseph for a happy death and the wee wooden cross to protect them from evil. It was a superstitious religion tied in with the whole Catholic nationalist thing, the theology of the just war.' In and out of the confessional he debated this issue with republicans, adhering to the principle of the sanctity of the individual conscience, and each person's right to make a personal moral decision. Rarely did members of the IRA use the confessional to seek absolution for murder. 'They didn't regard killing as a sin. They'd come into confession and tell you they'd missed their morning prayers or had sex with somebody other than their wives. They didn't confess to violence. They might say, "Look! I'm a republican, and I'm just saying that in passing because I don't regard it as a sin." I would say, "That's a moral issue, let's talk about it." '

It was, in any case, older, self-righteous republicans

who came to confession while the younger ones ignored the Church and rarely attended. According to Buckley, though, IRA veterans were inflexible men, unwilling to enter a debate about God and the gun. When he dispensed communion to men he knew were guilty of dreadful things, he was overcome with sadness.

As a young priest, Buckley felt isolated because he did not know where to turn for genuine debate or advice. However, he recalled an occasion when he first arrived in Belfast and was attending a Christmas party at the home of Bishop Philbin in North Belfast. 'The Bishop said to me, "Anything you can do to counteract the IRA, do it." It was a throwaway line and it was the only conversation I ever had with him.' The Bishop's advice was not unreasonable. He saw priests in the front line and believed it was their moral duty to advise their flock that membership of the IRA was sinful and that those who supported the organisation in its campaign of violence were acting against the moral wishes of the Church. Buckley did not consider the advice sincere. He saw it as typical of Church statements, which appeared to carry little authority and were intended to placate the British government.

Buckley's criticism of the role of religion in the conflict is not reserved for his own Church but all Churches, which he believed to be cynical and manipulative, preoccupied with power and controlling their respective communities. They played the tunes of prejudice in a society where bigotry was already endemic.

I first met Pat Buckley in the early 1980s when I was producing and editing a controversial current-affairs programme for BBC Northern Ireland. At our first meeting, I sensed that he was the kind of frank and outspoken priest who would soon find his way into the media. He was always prepared to talk openly about controversial issues, which I knew would exacerbate the deterioration of his relationship with his superiors.

Buckley soon found himself at odds with his fellow priests in Divis when he turned the parochial house into a haven for unruly teenagers. Suddenly the priests' lives were disturbed by the arrival of young people at all times of the day and particularly at night when the noise made sleep impossible. Buckley dismissed their objections, but there was a wider gulf between him and the other priests of St Peter's: 'During the hunger strike of '81, people in Divis were saying the rosary every day for the hunger strikers and I joined them in prayer. I remember my parish priest coming into the back of the church and ordering me out of there. When he got me into the sacristy he said, "What the fuck are you doing in there?" I said I was praying with the people. He said, "You can pray for those bastards but you shouldn't be *seen* to be praying for them." What he was really saying was that we should all feel sympathy for them on hunger strike but, after all, they were murderers. So we have to have our sympathy but be careful how we express it. As far as he was concerned, Bobby Sands and the others were in there for murders, crimes and stuff and they were our people. We felt for them, we didn't feel for the Brits, but we couldn't be seen to be too much on their side.'

He was forbidden to attend Bobby Sands' funeral but ignored the instruction: 'The Church said it would look bad in the eyes of the police and the authorities if a guy in a collar was seen walking behind the coffin. I replied that I didn't agree with the Provos but I had heard Sands' confession, given him communion and I knew

his family. I went to the funeral and was ostracised by
my fellow priests. They wouldn't eat with me in the
dining room. I had to eat in the kitchen with the
housekeeper. It was because I was becoming too
involved with the people, with their struggles, etc.'

His fellow clerics must certainly have felt uneasy
about his conduct, perhaps worried that by bringing the
events on the streets into their lives he was placing
himself and them in jeopardy. They also felt that his
behaviour compromised an agreed approach to dealing
with the problems in West Belfast: he ignored an
important Church principle that in ministering to his
flock a priest should not become involved in political
dispute. The bishops feared that one priest acting alone
was capable of changing public perceptions of the
Church's role in a society ridden with political violence.
He might present an image of disunity within the
Church, which would be exploited by the media, who
might represent his views as those of the Church. It was
dangerous to confront the IRA and priests who had the
courage to do so often found themselves rejected and
publicly humiliated by members of their flock. Buckley
asserted that the discord between him and his fellow
priests was reflected in behaviour that most Catholics
would not associate with the priesthood. When he had
been a seminarian, the priests who taught him were
regarded as gods. In the outside world he encountered a
different type of cleric: 'When I went into the dining
room, they gave me verbal torture. They used to get
pissed and sing songs outside my door at three in the
morning. Most of this I have never told anyone because
they would not believe me.'

He suggested that his fellow priests thought that his
behaviour was denuding the priesthood of its mystery

and power: priests believed that the pulpit gave them power, not direct contact with the people. 'One of the things which really infuriated them was that I organised a clean-up in Divis Flats. I put on a pair of blue dungarees given to me by the housing executive. I went out and brushed up dead rats, dirty nappies and stuff. Two of them were at the window knocking it and giving me the fingers. When I went in for my lunch, one of them, pretending I wasn't there, said, "What would you think of a fella who's ordained a priest and becomes a fucking bin man? What would you think of him?" '

I was surprised at the language he attributed to other priests but Buckley said, 'You haven't a clue. Most priests when it comes to sex are adolescents. They're at the experimental stage and mystified by the whole thing. That's why they're so very bad at being committed in relationships. They are human beings like the rest of us ... even more human. They have the same money thing ... the same power thing.'

From Buckley's description of the human frailty of priests, their difficulty in confronting some of the issues in a violent society is understandable. Some who stood up to the gunmen were traumatised and retreated into a world of mental breakdown and silence. I found them reluctant to discuss their experiences because they feared that they would show weakness in themselves inconsistent with the perceived strengths of the religious life.

Priests who publicly confronted the authorities were not only branded pro-IRA but privately reprimanded by their superiors. Buckley knew two priests in North Belfast who had delivered a verbal barrage at the British Army for destroying the street lighting in their parish. This had been done because the lights illuminated streets in which soldiers were vulnerable to sniper fire. The priests, though, felt strongly that the streets should be well lit because darkness enabled loyalist murder gangs to abduct their parishioners: the Shankill Butchers and other loyalist gangs were operating with apparent impunity in that part of the city, unhindered by the Army or the police. The priests accepted that the Army was always at risk from snipers but those at greater risk were innocent people. The arguments on both sides were equally valid but Bishop Philbin was more concerned about two of his priests being involved in a political debate. Buckley said, 'The priests were summoned to a meeting with Philbin and several Army officers. When the meeting ended, the Army officers were asked to stay for tea and the priests were asked to leave. It was a sign of the Bishop's displeasure with his priests.'

The priesthood had always been a seamless, tightly knit club, in which individuals were expected to conform and those who went their own way did so at their peril. Buckley remembered an occasion at the parochial house when the priests made fun of one of their group because he had appeared in a corridor late one evening shouting, 'Is there anyone here to pray with me?' Priests rarely prayed with each other, perhaps feeling that prayer was something to be undertaken privately or in large groups which permitted a degree of anonymity.

Politics was a topic for dining rooms and Buckley said: 'Northern Irish priests tended to be nationalist or republican. I had never heard priests talking like that in the South. I was in a dining room when a priest looked out the window and said, "There's the fucking Brits again." When you met soldiers in the streets, they

looked at you wondering if you were going to speak to
them. As far as I was concerned, it was probably an
eighteen-year-old from Liverpool and it wasn't his fault
he was over here. The people didn't approve of me
speaking to the soldiers and I was often reprimanded by
the people for saying "hello!" ' He went on, 'I was
walking down Leeson Street with Father Jimmy
McCabe, a fellow curate. A soldier came running after
us shouting at Jimmy McCabe, "Father, Father."
McCabe was storming along and whispered, "Fuck off
… Don't talk to him." The soldier caught up with him,
put his hand on his shoulder and from under his
uniform produced a miraculous medal of Our Lady.
"Would you bless that for me, Father?" he asked.
Jimmy McCabe refused.'

However, many priests would argue that the military
were often ill-disposed to the Catholic clergy, and in the
early years of the Troubles there was hostility between
the Church and the British Army. Pat Buckley once
found himself in a serious confrontation with an Army
patrol. 'One day a Provo on a balcony in Divis Flats
was shot by a military sniper. He was alive when I
reached him and gave him the Last Rites. Everyone
knew he was active in the Provos but on that day he was
unarmed. He was walking along the balcony when he
got it in the back. There was a lot of trouble at the time
and I got into the ambulance with him. On our way
along the Falls Road to the Royal Victoria Hospital, six
soldiers blocked the road and pointed their guns at the
ambulance. The ambulance driver told me to lie on the
floor and that he was going to drive through them. I
told him there was no way we were going through …
we would be riddled. The driver stopped, was taken out
and told to lie on the road. I was made to do the same

thing. I had a gun in my ear and I could hear the guy in the ambulance choking on his own blood. I told the soldier in charge that the guy was dying and he replied, "That's the idea, mate." They held us there for ten or fifteen minutes and when we got the guy to the hospital, he was dead.'

Pat Buckley made representation to police and Army chiefs and was told there was no case to answer. On several occasions soldiers tried to prevent him driving along the Falls Road, others would greet him with, 'Good day, Vicar,' while a minority saw him and other priests as chaplains to the IRA.

Naïve, humanitarian, vulnerable are words applicable to Pat Buckley. Malicious, republican, anti-British are not. His honesty led him to tell me of episodes that might bring others to condemn him as a dangerous cleric. One evening three Provisionals arrived at his parochial house and told him they had a wounded colleague. They asked Buckley to ferry him across the Border: if the man was treated in a Belfast hospital he would be arrested and charged after treatment. Buckley, acting on instinct, undertook the task and says he would have done the same for a loyalist, for anyone irrespective of their political beliefs. He did not know whether the man had been shot in a gun battle or had killed a soldier.

His involvement in that episode illustrated the problem he posed for fellow clerics and the Church. He was a loose cannon, an unguided missile. In the early 1980s he was transferred to the quiet town of Kilkeel, on the Co. Down coastline. His superiors undoubtedly believed that there he would fade into obscurity. They were wrong. 'For me it was another parish in a society at war.' He made that comment with his usual candour and his smile confirmed he had known that the move from Belfast was politically motivated.

In Kilkeel he was up against members of the feared INLA. He challenged their influence on the youth of the community and received death threats, but ignored the risks and began running a weekly disco in the parish hall. Late one evening when he was putting the takings in a safe in a back room of the building he heard people screaming. Suddenly there was a knocking at the door. When he opened it he was confronted by two armed men wearing balaclavas. A revolver was put against his head and he was told to hand over the night's takings. He leaped to one side, slammed the door, locked it, ensured the safe was secure, and escaped through a window. As he ran to a telephone to summon the police and the Army, the gunmen lined everyone against the walls of the disco demanding to know Buckley's whereabouts. 'Young people were crying and screaming. One of the gunmen told them he would be at ten o'clock Mass the next morning to shoot me. As the gunmen ran from the building, they met me on my way in. They asked if I'd phoned "the fucking cops". I told them I had and it would be better if they remained with me until the police arrived. As they ran to a car, I took down the registration number.'

The two gunmen were later arrested and he gave evidence against them in court. The parents of one were angry with him but those of the other were pleased that he had helped to take their son out of circulation. They said that his arrest ensured that he could not commit a more serious crime.

A HOLY CAUSE
FOR HOLY MEN?

O nly those who live in Ireland know the real significance of being born into one of the two traditions and the conditioning that automatically takes place. Des O'Hagan found himself in a typical Irish Catholic family that shaped him for conflict. His maternal grandfather had been first secretary of the Dockers' Union in Belfast and a friend and associate of James Connolly, the socialist leader and prominent leader of the Rising, executed by the British in Dublin in 1916. Though not a republican, Connolly was, in the minds of Belfast republicans, one of theirs. Des O'Hagan remembers his mother talking about Connolly and how his brand of socialism had found fertile ground within her Irish nationalism.

Her politics were not uncommon in West Belfast and she saw Éamon de Valera as the man representing the continuity of the republican tradition, but she told her son that de Valera betrayed the cause of freedom by signing the treaty with the British that led to partition.

Like many of her contemporaries, she was a devout Catholic though her attitude to the Catholic Church was unusual in nationalist areas of Belfast: she believed that the Church existed to preach the word of God and should not interfere in politics.

O'Hagan remembered that during the Spanish Civil War she castigated the clergy and the Church hierarchy for supporting General Franco and publicly blessing Irishmen who fought for him. She told her son that to be a true republican he had also to be a socialist. Like many Irish Catholic mothers of the first half of this century, she was the forceful dynamic in the family. Her husband, Peter, was a nationalist and a leading member of the Ancient Order of Hibernians, which many regarded as the Catholic equivalent of the Orange Order. The Hibernians traced their origins to a Catholic insurrection of 1641, though the title was acquired in the 1930s. Associated with the defence of the Catholic faith, it was organised in divisions and promoted Irish nationalism. It held its parades on 15 August, the feast of the Assumption of the Virgin Mary into Heaven, and its members paraded with banners and sashes, again like the Orange Order. But Peter O'Hagan and his wife were opposed to the sectarian divisions that character-ised life in Northern Ireland, and especially in West Belfast where the two communities had fought from the middle of the nineteenth century.

When the time came for Des O'Hagan to start primary school, his mother told him that she had chosen St Comgall's in Divis Street, which had once been an integrated school known as 'The Model'. It was located near the Catholic/Protestant divide but had been burned down in sectarian riots in the 1920s and was taken under the control of the Catholic Church. It stood in the shadow of the twin towers of St Peter's, the Catholic church that dominated the West Belfast sky-line. O'Hagan remembered his father having bitter arguments with local priests about the decision to rename the school and make it one-denominational.

O'Hagan believes that his developing awareness of society was supplemented by a Catholic ethos derived from his schooling. Yet of all the elements shaping his life, it was, he recalled, his mother who moved him towards the republican tradition. 'She read voraciously about the republican struggle in Ireland and there were books which presented a romanticised interpretation of history. Dan Breen's *My Fight for Irish Freedom* was one of the first books she put in my hands. It could be said she was a woman who believed that republicanism was for republicans and nationalism was for those who were not sure what they were.'

Her definition accurately reflected the political dilemma within Irish nationalism. Nationalists were often defined as those who were content to aspire to the ideal of Irish unity but were not prepared to go the whole way, with an armed struggle, to achieve it. Much to the annoyance of her husband, she voted against nationalist candidates in local elections. On his thirteenth birthday, her son joined the Fianna, the youth wing of the IRA. He says, 'It was practically automatic ... a part of my heritage. It was the boys' organisation with an entrée to the IRA. There was nothing particularly sophisticated about the Fianna. There were rudimentary lectures about the history of the 1916 Rising. Looking back, it's bizarre to think that at thirteen I joined an organisation which would eventually train me for conflict.'

Within two years he was told he was ready to take an oath and become a fully fledged member of the IRA. 'Looking back, I saw the issue as Irish freedom through a romantic tradition.'

At fifteen, his mind and language were imbued with stories of glorious IRA exploits and the figures lionised in his mother's stories, while his progression from the Fianna to the IRA gave him a sense of achievement. He was under the tutelage of men experienced in the ways of militant republicanism. The oath, the secrecy, the membership of an organisation with its own codes and hierarchy increased his self-esteem and made him feel more important than his peers. His mother's accounts of the past were supplanted by others told by men who were an integral part of the tradition and, much more significantly, could be, in their opinion, instrumental in shaping the future.

Once in the IRA, Des O'Hagan found himself under the influence of two important members, Seamus McCallum, the Belfast commander, and Frank McKearney, a senior operative. In particular, he was impressed by McKearney who was a republican in the Connolly, socialist tradition: 'McKearney was concerned about class issues while many republicans fitted into the romantic tradition, favouring leaders of the 1916 Rising such as Padraig Pearse. For them, republicanism was simply a matter of forcing the British out of Ireland and uniting it. McKearney was concerned about uniting the working class.'

Irrespective of the political divisions inside the IRA in Belfast, religion united all the republican factions. There was no perceived conflict between membership of an organisation committed to the violent overthrow of British rule in Northern Ireland and Roman Catholicism. O'Hagan went further: 'There was also no conflict in many of them being anti-Protestant. Being in the IRA and being a Roman Catholic, somehow or other, fulfilled obligations which were handed down. The IRA

wasn't a Catholic organisation though at yearly commemoration ceremonies decades of the rosary were said
and there was other symbolism of that kind. It must
have horrified any non-Catholic who wished to subscribe to the republican tradition.'

One of the senior IRA figures who featured prominently in the Belfast Brigade was Jimmy Steele, who
argued against socialism, defining it as a form of
communism: anti-Catholic and anti-God. He told the
young men joining the IRA that Padraig Pearse, unlike
Connolly, had been a devout Catholic and the real icon
of the 1916 Rising. Within twenty years men like Steele
had formed the Provisional IRA, renouncing any connection with an IRA that had moved to the left, and
defining the republican struggle as a holy cause. 'Steele
played up the concept of "Good and Holy Men for
Good and Holy Causes". They told me that the fight for
Irish freedom was a good and holy cause, not a class
struggle. The emphasis was on good and holy men.'

Steele had good reason to believe the cause was
blessed: the history he had learned had been acquired
through Catholic schooling and the teaching order, the
Christian Brothers.

Des O'Hagan accepts that the blood-sacrifice tradition of republicans before and during the 1916 Rising,
and the avowed willingness to give one's life in the fight
for freedom, was rooted in religious symbolism (Christ
on the Cross). The leaders of the 1916 April Rising in
Dublin had known they faced overwhelming odds, that
they would be slaughtered by the British, but it was a
sacrifice worth making to resurrect the revolutionary
fervour in the Irish spirit. Many accepted death in the
conviction that their cause was just and morally
defensible. That the Rising occurred when Catholics

celebrated the Resurrection of Christ strengthened the
religious connotation. O'Hagan believes that subsequent Easter Sunday IRA commemorations effectively
linked Christ's death and Resurrection with IRA myth-
ology.

He says he was lucky to be tutored by Seamus
McCallum, and not the faction represented by Steele. 'I
am eternally grateful to have known McCallum and
perhaps others like McKearney, Dixie Cordner and Joe
Quinn. They had a more realistic view of what we were
involved in. McKearney had a class antagonism
towards the people who owned his house, namely the
Catholic Church.' After a 'gun lecture', O'Hagan went
to McKearney's home, a tiny two-storey back-street
house with an outside toilet and rotting floorboards.
McKearney pointed to a fissure in the kitchen ceiling
and struck it with a hammer. The ceiling slowly
disintegrated with each blow. 'McKearney was screaming about "the fuckin' bastards" who owned his house
and other houses in the street. He didn't know that I
knew they were all owned by the Church. I told my
father about the house but not about me being at the
gun lecture and he said that he'd been offered the whole
street for twenty-five pounds and turned down the
offer. The Church bought it, did no repairs and
exploited people with unreasonable rents.'

The first gun placed in O'Hagan's hands was a heavy
.45-calibre Webley revolver of the type carried by the
police and the B Specials (see pp. 286–7). It did not take
him long to overcome his initial fear of handling such a
heavy weapon. He was a slightly built teenager who had
to use both hands to hold it. Knowledge of weapons, he
recalls, encouraged him to believe that he was 'special'.

At sixteen he was regarded as a fully fledged member

of the IRA surrounded by 'decent men' such as McKearney and McCallum. 'There's no doubt that at the age of sixteen it's difficult to cope with the concept of violence but, on the other hand, there were people of that age who died in Flanders and at the Somme. I wouldn't recommend anyone at that age or any age to take up the gun. I'm not a pacifist and I see the gun as a means of defence. People who read this will say I'm adding colour to my history when I say that the men around me were decent people. They didn't want to kill Protestants. They wanted an IRA who would have the support of all of the people. There is no doubt about that.'

It may be true that McKearney and McCallum had no wish to kill Protestants, and saw such a course as sectarian, but the reality of a divided society meant that any action against the forces of the Northern Ireland State resulted in the murder of members of the other community. Few Catholics were in the ranks of the Royal Ulster Constabulary or the Ulster Special Constabulary, whose purpose was the defence of the State and its single Protestant ethos.

Whatever the socialist pronouncements of McKearney, his role – and McCallum's – was to prepare teenagers for violence. This has not escaped Des O'Hagan: 'There's no doubt that you don't train people to use a gun to shoot pigeons. I'm saying they were decent people because they weren't into gaol culture. They didn't want to see me losing my youth and becoming part of an embittered "I have spent my life in the cause of Ireland" shit. They weren't like that. They enjoyed liquor, they'd all been in prison for three, four or five years. They were people who didn't want to see me exploited. They were loyal to the concept of the IRA as they were to the concept of the Republic and they were not going down the road with any romantic nationalist view.'

If that was so, what did these men think the future held for a sixteen-year-old trained to handle guns? Surely their own history of imprisonment should have convinced them that the teenage O'Hagan was embarking on a dangerous career. His chances of staying out of prison could not have been, in their experience, remote.

The political stresses within the IRA in Belfast impacted on Des O'Hagan at the beginning of the 1950s when a bitter dispute began between his mentors and those promoting a holy cause. O'Hagan had allied himself with McCallum but soon found himself charged by Steele with having behaved in a way detrimental to the republican cause. He had decided to find a job and applied to the Civil Service clerical section, which was one of the few institutions in which Catholics could achieve white-collar positions: 'It meant that I had to take an oath of allegiance to the British Crown. Steele said that taking such an oath was incompatible with membership of the IRA and dismissed me.'

That might have been the end of his terrorist career but political indoctrination is hard to erase, and O'Hagan joined Saor Uladh (Free Ulster, see p. 280), a militant grouping that attracted young IRA men who wanted action. The body was formed in October 1951 after Liam Kelly, a member of the IRA from Co. Tyrone, carried out an armed operation without IRA approval. At Easter the following year members of Saor Uladh took control of Pomeroy in Co. Tyrone and held their own commemoration service. Kelly was arrested, by members of the RUC and B Specials, was found guilty of sedition and imprisoned. From prison he won a seat at Stormont, was elected to the Irish Senate and was greeted by ten thousand people in Pomeroy on his release.

O'Hagan says that he was approached by members of Saor Uladh and agreed to join them because he believed Steele and his supporters saw the IRA as their private army – they regarded Saor Uladh members and Liam Kelly as a 'bunch of mavericks'.

At midnight on 11 December 1956, the IRA leadership in Dublin launched 'Operation Harvest', the codename for a campaign they believed would take Northern Ireland out of the United Kingdom. According to Des O'Hagan, with typical Northern-Irish humour, the campaign began at midnight and ended five minutes later. In 1957, O'Hagan was apprehended by police as he attempted to remove a Saor Uladh prisoner from a hospital bed. His arrest ended what he calls his *Alice in Wonderland* struggle and led to a four-year prison sentence, which provided him with opportunities for reflection and education. He read Wilde, Hemingway, Marx, Engels and what he calls 'a load of rubbish'.

He left prison in 1960, with remission, and asked himself one question: 'I said to myself, "What kind of a fuckin' eejit are you?"' He was not alone in his disillusionment with the IRA and its campaign, which was inexorably grinding towards defeat. The Catholic population was turning away from the politics of the gun and many IRA men released from gaol found no one to meet them at the prison gates. The nationalist consensus in Northern Ireland was that the gun brought misery and that the time had come for a re-evaluation of nationalist and republican politics. Political agitation seemed a better alternative in a society in which

Catholics were treated like second-class citizens, and prejudice and social injustice were endemic. The glamour had been stripped from the IRA and fellow Catholics saw them as losers and troublemakers.

O'Hagan did not at first fully recognise the extent to which prison life had changed him. In the 1950s, prison was harsh, and eighteen hours of every day were spent in a cell. Two hours were allotted for exercise in the prison yard, two for tasks in the workshop and two for meals. (In the 1970s, in the Long Kesh internment camp, inmates were permitted unchecked contact with each other, allowed to form a military structure and given the freedom to hold political education classes and to plan escapes.) 'On leaving prison, I didn't realise the great burden I was carrying, the impact of that kind of imprisonment on me. In effect you are a lethal cocktail. You can't cope with family or friends. If you drink, you over-drink. You have to get away from things. You can become very arrogant, very self-centred and possibly very violent.'

He says he did not blame anyone for his predicament or for the degradation he had experienced in prison. However, the images that remained with him of 'shitting in the cell, the spyholes in the door, having to accept the authority of the screws' were difficult to leave behind. He decided that England could offer him anonymity and work prospects: 'It presented an opportunity of breaking with the past and understanding self.' In London he found casual work and went to evening classes at the London School of Economics. Eventually he became a day student there and was awarded a degree.

However, while O'Hagan was changing his life, Northern Ireland was proceeding along a political road that would lead to conflict: in 1964 the signs were all too evident with the emergence of Paisleyism and its brand of sectarian politics, the refusal of the Northern Ireland State to grant civil rights to Catholics, and riots on the streets.

In London, though, he felt he was breaking with the past, particularly with Catholicism, and was committed to atheism and socialism. 'I'd begun to be aware of the tortuous, romantic character of what I'd been engaged in,' he says, with a certainty that has not wavered over thirty years.

In 1966, Des O'Hagan returned to Belfast. His homecoming coincided with the fiftieth anniversary of the 1916 Rising, and the re-emergence of the UVF. He went to Queen's University in Belfast to study for a diploma in education where he met a small coterie of people concerned about civil rights for nationalists. Eventually he became one of the founder members of the Northern Ireland civil-rights movement. 'I had totally rejected any concept of the republican movement being in any way a vehicle for progress. Yes, I knew the IRA was in there [the civil-rights movement]. I saw the IRA as a grossly reactionary, nationalist organisation but by that stage they weren't any of those things. I didn't know that then nor did I believe them.'

During his period of exile, O'Hagan had not known that the IRA had moved to the left and was involved in social agitation in the Irish Republic and had infiltrated organisations clamouring for an end to injustice in Northern Ireland. The IRA chief of staff, Cahal Goulding, and the Belfast commander, Billy McMillen, were committed Marxists. They had gone through a political transition similar to O'Hagan's in prison and on their release in the early 1960s. Their detractors blamed the

leftward trend of republican politics for its failure to
defend Catholics and claimed that real republicanism
was rooted within the blood-sacrifice tradition and its
romantic link to the 1916 Rising.

In 1969, romantic nationalism fused with the concept
of a holy cause, as Catholic clergy gave their support to
vigilante groupings that provided the genesis of the
Provisional IRA. One man who was central to that
period and wishes to remain anonymous is 'John', and
his account of the re-emergence of 'the holy men' at the
end of the 1960s dovetails with that of Des O'Hagan.
Now he lives in a mixed neighbourhood and constantly
worries about his safety.

John grew up in West Belfast in the turbulent 1920s
when Catholics and Protestants were virtually at war.
The 1923 report of an American Commission into
disturbances in Northern Ireland pointed out that 'no
examination of the Irish situation can ignore the
religious issue' and finally determined that religious
strife was rooted in economic and social problems.
Protestant manufacturers, fearing the solidarity of Catholic and Protestant labour, had instigated the sectarian
fighting. Both communities suffered during the killings
and burnings of the 1920s, and John remembers the
stories round the fireside and the fear that existed in his
community. In 1930, at the tender age of eleven, he
joined the Fianna, which, he says, was expected of him.
'One thing I remember from that time when I joined the
IRA's youth wing is that when you went to confession
and if you told the priest you were in the IRA, he was
liable to throw you out of the confession box. Those
were the days when excommunication of IRA members
was a real threat. The Church vacillated between
support and sometimes outright condemnation. It all

depended on whether the authorities in the Republic wanted the Church to move against the IRA. After the treaty with Britain was signed and the twenty-six-county State was established, it was easy for the authorities in the Republic to say to the Church, "Use excommunication ... that'll isolate them in the Catholic community and stop Catholics joining the IRA." You have to remember that when they got their freedom in the South and the IRA opposed it, they were opposing the State and the Church was an integral part of the State. Nowadays, I know of priests who when an IRA man goes to confession they lift their hands and say, "If you've committed murder, don't tell me about it. That's political." ' John went on to name priests whom he said were supportive of violence, believing it was morally justifiable in confronting a State that promoted injustice. Priests of his generation, he said, did not tell penitents that murder was something they need not confess.

John says that in the 1930s and 1940s the IRA exercised strict control over its members and insisted that they maintain a religious lifestyle in keeping with the requirements of the Catholic Church. He remembers the IRA's code of conduct for its youth wing: 'Fianna activities were largely to do with being a devout member of the Church. You were forbidden to swear or you'd be court-martialled; you weren't allowed to talk about sex or run after young girls. You went to Mass every Sunday and after Mass you went to the Falls Park and drilled. By and large, everybody associated with Fianna activities was closely connected to the Church. IRA men were part of the old Catholic tradition, and those of us in the Fianna were expected to bless ourselves when we passed a church.' The clergy, he says, were from two distinct backgrounds: 'Those from middle-class families tended to despise the IRA and those from a republican, working-class tradition were openly sympathetic and some encouraged the growth of the Fianna.'

He was aware of the Women's IRA, Cumann Na Mbann, which also had a youth wing but John saw no obvious connection between the junior organisations. 'I didn't know what the girls of my age did in their organisation. They were kept apart from us. I know that the women's organisation, Cumann Na Mbann, provided girls and women for carrying weapons and messages. They were also trained to use guns and explosives. It could be said that they were even more secretive than the IRA.'

The link between the Church and the IRA was inevitable: 'I know it was not stated but we all knew there was a close connection. It was merely a progression. When there was an attack by Protestants the IRA went first to the church walls to defend the building. Just think of 1969 when Protestant mobs were burning Catholic streets in West Belfast. What did they really want to burn down? Clonard Monastery. It was the heart of the community, the symbol of our tribe. And what did the IRA do with what few guns they had? They went to Bombay Street and to the monastery, and the priests there were happy with that. Who else was going to defend the monastery? It wasn't going to be the RUC or the British Army. And it was from that neighbourhood that the Provisional IRA was really born because some of its leaders came from there and they experienced the failure of the IRA to provide a proper defence, which was the IRA's traditional role right from the twenties. If you go back to my period in the IRA, there were many devout men in there in the thirties and forties. Take Billy McKee – he went to Clonard Monastery even in those days. He was a daily communicant and he was later a founder of the Provisionals. IRA men in the thirties and forties were sometimes the most prominent people in the Church.'

John identifies internment and imprisonment as having produced the socialist–atheist element in the IRA. 'The process of change for many of us in the forties began in prison ... it began with cynicism. You must remember that the IRA campaign of the late thirties began as Britain was about to go to war with Germany. There was a lot of pressure on de Valera in the Irish Republic to deal with the IRA, who were exploding bombs in Britain. Dev introduced internment, a big clamp-down, and so did the Unionists in Northern Ireland. Essentially the Catholic Church in Ireland had to support Dev and regard the IRA as a menace. That meant the Church rejected us and we rejected them. That was the beginning of the cynicism. The other thing that happened was that as members of the IRA we had an opportunity to talk to each other and read James Connolly's works on socialism. Most of us never knew the real James Connolly. For us he was just one of the dead heroes of the 1916 Rising. He was no romantic in the sense in which we saw ourselves as part of the blood-sacrifice tradition of other leaders of the '16 Rising, such as Pearse who was a devout Catholic and loved his mother as much as Mother Ireland. Our minds were being opened to other politics, the politics of a different reality. Looking back, the divisions were there in the discussion groups – one cell would be communist, another would be the GAA [Gaelic Athletic Association]. Discussions went on night after night and people

passed round books and pamphlets. It was benign, there
was nothing malicious about it, but the seeds of change
were there in many of us. By the end of the forties,
people like me who were interned in either the North or
the South became members of the communist party or
joined labour groupings. That left the IRA with a
leadership of the devout Catholic type, who have
always been there and are there to this day. Generally
you find that if IRA men drift towards socialism or
atheism, they leave the IRA or try to change it.
Changing it had always proved impossible because its
roots are that romantic tradition with the Church or a
sense of our God in there. People say, "They're all
Catholic in the IRA", and maybe they are in name
because they all come from that community, and it must
be said that they see themselves as defenders of their
community, which by definition means defenders of
their faith. Look at the IRA which went to the left in the
sixties. It was hated by the Church because it was
Marxist, it was feared by the right wing in the Irish
Republic and it didn't survive after the violence of '69
because it didn't fulfil its chief role in Northern Ireland
to defend Catholics ... to defend the faith. I'm not being
cynical. I'm just trying to explain what it's all about.
Many people like me who left the IRA in the forties
were the first to demand guns to protect our people in
'69 ... The problem was that there were other people,
the romantics who were ready for a resurrection.'

In the 1960s John watched the IRA lurch towards
Marxism, while many people still believed, in both parts
of the island, that it was a Catholic movement with no
need to rely on atheistic doctrines. But the socialists
won the day and their opponents moved into Sinn Fein,

which controlled the political outpourings of the republican movement.

'When Catholic areas were attacked by the police, B
Specials and Protestant mobs in August '69, everything
began to change in terms of the IRA. The Church was
happy to see the emergence of defence groupings which
would soon form the basis for a new IRA, the Provos. A
lot of bad elements got into those groups, guys who
would never have been admitted into the IRA. The
Church encouraged people to join the defence organisations. If you look back at the formation of the Provos,
you find that guys sprout up from nowhere and set up
the Provos in lots of areas. There were bad elements in
there. A lot of them were involved in all sorts of
criminal activity and were bad eggs. Let's be clear, the
Church did not want the Marxists or anyone associated
with them for the same reason that the Irish government
of Charles Haughey didn't want them. The Church –
and I don't care what anybody says, I saw it, I knew all
these guys who were in there – the Church supported
them because they were anti-Marxist.'

I asked John if his assessment of the role of the
Church between 1969 and 1971 was based on his
dislike of the Provisionals.

'Look, the Church gave them support.'

'Are you certain that's historically accurate?' I asked.

'I'm telling you it's historically accurate,' he replied.
'The Church gave the Provos benediction, sprinkled
them with holy water and blessed them the way they did
those who were going to fight for Franco in Spain.'

In the aftermath of the violence in Belfast in 1969,
priests from various parishes attended meetings of the
Catholic Citizens' Defence Committees, the controlling

organisation for defence groupings throughout Northern Ireland. Their presence had been ordered by Bishop Philbin, of the Down and Conor diocese, to ensure that he was properly informed about events, and that things did not get out of hand. John says, 'Philbin didn't want the Marxist IRA controlling the main defence body because at the outset leading members of the Marxist faction of the IRA were in there. A friend of mine left the defence set-up when it became clear that the Church wanted its own people in there, and the people it put in were people it approved of and they were the people who were about to form the Provos. The Provos took over the controlling body, then the committees in all the areas and they had the basis of a new IRA which became the Provisionals. That lot had the Church's blessing. The Church didn't know what it was messing with. Those of us who'd been in the IRA in the thirties or forties, men who'd watched the changes in the IRA in the sixties, knew what was going on. We saw these guys, like Jimmy Steele, Billy McKee and the others who'd never changed their politics, having a major say in what was happening in Catholic districts, who should have the guns and the money for guns which was coming from the Irish government. We warned the Church but as socialists we were not listened to. The fact that these guys who formed the Provos had the backing of the Church when they took over the defence committees meant a lot. After the Provos were formed, a friend of mine went to a meeting of the defence controlling body and discovered that Provos were hidden in another room listening to discussions.'

John's overall analysis of the conflict was that informally it is a holy war and he attributed its significance partly to the support throughout Ireland for the Provisionals at the expense of the democratic nationalist party, the SDLP, led by John Hume. In his view, people in the Republic of Ireland are drawn to the Provisionals because they have dominated all initiatives. 'The difference between the communities in Northern Ireland is religion. For God's sake, where is the Border? Drive up from the South and where is the border?'

He identified Protestant fundamentalism as dangerous to the future of Northern Ireland and he pointed an accusing finger at Unionist leader David Trimble. 'When Trimble walked hand in hand with Paisley in Portadown in 1995 and the following year was seen in the company of the extreme loyalist Billy Wright, that crystallised the divisions between the two communities. It was irresponsible.'

His vision of Northern Ireland's future was bleak: a society drawn deeper and deeper into sectarian conflict around the political axis of Sinn Fein/SDLP versus Unionists/loyalists. A recipe for disaster.

WOMEN AT WAR

On a warm summer night in 1972, my news editor sent me to a Catholic neighbourhood in North Belfast following reports of sectarian clashes. I was a young reporter, willing to go anywhere and without the sense to recognise then that in Northern Irish society violence was often indiscriminate. Carrying a press pass appeared to confer on the bearer immunity to danger, particularly in republican districts. When loyalists had attacked Catholic neighbourhoods in August 1969 the world's media had saturated those areas, portraying Protestants as the aggressors. Protestants now resented the media and journalists were not welcome in loyalist areas. Much reporting was conditioned by perceptions acquired in one part or the other of the political–religious divide. I was fortunate to be able to enter loyalist districts because although I worked for the mainly Catholic daily newspaper, the *Irish News*, I was respected by loyalists for having tried to reflect their view of the conflict.

On this particular night I arrived, notebook in hand, identified myself to people I knew were republicans, and joined a group of journalists on a street corner. They were watching a battle in which crowds of youths were hurling stones and petrol bombs at each other. A hundred yards from my vantage point I saw policemen mingling with the Protestants and watching as a man emerged with a shotgun and fired at the Catholics. Several young men were struck by pellets and dragged from the roadway.

Suddenly I heard a commotion behind me and a young man in his early twenties pushed through the circle of journalists carrying a Thompson sub-machine-gun with a stick magazine. The barrel rested over his shoulder and he exuded a terrifying casualness. He looked down the road, and the journalists, myself included, retreated. He turned and walked away.

Catholic youths shouted at him, 'Why don't you shoot the fuckers?'

'I'm waiting for orders,' he replied.

As darkness descended, my fellow journalists left and I found myself in a deserted street, frightened to cross the main road that would lead me out of the district. The distinctive crack of rifle fire sent me scurrying towards a house where the door was firmly shut just as I reached it. I lay down as tracer bullets peppered the street, began to crawl towards the end of the street and the safety of an alleyway. It seemed to take an eternity but when I reached relative safety I found myself staring into the barrel of a Mark I carbine.

'I was gonna shoot you,' laughed the young man holding the rifle.

I eased myself upwards, using my back as a support against a brick wall.

'Leave him alone.' It was a woman's voice and I strained to identify her among a sea of blackened faces and balaclavas. 'C'mon, son, you need a cup of tea. If you stay here you'll get yerself killed.' A hand reached out, took my arm and dragged me deeper into the alleyway. 'You should have got yerself out of here hours ago,' she said, as we entered the backyard of a two-storey house. 'Watch the bin.'

It wasn't the bin I was worried about but a menacing growl. 'Don't worry about him,' she said. 'That dog only eats the Brits.'

It was not uncommon for soldiers and dogs to find themselves at odds. The soldiers hated dogs because they warned people of their presence, and dogs hated soldiers because many had felt the force of a steel-tipped boot or a rifle butt.

'This way, son.'

Her voice was reassuring and she led me into an untidy kitchen. 'Take yerself in there,' she advised, pointing to a small living room. 'And what you see, you don't see, if y' know what I mean.'

I thought I knew exactly what she meant.

In the light of the kitchen, I saw Eileen, whose name I learned later, for the first time. A large woman, with a reddened face and greying hair, she had bright blue eyes and a welcoming smile. 'Go on,' she said, noticing my hesitation. 'All right,' she said, moving me gently to one side. She took my hand and led me into the living room. 'This young fella's a reporter with the *Irish News*,' she announced.

I wasn't prepared for the scene in that room. Three men in black-knitted balaclavas were seated on a shabby couch, one was in an armchair while another lounged in a corner. Eileen pushed me towards a wooden chair near the window, which had a blind drawn to prevent light reaching the street and to conceal the presence of those in the room.

The men in balaclavas grunted as a slightly built man

in middle age, walked towards me. 'I'm Sean. I'm her husband,' he said, reaching out a hand in greeting. 'You'll be okay in here. Out there you're liable to stop a bullet.' His voice was raised to compete with bursts of information emitting from the television set, which had a white screen. 'We've it tuned in to the police and Army radio.' He laughed and sat in front of the set manipulating the sound.

I wanted out of there but I felt frozen to the wooden chair. I was aware of eyes fixed on me from within the slits in the balaclavas and I kept my gaze on the ceiling. The only person who spoke was Eileen's husband, who occasionally identified a police message he thought significant.

I saw an opportunity to depart as Eileen came in with a tray of tea. My fear was that if the Army or the police raided the house, and I was found in the company of men in balaclavas, I would have a lot of explaining to do. As I got up nervously, Eileen stared at me and I sensed that at that moment I was not free to leave her house. My eyes wandered to the man in the corner, who was being handed a mug. As he reached for it, I caught a glimpse of rifles behind him. Eileen returned to the kitchen and came back with a tray of sandwiches the like of which I had rarely seen. They were constructed like a double-decker bus: several layers of bread interspersed with ham and cheese. There was a murmur of approval round the room as the gunmen competed eagerly for the largest. 'You're next.' She smiled, looking in my direction. 'The boys need feed ... They've work t' do.' 'The boys' was a term used by locals to describe the IRA, and 'work' meant only one thing. Killing. When it was my turn to be fed, the living-room door opened and the young man I had seen earlier with the Thompson sub-machine-gun walked into the middle of the room. His presence acted as a signal to the others, who stood up, took the rifles from the corner and filed past me, one man grunting in derision as he looked down at me.

I breathed a sigh of relief at their departure and Eileen smiled and handed me a cup of tea.

'Why was the young guy with the Thompson not wearing a balaclava?' I asked.

'He likes t' strut around. He's only a messenger. The others are the real men. Drink yer tea and don't be askin' too many questions.' The warning came with a change of expression which signalled that this woman might be kind but she could also be hard.

'Get yer arse out there,' she said, tapping her husband's head, 'and let me know what's happenin'.'

He moved quickly and left the room just as a pretty teenage girl arrived.

'Who's he?' said the girl, pointing at me.

'He's a reporter.'

'What's he doin' here?'

'What's it look like?' barked Eileen. 'He's gettin' fed like everybody else. Now you get to bed.'

As the girl left the room, casting a disapproving glance in my direction, Eileen laughed. 'That's my daughter Bronagh. Y' can't keep the young ones off the streets. They're all wound up. She's sixteen and I can do nothin' with her.' Which seemed odd, coming from a woman who could control her husband with a pat on the head. I was about to leave when one of the gunmen returned and, ignoring me, reached behind the sofa and retrieved something. As he left again, I saw that he now held a bomb composed of sticks of gelignite surrounded by nails with a fuse wire protruding from the top.

That's it, I thought. I'm out of here.

'You watch yerself out there,' warned Eileen. 'It's about t' get hot and heavy.'

As I made my way along the street, hugging the windows and doorways, her warning became reality.

A loud explosion was followed by bursts of rifle and pistol fire. As I ran for safety, I heard other feet pounding the pavement and men shouting instructions. Suddenly the sharp report of an automatic rifle sounded close by me, followed by a thud and a gurgling sound, which has never left me. I sheltered in a doorway as four men ran past carrying a body. I learned later that a British Army sniper with a night scope had shot an IRA member. The bullet had struck him in the chest and had torn a hole the size of a pineapple in his back.

In the months ahead, I contacted Eileen whenever I reported events in that neighbourhood. When I joined Northern Ireland's leading daily newspaper, the *Belfast Telegraph*, I continued to see Eileen if I needed first-hand insight into events in North Belfast.

It was a long time before I finally persuaded her to discuss the events on that night I had first appeared in her home. She looked more than her sixty-four years, but the deep lines on her face were due to constant stress rather than age. She was addicted to Valium as much as she was addicted to the conflict. She admitted that during lulls in the violence, she 'didn't know what to do with herself'.

'What do you really want to know?' she asked one evening, looking at me with her piercing blue eyes.

I said I wanted to understand the role of women in conflict.

She was never anything but direct. 'What you really

mean is that you want t' know about women in the
republican movement.'

I nodded. It was the beginning of an association that
enabled me to understand the most secret arm of the
IRA, Cumann Na Mbann, the young girls' and wom-
en's organisation.

Eileen had learned her history on her grandmother's
knee and like many Catholic women, her heroine was
Countess Markievicz (Constance Gore-Booth) under
whose auspices a Republican Boy Scout movement,
Fianna Eireann, had been launched in 1909, the
organisation that became the junior wing of the IRA.
'My family was republican, not that everybody was in
the "RA" but they talked about Irish freedom and the
heroes who fought the British. My granny told us
stories about how the IRA protected us against the
Protestants and the Specials. By the time I was fifteen I
knew the poems of Padraig Pearse, his speech at the
grave of O'Donovan Rossa and all the lines in the
Proclamation they read on the day of the Rising in
1916. My granny said the republicans in the north were
the real republicans because the others sold us out to the
British, left the country partitioned and us at the mercy
of the Prods. We were a decent family. My mother and
father were republicans in name but my mother's sister
Bridie was the real thing. She hated the peelers and the
Specials, and I heard stories of how she hid guns in a
pram and wheeled it through the Falls under the noses
of the peelers. I knew about the Fianna and when I was
seventeen, I wanted t' do my bit for Ireland. My father
had taken me on his shoulders through Glasnevin
cemetery in Dublin when I was a child and that memory
and stories of Countess Markievicz's role in the struggle
made me want to do somethin'. I talked to my auntie

Bridie and she wasn't keen but after a while she put me in touch with a woman I'd seen sometimes at Mass on a Sunday. It was as if Bridie didn't want t' have first-hand responsibility. The one thing she told me was that I'd better be sure of what I was doin' and not t' tell my mother. I imagined that being in Cumann Na Mbann meant that we would be fightin' alongside "the boys" but that wasn't the case. It was as if the two organisations had their own command structure. I was given political lectures, learned about guns and explosives and how to conceal things about my person. It wasn't quite what I expected it to be. Looking back there was that thing about women not bein' strong enough t' fight and that just wasn't true. There were girls and women who would have done just as good a job. When the campaign started in Britain in the late thirties, many of us expected to be sent there but the Dublin leadership thought the IRA in the North was full of hotheads and didn't involve them to the extent they should have done. There was always a resentment in republican circles in the North that Dublin was runnin' the show yet we were the people sufferin' ... They'd won their freedom. Even in the fifties, we were only used for transportin' guns and carryin' messages. We were dedicated and a lot more security-minded than the men. That was the one thing always impressed on us, keep yer trap shut, and if there's one thing about a woman, she can keep a secret. The peelers never got as close to us as they did placin' touts in the "RA". By the time the Provos were formed in 1970 my days were over. I was too old t' go runnin' around – though, mind you, I still carried clout because those in the know knew I was sound. The Provos ... well, maybe times were changin' ... the Provos saw the importance of a strong Cumann Na

Mbann. Girls and women could get things through Army roadblocks hidden in their knickers. They could get messages int' prison hidden in other places which I'll not mention. Cumann Na Mbann wanted a bigger role and it was Provisional IRA intelligence that recognised their worth.' At this point, Eileen reminded me that she was using 'Provisional' for my sake, whereas the correct term was Irish Republican Army. The Provisionals were the true Irish Republican Army. She pointed out that the remnants of the commies who ran the IRA in the sixties, known locally as Stickies or Officials, were traitors.

When I asked her about her commitment to republicanism and how she related that to her Catholicism, she laughed. 'All good republicans have been good Catholics,' she said, with a malevolent grin. 'Now that can't really be said about James Connolly. I think he would have given us communism. The republicans of my time were churchgoers and the two things were separate. There was no question that being a republican was a sin or fightin' for Irish freedom was a sin. Y' must remember we'd been fightin' the British for hundreds of years because they wouldn't let us speak our own language, they closed the schools, they persecuted us because we were not only Irish but Catholic, and then they handed part of the island to a bunch of ascendancy Prods who hated everything Catholic. So, to be a republican was to be someone prepared to defend your faith and your culture. The two things were one and the same. I hear all these people beatin' about the bush, sayin' this is a constitutional this or that issue, the Protestants think we're ruled from Rome. Little do they know that nowadays you can hardly get the young ones t' go t' church. The closest they get t' Rome nowadays is one of those Italian take-away pizzas.'

I asked her whether the role of the Church had changed compared with the closeness she implied was in place in her youth.

'The Church can't just wash its hands and walk away. Most of us have learned our history from nuns, priests or brothers. Everybody knows the big-wigs in the Church have always shilly-shallied, playin' politics when it suited them. When the bishops or the Cardinal needed somethin' from the Unionists, even at a time when we were second-class citizens, they played ball. The priests know that if they walk away from us, then who are they gonna preach to? The Prods talk about excommunication. That's all hot air. I never went t' confession and said, "Bless me, Father, I'm a member of Cumann Na Mbann." If I did and he said, "Y're excommunicated", I'd have gone to another priest who was sympathetic to the cause. Anyway how could the Church, whose people have always been under the boots of the British and the Unionists, tell many of its people that they can't receive the sacraments? If some-body goes int' confession and confesses t' murder, it's under the seal of the confessional. No priest has the right t' refuse absolution. Excommunication. How could they put it int' practice? Would they walk around the streets, look at newspaper photos of riots, announce that the whole IRA leadership has been excommuni-cated? There was a time when I was young that people expected it – but nowadays? People would tell the bishops and the Cardinal t' go get stuffed. The Church is only there because people are there and their politics are their own.'

Eileen talked to me at a time when loyalist murder gangs were carrying out gruesome atrocities. I asked her whether she understood that loyalists believed, just as strongly, that they were fighting for their political, cultural and religious survival, and that God was on their side.

'Sure. But why are they killin' ordinary Catholics and not only killin' them but torturin' them? Killin' I understand but butchery? That's for people who have no politics.'

She could not grasp the concept that loyalists, with their slogan of 'For God and Ulster', equally felt justified in waging war.

Eileen died in the late 1970s. Years later I met her daughter again, whom I had only glimpsed that night in her home in 1970. She had grown into a pretty and intelligent young woman with a nine-month-old baby and was living in the west of the city. Married to a carpenter, she appeared to be living a conventional lifestyle with none of the trappings of the republicanism of her late mother. At least, that was my impression when I first talked to her about the night we had met and how suspicious she had been of my presence.

Three months after that encounter, I was investigating an episode in Belfast in which an IRA unit, with a woman in tow, had carried out an attack on a British Army patrol. In conversation with a security source, I received a description of the female, and immediately identified her as Eileen's daughter. A year later I approached a leading member of Cumann Na Mbann for an interview with some of its members but was refused. But Eileen's observations about the women's organisation and its importance in the conflict proved accurate. IRA intelligence quickly recognised the value of young women in information-gathering. They employed them to spy on pubs used by policemen or the Army. They carried guns and explosives and, in one instance, I saw several fire weapons during a gun battle with troops.

Significantly, though, it was in intelligence acquisition and as part of bombing teams that their role increased. The exposure of the Price sisters as members of the IRA bombing team that had targeted London in the 1970s showed the type of women recruited into Cumann Na Mbann and seconded to work with IRA units. The Price sisters were pretty, intelligent and trained as terrorists. In the late 1980s, Mairead Farrell, shot dead by the SAS in Gibraltar, reinforced the theory that women terrorists are as effective as their male counterparts. These three women were among many others who came from respectable Catholic families and saw themselves as working in support of a morally justifiable cause.

I renewed my acquaintance with Eileen's daughter when I was researching this book. She was no longer involved with terrorism, was considering doing an Open University degree and had settled in a peaceful neighbourhood in Co. Down. Her story is best told in her own words.

'I loved my mum even though she was sometimes hard but that was her life. She grew up not knowin' anything better and my father ... well, he was a bit weak. He knew what my mum was involved in when they got married but he was never able to ask her anything about her other life. She was strict with me, sending me t' church to confession every week and Mass every Sunday. When I was a child I remember her having meetings in the house with other women. The blind would be drawn on the window and my father stood at the front door – some guard he would have been. That was at the time of the civil-rights marches in the late sixties. Politics was always bein' discussed in the

house and my father was always glued to the news on
the radio or television. I think my mother knew that all
that marching would lead t' violence. I remember her
sayin' that there was no way the Unionists would let us
have civil rights and that there would be a backlash. She
hated the IRA leadership in Dublin because she thought
they were communists and all they wanted t' do was t'
play politics at our expense. My father agreed with
everything she said and when he was talkin' t' neighbours, he'd repeat everything she told him. When the
backlash came in '69 and the IRA in Dublin wouldn't
send the guns north, my mother swore that the IRA was
finished and she was right. When the Provisionals were
formed she was over the moon. She used t' sing the song
"Take it down from the mast, Irish Traitors, it's the flag
we republicans claim". I later found out from other
people that, though she was no longer active, people in
the Cumann sought her advice. For me it was a weird
period ... there was so much goin' on. Everybody was
livin' on adrenaline. Lookin' back, it was as if everybody was makin' the news and livin' it. When there was
a lull, people seemed depressed. There was a great
comin' together in all the areas, people felt closer to
each other because there was a common cause. It was
fashionable to be a republican and a lot of people who
had nothing t' do with the "RA" paraded around as
though they had and talked to all the foreign journalists
who came into the area. God knows what stories some
of those journalists must have written. I remember
listenin' to my father givin' one of them a lot of shite
and he took great delight in doin' it. One of the things
which maddened me was the fact that the Army and
police favoured the loyalists. We were the enemy and
once they started t' saturate our areas and lift men and

boys we all knew, that made things worse. It was indiscriminate and it was deliberate. It was a policy of squeezing the Catholics. I remember internment when they lifted a lot of men who belonged t' nothin' and all the mothers and wives crying. Soldiers would make suggestive remarks, stop girls at roadblocks and remove tampons from their handbags and laugh. I hated them because they hated us. I grew up in a house where the IRA was held in high esteem but not where killing was promoted. That changed when people wc knew were killed by the Army or the loyalists. We all felt, in all Catholic districts of the North, that we were under siege. I decided just before you first saw me in 1972 to join Cumann Na Mbann. I was approached by a girl in our area who saw me manning a barricade and throwin' a petrol bomb at the Army. I told her my mother would not approve and she fell about laughing. That was the first time I realised something about my mother's past. I began to look back on the things I remember from my childhood like the meetings in our house. My mother until the day she died knew nothin' about my involve- ment. In some ways I knew she would disapprove because she wouldn't have wanted me t' take risks and in other ways I'm sorry I never talked to her about it. It was as if I was gettin' my own back on her by concealin' it from her. Also, there was that code of secrecy which implied that it was better not to involve even those closest to you. Maybe she suspected and decided that she was in no position t' lecture me about something which she herself had done. As a member of the Irish Republican Army – that's what we all were even though I was in the women's wing – I was given political lectures, took the oath of allegiance and was trained in the use of weapons. It was hectic for the first few years and people of my age learned a lot by doing jobs, like building surveillance on policemen and places frequented by the Brits or members of the [Ulster Defence Regiment]. Unlike my mother's day, a lot of members of Cumann Na Mbann were well educated and well trained. We were a smaller organisation than the men and we were more tightly knit. Our services were requested through contact between our superiors and battalion or brigade commanders of the "RA". It meant that our security was much better because we did not have the high profile of young men of our age who were associating with a lot of our people in units in a battalion area. We never talked to the media and British intelligence was never able to get near us. Of course, we lost a lot of good operatives who were caught on an operation or betrayed, but generally we kept things very tight. You asked me about God and I have t' tell you I did pray for my own safety when I went on an operation and I did go to Mass, though not as frequently as I did when I was younger. I didn't regard anything I was doin' as sinful though I have t' say that there were times when the bombing campaign was in full swing that I asked myself whether it was right to be part of an organisation which was killing ordinary people. When it came to the Brits, the RUC, the UDR and loyalists like the UVF/UDA [Ulster Volunteer Force/ Ulster Defence Association], that was war and I believed it was justified. If you're askin' me if I went t' confession and told the priest what I was doin', the answer is no. None of us talked about religion in those terms, it was a private thing, it was yer own conscience, though it was clear we all believed that what we were doin' was right. After all, who said it wasn't? There were some priests who gave off from the pulpit but everybody ignored them. We all knew that was instigated by the Bishop or the Cardinal. On the ground, the priests were not sayin', "The IRA is the Devil." Anyway, young people were beginning t' see the Church for what it was. I remember a woman standin' up during a sermon and tellin' the priest t' get lost and people cheered her. Some priests forgot that if it hadn't been for the IRA the loyalists would have burned Catholic churches. If it hadn't been for the IRA, the Brits would have let the Unionists continue t' run the place and walk all over us. It's all very well for these so-called liberals t' say that violence changes nothin' ... It brought down a corrupt government after forty years and it made the Brits and Unionists realise that any deal in Northern Ireland can't be done without republicans bein' involved. Marriage changed my life and maybe the birth of our first child was a big factor. You begin to see life in a different kind of way. My husband was never involved in anything and I felt that if I continued, without his approval, which I knew I would never get if I told him the truth, that I could wreck his life and that of our baby. It's strange that when you're single it's much easier t' make decisions for yerself. Many of the girls and young women who joined like me didn't have commitments. You also don't see the whole picture. When I decided t' get out of Cumann Na Mbann, it was hard because I'd established good friendships and respect for people in it. They're not all marvellous people. Like all organisations, there are real bastards in there, women hardened by bein' there too long and who have nothin' else in their lives. My husband is such a good man that I couldn't have led a secret life while married. When I got out, I have t' say, I felt a weight had been lifted off my shoulders. It was the first time in my life that I really sat back and asked m'self what I'd been involved in. You asked me if I'd regrets and I suppose I'd have t' be honest and say yes. I'm not goin' to tell you what those things are but I'm not sure if they were right.'

I asked her if she had gone to confession to clear her conscience.

She paused briefly. 'Well, that's a strange thing. It's only since I left that I've begun t' wonder if what I did was sinful. That was something I'd not really considered. Let's put it this way. If my daughter was growing up and asked me if those things were wrong, I'd probably tell her they were.'

I suggested that, just as her mother's politics had influenced her, perhaps her own would eventually impel her daughter to become involved in the conflict.

'That's why I insisted that we move to a district which, though it isn't quite mixed, at least it's not in the heart of republicanism. There's nothin' wrong with bein' a republican but I'd like her t' grow up without the same influences. I never really had a choice. It was all round me.'

I felt that Bronagh was bound for a journey of discovery, uncertain at the outset about her past, confused by her conditioning and worried by the moral dilemmas finding their way into her thoughts. I asked her whether the conflict in Northern Ireland could have been avoided if everyone had been taught from the cradle that violence was morally unjustifiable.

'Maybe. We've all grown up in our own traditions with a belief that God is on our side. My mother portrayed the Protestants as heretics and the English as godless. It's all that Reformation stuff. I'm sure the Protestants were taught t' regard us as heretics ruled by the Pope. Paisley was forever preaching that the Pope was the devil, and what did that make us? When I was a child, I knew the Orangemen hated the Pope and all Catholics. I'd like t' be moderate but that isn't easy. There's always the threat from the loyalists and Unionists that there will be a bloodbath if they don't get their way and the British ... they couldn't make a decision in a fit. That leaves us – Catholics, that is – always thinkin' that it's better t' have the IRA because without them we'd be defenceless. Nothin' can change that.'

There is no real parallel between Cumann Na Mbann and women involved in loyalist paramilitarism. Many women have been involved in loyalist violence but in a less structured way and without the same historical lineage. Also, like members of Cumann Na Mbann, some loyalist women have been involved in loyalist politics, others in concealing weapons but not in the gathering of intelligence or weapons and explosives training.

Incidents of violence instigated by female loyalists have been gruesome: they have killed women suspected of having affairs with their husbands, or they have witnessed macabre killings. During the 1970s, when innocent Catholics were snatched off the streets and taken to illegal drinking clubs to be tortured and killed, women were often present among the revellers who watched the murders.

The late John McMichael, leader of the Ulster Freedom Fighters, told me he would have liked to have formed an organisation such as Cumann Na Mbann. He recognised the importance of women in conflict. McMichael was murdered by the Provisional IRA, and one of those who carried out surveillance on him was a member of Cumann Na Mbann.

CHURCH AND STATE

In the early 1970s, elements of British military intelligence bugged confession boxes in Catholic churches. The operation had not been sanctioned at the highest levels, and came to light after a device was discovered in a Belfast church. The find was kept a closely guarded secret within the Church and the matter was dealt with by Bishop Philbin and one other priest. Cardinal Conway was informed and it was decided that he alone would talk to the British government. He and Philbin knew that the issue could not be made public because of the damage it would do to belief in the Church's guarantee of the secrecy and sacredness of the confessional. The damage was potentially incalculable. Another bugging device was discovered in a radio in a room in the St Peter's parochial house.

A retired Army officer told me that the bugging was a 'disgraceful business' and had been carried out by 'rogue elements'. He added: 'At that time there were few controls on the operations of intelligence organisations, particularly military intelligence. Ulster was a new situation. No one was able to scrutinise all the undercover operations which were taking place. There was no imperative to seek permission for surveillance operations. The targets were widespread, priests, teachers, journalists, anyone who was a suspect or was in possession of information which was necessary in the war against the IRA. I was not surprised that confessionals were bugged. There was no better target. It is not something I would condone and would not be permitted now. It must be placed against the extreme circumstances of the period.'

I asked what mechanisms existed to prevent such a thing happening in the 1990s. He replied that MI5 would never sanction such an operation: the fall-out would be politically catastrophic. He was unable to confirm that bugging of confessionals had stopped after representations by the Cardinal in the early 1970s, but he admitted that mail intercepts, surveillance and phone taps increased – and were not only directed at suspects or known terrorists.

A priest at St Peter's in the early 1970s confided in me that the discovery of a listening device in the parochial house had shocked the Church hierarchy to its foundations. The whole matter had been hushed up because the British Army and the Church knew that neither would benefit from public exposure of the affair.

In 1972 Cardinal Conway used it as leverage in persuading senior British officials to drop charges against Father Jim Chesney, who had been involved in the bombing of the tiny Protestant village of Claudy in which five people had died. The priest was sent to a remote part of the Irish Republic and later died in an institution in Donegal.

Cardinal Conway was an astute politician, whose family had lived through the terrible violence of the 1920s. He worried that if the Church openly confronted the State and supported the republican cause, a violent reaction would cost the lives of many Catholics. In the early 1960s when young Catholic couples were denied access to newly built homes because of religious discrimination, Conway asked the newly ordained Father Raymond Murray to investigate the issue. Murray was surprised at the request because priests were not normally allowed to be involved in social matters or publicly identified with a campaign for social justice.

Murray says, 'When the suppression came after the Troubles in '69, I learned a number of lessons. I lost this awe of the State and I have never recovered it. I will be polite to the State, courteous to the State and co-operative so far as I can, but I do not give one hundred per cent trust, confidence and obedience to the State. I would no longer term it as it was in my old sociology textbook, "the perfect society working for the common good". The ideal may be there in sociology but in the modern world so many problems happen within states, and therefore there is this necessity of watchdogs, civil-rights groups and human-rights groups.'

He claimed that the Northern Ireland State had been guilty of injustice and arrogance in making Catholics second-class citizens, which it did to maintain the monolith of Unionism. He felt that Cardinal Conway's childhood experiences had led him to conclude that opposition to the State would lead to the murder of Catholics, collusion and the use of its power in 'door-step' killings. He feared, too, that civil-rights protests would mark the return of 1920s-style turbulence, which made him cautious and nervous. He carefully weighed every phrase he uttered so that not a single word would lead to the death of any individual. Father Murray said that the Cardinal knew it was probably too much to hope that those who had the power and privilege would ever agree to share it.

Like many other priests to whom I spoke, Murray branded the British Labour government of the 1960s for having failed to address basic human-rights demands which, had they been granted, might have averted the Troubles. He conceded that, after the trouble began in August 1969, priests were sympathetic towards their community because they remembered the 1920s. When Catholic areas of West Belfast were invaded by Protestant mobs, with elements of the police force and B Specials, the priests supported the Catholic defence organisations, but he also contended that Conway saw the danger that the defence groupings might become an offensive organisation. Of the British Army, Raymond Murray said, 'The British Army is completely naïve. You have a situation where these people are coming over from Britain, whether it's Wales, Scotland or England. They know absolutely nothing about Ireland. They know nothing about its history, its feelings, its culture, its traditions. They don't know the backward glance that every nationalist Irishman has. He's been here for thousands of years. He's mixed with Danes, Vikings, Celts. In a sense Ireland was never really conquered and in a sense they come with arrogance, an assumption that this belongs to them and that you are a rude boy. So from Elizabeth I's time to the rapparees, to the rebels, to the terrorists, they find a name for you because you are the illegal, unlawful person. They always assume that legality and morality and what they regard as right is legal and moral.'

Father Denis Faul said that from the outset of the Troubles relations between the Church and the Army

were 'very bad'. The Army arrived with the impression
that in every parish the priest was the leader of the IRA,
and he discovered that soldiers sent from Germany had
been briefed to this effect. 'Those briefings, I was told,
were very anti-Catholic Church. At the hunger-strike
stage, the policy changed. After the hunger strike they
were very nice, particularly to the Catholic professional
classes because before that all Catholics got the stick in
the seventies. Priests, doctors, dentists got a very bad
time on the roads in the seventies. If you'd a Catholic
name and address you got stick. In the eighties they may
have realised they were losing out and changed the
policy.'

Father Murray told me that soldiers arriving in his
parish would have known as much about the tradition
and culture of the people as they would have known
about Mexicans. 'They thought you should be like
them. They were coming from a history since the Tudor
times when Britain became a power state to contest with
the other European power states. Ireland became a
vulnerable part of that concept of the power state as
well as Scotland and Wales. Everybody had to be
suppressed. They had wiped out the psychology and
mind of the Scots and Welsh to a great extent and,
having destroyed them, pulled them into their armies to
do their work abroad in imperial expansion. And after
making these people die for them, they created a new
tradition of a kind of shallow imperialism and British
Empire stuff. All that came apart but they assumed that
Ireland fitted into that. They had little rapport, little
understanding.'

I pointed out that, if the British Army knew little, the
Catholic Church had a wealth of knowledge about Irish
conflict. Had the bishops made incorrect assumptions

about how republicans would react to the presence of the Army?

'There was a wrong assumption on the part of the bishops that there was British justice and it [the conflict] would not go as far as it did.' In the 1970s, Father Murray said, corruption was rampant in the courts, and that, linked with the brutality of the State towards the Catholic population, made it difficult for the Church to convince people to turn away from violence because they did not want to hear that message. 'People who were at the receiving end of their houses being wrecked by the British military, who had people belonging to them shot, who were at the receiving end of the injustice, when they were manipulated into offensive war, they didn't want to hear, or let on they heard, condemnation of them or condemnations of the police and Army. Changes weren't coming, justice wasn't coming, redress wasn't coming, and they did not want to hear condemnation of their own violence. Father Faul and myself told them time and again, "You keep the law yourselves. You have eroded the confidence of the law. You have eroded the confidence of those who are supposed to uphold the law, and you are wrecking the whole psychology and morality of the place also." '

He was quick to praise Protestant clergymen who took a stand against the State in the 1960s and were forced out of their parishes: some had to leave for England. But on the big issues, like internment, ill-treatment of prisoners, the courts and the shoot-to-kill policy, he said, 'They never came out strong. No matter how unsuccessful the Catholic Church and its priests were in that massive condemnation, which embittered many of our deprived people, you did not find on the

Protestant side their Churches making a massive condemnation of loyalist violence in the early seventies
when they killed five hundred people.'

In this criticism of the majority of Protestant clergy,
Murray was correct: they were reluctant to confront the
terrible killings by loyalist paramilitaries from 1972
onwards.

Denis Faul said, 'The Protestant Church were very
bad in the seventies. The Anglican Primate in Ireland,
Archbishop Simms – poor Simms ... he did his best. He
was such a decent man but there was very little
sympathy from them on the points we were making
about the torture of prisoners. The recent leaders are
very good and speak up about fair play and justice for
everybody.'

Father Murray is convinced that as the long war
progressed, the Church faced short-term moral dilemmas because it could not convince the State to drop the
shoot-to-kill policy, the use of plastic bullets, strip-
searching of prisoners and their visitors, and other
police and military strategies. 'It went from bad to
worse. You tried to do your best to bring the State to
heel, to stop them doing these things, not to be breaking
the law. So, on the one hand, those who looked upon
themselves as insurgents who were using violence as a
method, the actions of the State gave them a grievance
and a justification in people's eyes to use violence. One
was paying the penalty for the actions of the other.
Priests did not give in to the thesis that armed resistance
was justified, because they saw also the suffering, the
loss, the emergence of politics and a manipulation of
people, and how vulnerable young people were in being
caught up in violence.'

The majority of priests were not republicans but the

British Army was not convinced of this. It saw the Catholic Church as an integral part of the problem, believing that it was linked to the republican movement. It was a blanket assumption without foundation and, dangerously, it defined all priests as potential terrorists. But a retired Army officer told me, despairingly, 'How could we get it right from the outset when we were looking at a community which was opposed to us, and that included priests? The Protestants did not express the same hostility or animosity. Our intelligence confirmed that priests were aiding and abetting the paramilitaries on the Catholic side. Of course that was not something every priest was doing but we could not be sure. We had to treat them all as a potential enemy.'

In fact, the Army had arrived as the saviour of the Catholic population, and in the autumn of 1969 their first real confrontation was with loyalist paramilitaries in a fierce gun battle on the Shankill Road. However, in the Clonard areas of Belfast the Army had already attracted bitterness because on their arrival troops were ordered not to fire at or confront loyalists who burned all the houses in Bombay Street. They failed to act when priests from Clonard Monastery pleaded with them to stop the burning and looting of Catholic homes, and to offer protection to the monastery. It was from the Clonard area that the Provisional IRA leadership emerged.

The Army's problem, though, was that the Stormont government was still in power, and within eleven months a Conservative government, led by Edward Heath, had been elected in Westminster. Heath and his cabinet colleagues looked to the Army to resolve a situation in which British politicians had met with resounding failure. The Army chose an enemy: it could not be the Protestants because their government was still running Northern Ireland and they regarded themselves as British.

Nineteen-seventies Army leaders now place much of the blame for the mistakes of that period on Edward Heath and his cabinet. In one secret cabinet meeting the chief of the defence staff, General (later Field Marshal) Michael Carver was told that the soldiers on the ground were entitled to shoot anyone who opposed them, particularly protesters who, by their actions, were enemies of the Crown. He replied that he had no legal right to enforce such a policy and asked if one member of the cabinet would be willing to appear in a courtroom to defend his soldiers if as a consequence of such a policy they were subsequently charged with murder. But the British Army reluctantly took on the task of finding a solution, using stratagems like the bugging of confessionals, dubious undercover operations, military counter-insurgency assassinations, the hooding and in-depth interrogation of innocent people – sanctioned within the Ministry of Defence and kept secret even from General Carver and the British cabinet – the Lower Falls Curfew, the disastrous one-sided policy of internment without trial, which again targeted many innocent people, and the definition of the Catholic population and its Church as the enemy. One officially sanctioned operation was aimed at a priest in the Dungannon district, whose identity must remain anonymous because some people might misinterpret aspects of his story. He was never a supporter of the IRA and did not provide an escape route for terrorists wanted by the security forces. His crime, in the eyes of military intelligence, was that he constantly identified episodes of military brutality.

A plan to compromise him was hatched by the Intelligence Corps at Dungannon. It was decided that a youth should be recruited from within the local Catholic community and, under Army tutelage, would be encouraged to join the IRA and attend a terrorist training camp. They selected seventeen-year-old Columba McVeigh who had recently been questioned by the Army during a screening operation in the area. It is unlikely that anyone will ever know what pressure he underwent before he agreed to become an informer. Once McVeigh had been persuaded to join them, his handlers deviated from what might have proved a long-term plan to get him into IRA ranks. Instead they gave him ammunition and told him to plant it in his own house, which they would raid on a given night. Before they arrived, McVeigh was to 'escape' and seek sanctuary from the priest they wished to compromise. They hoped that the priest would take pity on the boy and ferry him to safety, knowing that McVeigh was not a member of the IRA and that he was being used by them. Later the British Intelligence Officer responsible for recruiting McVeigh justified his actions to a fellow operative by claiming that the priest ran an escape route for the IRA, which was untrue.

When the Army raided McVeigh's home they found the ammunition in a prearranged place in his bedroom, and a warrant was issued for his arrest. Everything seemed to be working according to plan. However, three days passed and McVeigh had not communicated with his handlers. His senior handler later said that the boy had gone to the priest, had asked him for shelter and help to get him across the Border, but the priest had refused. If he had agreed, even for humanitarian reasons, the military intended to use McVeigh in open court to identify the priest as an IRA activist running an escape route to the Irish Republic.

Eventually McVeigh, frightened and lonely, went to Dungannon police station and asked for his handler. He was turned away. A week later, he was arrested and charged with possessing ammunition. I believe that before McVeigh went to court he met his intelligence bosses, who were intent on using him in prison. I also suggest that they gave him the names of innocent people, who they alleged were working for the Army, and told him that if he was interrogated by the IRA in prison he was free to divulge them. This ploy had been used already on two other young men who were in prison at that time and was a strategy used to create paranoia in the ranks of the IRA and make them believe that many local people were informers. In prison McVeigh was beaten up by the Provisionals and told them the names he had been given, among them those of a respected solicitor, the McVeigh family's milkman and an SDLP politician.

A short time later a milkman doing relief work for the regular McVeigh milkman was shot dead. Several weeks before the killing, McVeigh was released from prison with a suspended prison sentence, which hardly fitted the crime of possessing ammunition, and went to live quietly in Dublin with his brother. The IRA discovered his whereabouts, abducted him, and took him to South Armagh where he was shot and secretly buried.

If that was Army policy, how many other such operations occurred during what was a very dirty war?

It should also be said that Charles Haughey's government in the Irish Republic was, to say the least, unhelpful. In those early years, it acted in support of the

Catholic defence organisations and the emerging Provisionals, which encouraged many in the British Army to conclude that they were also dealing with the Irish State and the Catholic Church, an integral part of the ethos of that State. The retired intelligence officer I quoted earlier sums it up: 'People conveniently forget that the British perception of the situation was that the government of the Irish Republic was up to its neck providing money and guns, and was putting them in the hands of people who were, by definition, citizens of the United Kingdom. Our ambassador in Dublin warned Haughey that people close to him, in and out of government, and within the Irish Army, were conspiring with the IRA and other republican groupings. If you place that in the context of the time when the perception of the Republic was that the Church and State were indivisible, then you can understand the dilemma faced by those obliged to make a military assessment. No one got it all right. With the benefit of hindsight, mistakes were made and people are quick to lay the blame at the door of the British Army. The British Army did not create a situation in which a government in Belfast was allowed to behave without proper scrutiny. It was up to the politicians to have anticipated events in Northern Ireland. The Army was in a no-win situation. If we had taken on the loyalists we would have faced the same problems, perhaps even greater problems because they had a hundred thousand legally held weapons in private hands, not to mention the police and the considerable armoury of the B Specials. The B Specials' armoury was something to see. No one could have guaranteed that if we had faced down the loyalists the IRA would not have opened up their own front against us. A major difficulty was that our role was to defend the State, and

Northern Ireland was part of the United Kingdom. The people who were intent on wrecking the Northern Ireland system were the Catholics. I am not saying they did not have justification for wishing to rid themselves of Stormont but our job was to protect the State. Perhaps if Stormont had been dispensed with at the outset it would have been better for all of us, particularly when we first went in. There certainly was a view at the highest levels that, without Stormont, the Catholics would have had no target and the Protestants at the outset were in a political limbo. They would probably not have posed the military threat they later posed. Martial law might have done the job until the society was able to rationalise its problems and the two sides reach some form of accommodation. I admit that there are a lot of "if only's".'

FOR GOD AND ULSTER

From the formation of the Northern Ireland State in 1920, Protestants adopted a siege mentality, characterised by the belief that the Catholic threat from the South was compounded by the Catholic enemy within. This was symbolised in the slogan 'For God and Ulster'; a principle that the Protestant faith and the State were indivisible. Over the years, Unionist politicians made no effort to curb the extreme behaviour of some of their supporters. Every year during Orange celebrations, the rallying cry of 'For God and Ulster' was linked to anti-Catholic sentiment.

In 1922, the Northern Ireland government introduced a Bill, which became the Special Powers Act, giving the minister for home affairs absolute powers of arrest and detention. It remained in place for fifty years and was aimed at the Catholic nationalist population. The forces of law and order, the Royal Ulster Constabulary and the B Specials, were predominantly Protestant, the latter virulently anti-Catholic: in the 1920s, the Specials were involved with loyalist fanatics in the killing of Catholics.

The creation of the State had been followed by the ending of proportional representation at a local level and an Act was passed to enable the minister for home affairs to redraw electoral boundaries. This gave Unionists political control in areas where they were in the minority, which encouraged discrimination in housing and employment and reduced Catholics to second-class citizens.

Even so the 'special powers' and discrimination did little to temper the language of bigotry or to dilute the myth that Protestantism and Ulster were under serious threat. In the 1930s, the Ulster Protestant League, a fanatical, pro-Nazi organisation, held mass rallies and issued anti-Catholic statements. Strange, dangerous organisations mushroomed within the Orange, loyalist and Unionist tradition, all claiming to be the true defenders of the 'For God and Ulster' tradition. Some came under the influence of British intelligence and were exploited in favour of British political interests, and threads of religious fundamentalism, homosexuality, perversion, violence and odd alliances stretched into the heart of the British establishment.

During the 1950s, when the IRA was involved in its Border campaign and part of the organisation was advocating Connolly socialism, Cold War theorists in MI6 kept their eyes on Ireland. At the time, MI5, which existed to scrutinise problems within the United Kingdom, was preoccupied with rooting out Soviet spies in Britain, which was why MI6 had been left to watch the IRA. On the books of MI6 was a Northern Ireland agent, William McGrath, a leading figure in the 'Christian Fellowship and Irish Emancipation Crusade'. McGrath was a homosexual paedophile, who believed that Ulster could only be defended with violence. In later years, commentators dismissed him as a 'nutcase' but that was far from the truth: he was deeply

embedded in the fabric of Unionist politics, working at
that fundamentalist level where he could define a violent
future for Ulster even in those Cold War days of the
1950s. Then, many people laughed when McGrath
warned that the future would be blood-spattered, but
he knew his own tribe, its strengths and weaknesses,
and he had studied the history of republicanism, which
moved through a cyclical form of violence: periods of
internal wrangling before another campaign. The fear
that, sooner or later, the IRA would mount a vicious
campaign of violence was rooted in the consciousness of
Britain and Northern Ireland. There were deeply
engrained ritual patterns of violence throughout the
history of Ireland, and events in the North during the
twentieth century convinced McGrath that the campaign of republican terrorism in the 1950s was the
forerunner of worse to come. As an amateur historian,
he would have detected those patterns in the history of
the nineteenth century. Through catch cries, slogans
and political principles, he would have seen the patterns
re-emerge in the 1950s and early 1960s. For McGrath,
land and faith defined 'For God and Ulster'. In history,
the land vendetta often arose from a Protestant determination to march in Catholic territory. For Protestants
the defence of Ulster was of primary importance, and to
nationalists the loss of part of the island to Unionists
was the grievance that led to violence. The inability of
the Northern Irish to decide where the past ends and the
present begins makes history an important element in
their assessments of the State. Thomas Carlyle wrote
that the beauty of the past was that it had none of the
problems of the present: that could never have been
applied to Northern Ireland.

The renowned historian A. T. Q. Stewart also quoted

Carlyle, that history was a letter of instructions handed down to us, and said, 'The problem with Northern Ireland is that the letter comes to us burned and charred, bits are missing and the instructions are difficult to read.' Today that applies to loyalists and republicans.

Men like McGrath never used the term 'loyalist' to describe themselves: they preferred to describe themselves as British and loyal. The term 'loyalist' emerged from the media in Britain after 1969, and was used to define extremists similar in behaviour to republicans. McGrath's loyalty was contractual, central to the Unionist thesis that if the Sovereign, namely the Queen through Parliament, treated her subjects well she deserved their allegiance. But loyalty was conditional upon Parliament upholding the constitutional position of Northern Ireland as part of the United Kingdom. Any attempt by Parliament to change that contract would, in the eyes of loyalists, make it invalid and Parliament could be defied.

Within the context of loyalty, secret or semi-secret organisations were always prepared at any time to defend the contractual position and to counter the nationalist threat. Like nationalism, the Protestant tradition always displayed a tendency to organise on the boundaries of the law. The Orange Order comes into the category of the semi-secret organisation and its roots spread outside Ireland. Early in the nineteenth century, members of the Order could be found in the Army and among royalty, until it was outlawed in the 1830s by the British Parliament. As a secret society with members in every arm of government it was regarded as a threat to the State, capable of exercising control over both Army and government. The Order resurfaced in the 1860s to defy a government ban on Orange marches and after 1886, when Gladstone introduced his first Home Rule for Ireland bill, it became a predominantly Ulster-based organisation.

People often define Orangeism as Unionism, which is inaccurate: Protestants invariably viewed the Order as a religious organisation, while nationalists saw it as the cutting edge of anti-Catholic policies. Its position within Northern Irish society was constantly exploited by politicians who wished to be identified as defenders of the Protestant faith. Within the Order men like McGrath set up their own lodges to further their personal political ambitions. The Orange Order never attempted to exclude fanatics who used violence to uphold Protestant interests. The siege mentality was rooted in Orangeism, with good reason, because despite the Plantation of 1641, which was the settling of Scottish Presbyterians, English Colonists and Episcopalians on lands confiscated from the Irish, Protestants were a minority in Ireland. They were unable to relinquish that fear, and the Orange Order was the one organisation that bonded all elements of opinion in the cause to defend God and Ulster.

At the beginning of the 1960s, McGrath, the IRA watcher for MI6, warned his handlers in London of a communist threat from the IRA (see pp. 274–8), and conveyed the same message to Protestant evangelical groups. He told them that Marxists within the IRA were planning to destroy 'our faith' throughout Ireland and that Ulster would be the battleground. Defining the enemy as godless was the classic way to engender hatred and the evangelical pamphlets circulating in Protestant districts in the mid 1960s carried dire warnings of battles between the children of God and His enemies, and stating that blood was always the price of liberty.

It was a tense period, with nationalist parades commemorating the 1916 Rising. McGrath's contacts stretched into the heart of Unionism and Orangeism and during 1964 and 1965 he persuaded senior figures to reactivate the Ulster Volunteer Force.

The UVF was perceived to centre on the Shankill area of Belfast, where the unit was led by Gusty Spence. In 1966, it was responsible for shooting four innocent Catholics, killing one, Peter Ward. Contrary to public opinion, though, at the time the UVF had a Province-wide network, and those controlling it included hard right members of the Unionist Party, politicians, members of the Orange Order and the B Specials. Their initial strategy was to generate political instability that would topple the then Unionist prime minister Terence O'Neill, whose cardinal sin had been to suggest that Catholics were entitled to basic reforms.

McGrath's role in the UVF was that of strategist: he defined the cell structure and brought into his circle those with powerful attachments to the defence of the faith. He saw the Marxist IRA as part of a global communist threat, and during the Cold War his views would have been shared with his handlers in MI6. They turned a blind eye to his sexual proclivities but their knowledge of his private life increased their control over him. McGrath also had his own paramilitary organisa-tion, Tara, organised into platoons of twenty men who were encouraged to join the UVF too. He told his members that the enemy should be shot if they could not be converted. Among those close to McGrath was John Bryans, a Grand Master of the Grand Orange

Lodge of Ireland, a secretive homosexual, and a member of the British Israelites. Many within the Unionist Party and the Order knew about and chose to ignore McGrath's and Bryans' secret sex lives and their preference for under-age boys. (The British Israelites claimed that Ulstermen would play a role in the rebirth of Britain, which was wilting under the communist menace, and alleged that the Jews were behind both communism and capitalism. The Ulster members believed that the Queen was descended from the House of David, that one of the prophets was buried in Ulster and that sustainable evidence showed that the British Isles would return the world to Christ.)

Tara was accepted within Unionism because some of those close to McGrath were well-educated young men from respectable families. He told them that the principle of civil and religious liberty was a nonsense. McGrath's Tara 'lieutenants' sometimes delivered semi-religious sermons to UVF recruits, and the relationship between the two organisations flourished until 1971, when the UVF decided to go its separate way because McGrath had failed to deliver large supplies of weapons and explosives as he had promised.

The split embittered McGrath and made him even more useful to the British intelligence community. Following the fall of the Stormont government in 1972, there was fierce loyalist paramilitary reaction, and two years later loyalists lined up to confront the British government's creation of a power-sharing administration. McGrath was used to disseminate black propaganda within Unionism, which claimed that the UVF was being taken over by Marxists, and that Unionist politicians were either homosexuals, wife-beaters or con men. His influence extended into the ranks of Ian

Paisley's Democratic Unionist Party, the Free Presbyterian Church, and the Vanguard movement, led by
William Craig, the former Unionist politician and
former home affairs minister during the 1960s in the
Stormont government.

McGrath was a frequent visitor to Paisley's church,
as was his associate, John McKeague, a homosexual
paedophile who ran the Red Hand Commandos.
McKeague recruited young boys, some for his personal
pleasure, and was involved in torture and gruesome
killings. Like McGrath he was accepted into the
Unionist family, and his homosexuality was ignored
even at this time of homophobia in Ulster. The fact that
McKeague, like McGrath, held the appropriate views
on the defence of the faith and the land was enough to
protect him from ridicule or condemnation.

In 1974 when it appeared that the UVF was under-
going a political rethink, which eventually took it into
serious dialogue with nationalists, Tara publicly
accused it of being run by communists. It is worth
noting that McGrath's assertions of a 'communist
menace within the UVF' were made at the beginning of
1974 when a coalition of nationalists and Unionists was
running the power-sharing executive. Perhaps McGrath
alone, or under the influence of his handlers, believed
that in wrecking the UVF a major threat to the
executive would be removed, but in the summer of that
year, under pressure from loyalists, the executive collapsed. However, McGrath's efforts did not go to waste
for in the autumn the UVF leadership was overthrown
and replaced by men who were not interested in a
political way forward. Like McGrath, they favoured
bloodshed and wanted to rid the UVF of those McGrath
declared Marxist-Leninist.

McGrath also targeted the UDA, and was ably assisted publicly by the Independent Unionist MP Jim Kilfedder, another closet homosexual. An overview of that period shows a serious fracturing between Unionism and loyalism, and a return to sectarian killing, which dragged the Provisionals into a tit-for-tat war. There is sufficient historical evidence to demonstrate that British intelligence were then working to detach the Provisionals from their 'armed struggle' and weaken them by depicting them as sectarian murderers, and the means to achieve that were now in place with the UVF's new leadership. The same applied to the UDA, some of whose leading members were beginning to consider the value of a dialogue with nationalists. With loyalist paramilitaries on the rampage, the Provisionals were caught up in a sectarian war which they later described as their 'darkest hour'.

In the context of the United Kingdom, other factors were at work which had an impact on Northern Ireland. The ultras within British intelligence circulated black propaganda about the Labour prime minister Harold Wilson and some of his cabinet colleagues. Against the background of the Cold War, British Labour leaders were branded communist spies and sympathisers.

Conspiracies abounded and McGrath became a tool for different parts of the British intelligence apparatus, including MI5 and military intelligence. Many intelligence operatives worked unsupervised, and whether he was used against the loyalists or the Unionist Party, McGrath was a useful tool. When Ian Paisley became a thorn in the side of the British political establishment, McGrath was employed to circulate scurrilous stories about him and his deputy, Peter Robinson.

The political chaos of the period, the terrorist war, the existence of secret bodies with conspiratorial people within them, ensured that it would be difficult to unravel the role that men like McGrath played. Even so it is hard to understand why he was protected after the news broke that he had been the central figure in a paedophile scandal at the Kincora Boys' Home, in East Belfast, where he had been the warden. In 1979 when RUC officers attempted to investigate McGrath and how he had abused his position at Kincora, the inquiry was frustrated by a British military intelligence officer.

Over the years McGrath established many useful contacts, and among them was one of the central Unionist figures at Westminster in the 1960s, Sir Knox Cunningham, a homosexual and friend of the Ulster writer Forrest Reid, whose explicit books about homosexuality Cunningham and his friends admired. Cunningham was part of a circle, provided with young Ulster boys for parties in England. Among those who availed themselves of McGrath's procurements was Anthony Blunt, Keeper of the Queen's Pictures, eventually unmasked as one of a group of Cambridge graduates recruited in the 1930s as spies by the Soviets.

In 1973 the Office of the Director of Public Prosecutions had been provided with information linking McGrath to a paedophile ring, but nothing was done about it because Blunt, who would have been implicated, was still at that time considered to be an upstanding citizen, close to the monarch and to several royal figures. Blunt knew several members of the Northern Ireland ruling class from his Cambridge days and had continued his association with them. Their contacts stretched into the echelons of the British Establishment and a circle that enjoyed 'young boys'.

Young men had been taken, against their will, from institutions in Northern Ireland to orgies in London long before McGrath took over as warden at Kincora. The latter role provided him and his friends in Northern Ireland and England with another group of victims.

While I was researching an earlier book I interviewed someone of seminal importance to the events that led to the exposure of Blunt as a Soviet agent, who also threw light on the perverse and shadowy world in which McGrath operated, and why important people cloaked his activities. I asked my source about the history of the McGrath–Cunningham–Blunt connection.

A. It is wrong to pinpoint Kincora. There were other homes in Northern Ireland from which rich people could pick up young boys and take them out. The person who knew most about the procedure was Sir Knox Cunningham.

Q. Was money exchanged? Were these boys paid?

A. They were given beer money at a weekend for sex.

Q. Blunt was involved in an attempt to discredit Paisley, isn't that correct?

A. Yes. No one could ever accuse Ian Paisley of being gay. This was a smear campaign by Blunt.

Q. Was it devised to take the heat off the Kincora investigation?

A. Absolutely.

Q. A police investigation concluded that British intelligence never knew about McGrath and his activities at the Kincora Boys' Home. Did they know?

A. From 1972 there were police files detailing the activities of —— [name withheld for legal reasons] and his rich friends in Northern Ireland. For anyone to say this matter was hidden from view is nonsense.

Q.   There was a theory that elements of the intelligence apparatus permitted McGrath to abuse boys and provide them for others in the hope that they would be able to discredit or blackmail leading Unionists and loyalists. Does that theory have any validity?

A.   Yes. Of course they knew about people who would have been useful. They knew about the son of a member of the judiciary who brought —— [a young man who worked in a garage] to orgies in the south of England at —— [name and place withheld for legal reasons]. Young boys often appeared at these orgies.

Q.   What age were the boys?

A.   Sixteen and over. They were picked up by —— [name withheld for legal reasons] and taken to England for orgies.

Q.   Why was McGrath protected for so long?

A.   Because he worked for the intelligence community. He knew people who were very powerful. If McGrath had been unmasked at an early stage, Blunt would have been named as a paedophile and no one could have been sure who else would possibly be named. There were top hats and royalty in that circle.

The Northern Ireland public was not satisfied with the official report of the Kincora inquiry, and neither were many journalists who tried to pursue the story and often found themselves frustrated by the web of intrigue surrounding it. Eventually McGrath was sent to prison for two years, but it would not be unreasonable to conclude that, considering the seriousness of his crimes and the number of young lives he destroyed, a deal had been struck. I was given access to notes of a police interrogation of McGrath and it was clear that he was not prepared to reveal any of his secrets or compromise those who protected him.

Before John McKeague, McGrath's associate, could be called to give evidence at the Kincora inquiry, he was assassinated. The INLA claimed responsibility, and because of the conspiracy theories that surrounded the affair, some people concluded that McKeague had been a sacrificial lamb. They pointed out that McGrath would never give details of his background as a spy or about prominent people in his paedophile ring. McKeague knew a great deal about McGrath and might have struck a deal for immunity with the Director of Public Prosecutions in return for information about him. It was said that McKeague was assassinated to stop that happening. It is also quite possible that the INLA killed him because he was an easy target – and a murderer.

In the 1980s UVF intelligence took a hard look at the evidence of British intelligence penetration of loyalist paramilitaries. They concluded that the British were adept at exploiting those who were most fervently committed to the defence of all that was British. Where religion and politics combined, the consequence was fanaticism, which was easily moulded for other purposes. The present UVF leadership knows that, since the early 1970s, many of its members have been agents for various British intelligence agencies, sometimes in an offensive role against the IRA, always as informers who were prepared to tell what they knew about loyalism. The connections that existed between the Orange Order

and paramilitaries continue to exist because many
loyalists see the Order as an important symbol of their
traditions. Others within the present UVF leadership,
though respectful of the Order's place in their history,
are reluctant to respond to its forays into politics and its
tendency to confrontation. The politics of dialogue
found their way into UVF thinking in the early 1990s
and culminated in a joint UDA/UVF ceasefire, but few
in the UVF or UDA leadership doubted that within their
ranks were men who preferred the old militant stance
and military response.

In the autumn of 1996, when the IRA was preparing
a new offensive, many loyalists at grass-roots level were
arguing for a return to the old days of tit-for-tat killings.
Some, like Billy Wright, were trying to damage the
leaders of both organisations with smears, claiming that
the UVF leadership in particular was Marxist and
godless. This time it was not the ultras in British
intelligence who were spreading false rumours: the
hard-liners of the 1990s were familiar with the history
of militant loyalism over the last twenty-five years and
how the mention of Marxism or socialism produced
political apoplexy among Unionists, and in the 1970s
the overthrow of an organisation that was redefining
itself. Like the IRA that emerged in the 1960s, the UVF
leadership in 1996 was concerned to maintain its
presence in the peace process. Some attributed this to
Gusty Spence, sentenced to life imprisonment in 1966,
who, like republicans of the 1950s, had gone through a
political re-education process in prison. The inherent
dangers of this for the UVF and the UDA are to be
found in the history of the IRA and how in the 1960s it
moved to the left, finally creating the Workers' Party in
Ireland, which left a vacuum for the traditionalists who

formed the Provisional IRA. Now dangerous parallels have arisen within loyalism, and the UVF/UDA leaders know this only too well. In the shadows are the paramilitaries of the ultra right with the traditional cry of 'God and Ulster', whose fundamentalism reflects the two principles of faith and fatherland and the defence thereof. Fortunately, in the mid 1990s, the ultras in British intelligence have been consigned to the quagmire of history, and without their input the UVF/UDA may be able to carry through a reforming process that will lead eventually to meaningful dialogue with the other community. However, slogans, vendettas over territory, the source of the confrontation at Drumcree, reproduce the engrained patterns of history and provide the traditionalists with the means to reassert themselves through violence.

BIGOTS AND GUNMEN I:
LOYALISTS

Hunger and the Border were the issues central to the childhood of Augustus Spence. Gusty, as he was known to friends, was born in 1933 in the Shankill area of West Belfast. Everyone was hungry in the 1930s but it was the Border that featured in the politics and conversations of his neighbourhood. Many Ulster soldiers had fought and seen terrible killings in the First World War: they were pro-Union and opposed to cynical political manipulation of the Protestant working class. Notwithstanding that, anyone who was not hard on the issue of the Border was labelled a socialist or closet republican. Spence remembers that people in his area were politically muzzled and the social issues were sacrificed at the altar of Unionist politics which thrived on fear: the fear that republicans were about to overrun Northern Ireland.

The Spence household was unusual in that to its members faith and politics were separate concepts. Its members voted Unionist because, as for most working-class Protestants, it was expected of them. When politics was discussed, Gusty's mother would comment that God did not have a political view. Their neighbours were orthodox Unionists, who believed that Christianity and Unionism were interconnected. The Orange Order was important in that those who led Unionism were in the higher echelons of the Order. Later in life Spence asked a judge in the Orange Order when his life had not reflected a political preoccupation with Orangeism. The judge replied that membership of the Order was the only way to ensure selection to the Bench.

There was political advantage to be gained from membership of the Order but not for the working-class man. In the Spence family, no attempt was made to link God, Orangeism and Unionism. Spence Senior was not in the Order and often remarked that it would be better if Orangemen went to church more often. He explained to his son that he could not understand how Orangemen could shake hands with each other on the morning of 12 July and spend the rest of the year 'stabbing each other in the back'.

Yet however unconventional in hindsight his family might appear, Gusty Spence admits that he was 'born with the God and Ulster' concept. His father had been a veteran Ulster Volunteer who had fought in the First World War, who saw himself as a fringe Unionist and perceived a separation between faith and fatherland. In that respect, he was unusual in his community. The majority of Protestants in Spence's boyhood believed that Protestants were God's chosen people. Instead of calling themselves loyal or loyalists, they described themselves as Protestants.

The B Specials were regarded as God's instrument in maintaining Northern Ireland as part of the United Kingdom. In his youth, Spence was what he now calls 'an unconscious bigot'. He told me that that was a 'cultured state of mind'. Unionist politicians shaped

their own community for bigotry and, with no formal
education, many Protestants fell into the trap of
responding to the clarion cries of 'No surrender'. Spence
knew the dates of the battle of the Boyne, the Dublin
Rising and the battle of the Somme, which constituted
his knowledge of history. Every election was characterised by the catch cries of IRA conspiracies and assassination plots, and no one questioned the politicians.

After a spell with the British Army in Cyprus and
West Germany, Spence returned to Northern Ireland at
a time when Captain Terence O'Neill, then prime
minister, was talking of reform. In an effort to portray
himself as liberal, he shook hands with nuns, much to
the dismay of many Protestants and to the anger of Ian
Paisley.

Spence became aware of 'the hark back to the old For
God and Ulster thing' because some Unionists were
dissatisfied with their leader and wanted to destabilise
his government. He found himself drawn towards a
reconstituted UVF without knowing much about the
shadowy figures who were behind it. Few would dispute
that Ian Paisley's vicious rhetoric of the early 1960s
helped to create a climate in which men like Spence
were drawn towards the traditional cries of 'No
surrender' – no surrender to reform, to the Church of
Rome, to the IRA, to ecumenism. Paisley was the
cynical purveyor of fear and hatred and used biblical
texts to support his contention that the Unionist prime
minister was prepared to sell Ulster Protestants into
'slavery'. In his news-sheet the *Protestant Telegraph*,
Paisley printed scurrilous stories about priests and nuns,
and the love affairs of popes. Journalists who did not
support him were described as 'scribbling rodents', or

homosexuals who kissed holy medals and were members of the Communist Party. In the 1960s, Paisley's preaching and writings were a powerful catalyst for bigotry, easily accepted by those with a rudimentary knowledge of politics and history, like Gusty Spence, who with others willingly swore the oath to join the UVF. It was similar to the one he had uttered when he joined the British Army, in which he had sworn that, by Almighty God and Her Majesty the Queen, he was prepared to defend his country against enemies foreign and domestic. According to him, 'invoking the name of God gave comfort and suggested a higher calling'.

Later he reached the conclusion that in the 1960s, the cloud of sectarianism was heavy within the Protestant community but camouflaged among nationalists. Passions and feelings were exploited for political advantage and the Unionist Party were, in his words, 'past masters' at the art. As for the Churches in the 1960s, Spence concluded with hindsight that the Church of Ireland was 'the Unionist Party at prayer'. In contrast, the Methodists stayed out of politics as did the evangelicals in the Church of God and the Plymouth Brethren. He said, 'Paisley arrived on a wave of anti-Catholicism, and to a large degree he hasn't changed that much. His delivery is a little bit more reasonable until such time as he is scratched and then we get the real Ian Paisley. In the evangelical Protestant groupings there was about twenty per cent who said we are Protestants and all that. However, eighty per cent said it is our job to bring our brothers back to the fold. Paisley, on the other hand, had this searing, acerbic approach to religion ... his religion. People forget that Paisley has disagreed with every Protestant Church which exists in Northern Ireland. His message was powerful because it was sectarian. Paisley appealed to a particular group of people who were sectarian. It was not so much a Christian message as a sectarian message through all the ritual incantation of Protestantism, the hymns, the God of wrath.'

Spence says that the society was always sick: Catholics and Protestants were buried in different cemeteries, taught in separate schools, and teachers were trained in different institutions. He now compares the nationalist opposition to a safety valve that was locked off. 'It has to be said that from 1922, even after Eddie McAteer led the Irish Nationalist Party into Stormont and took on the mantle of Her Majesty's Opposition, the only thing they got was an amendment to the Wild Birds Act. If you have that whole boiler with all the steam rising in it and you screw the valve down there is going to be the inevitable. We were never a wholesome society. It was an unholy war.'

He agrees that the conflict is still spoken of as a constitutional issue and it is often forgotten that the political, religious and social issues are always interconnected. 'We should all have been out fighting for civil rights. I came home from the British Army after fighting a war and had no house, no job and no vote because in those days at local level I couldn't vote because I was not a householder. The realisation of that was probably one of my first awakenings in politics.'

But Gusty Spence had not recognised the true nature of the State when he joined the UVF. In 1969 three-quarters of those disenfranchised were Catholics. In 1945 when the Labour government in Britain introduced universal suffrage, the Northern Ireland parliament, which was understood to be subordinate to Westminster, refused to follow suit, and introduced its own law restricting the franchise. The directors of companies were often entitled to as many as six or ten votes, and as many adult Catholics were not household-ers, a quarter of them were disenfranchised. Political boundaries were redrawn, and control of councils in areas where there was a Catholic majority passed into the hands of Unionists. Through a selective housing policy, Unionists ensured that Catholics were low on their list of priorities. It was aimed at maintaining a political balance so that, in critical areas, Protestant householders represented a majority vote.

In public-sector industries, Catholics experienced difficulty in finding employment, while privately owned companies were encouraged to employ Protestants. The vast majority of them were, in any case, owned by Protestants, who were either affiliated in some degree to the Unionist Party or were members of the Orange Order. In 1933, Sir Basil Brooke, parliamentary secre-tary to the Northern Ireland government, had stated publicly that he would not have a Catholic 'about the place' and that private companies should employ 'good Protestant lads and lasses'. In 1934 he reiterated his plea to discriminate against Catholics, citing his contention that 99 per cent of them were 'disloyal'. He warned that if Catholics were given employment, they would eventu-ally become the majority. It was a clear reference to the fact that Catholics had large families, and a prosperous Catholic population would be dangerous. In a public statement in 1961, Robert Babington, a lawyer and later a Unionist MP, said that loyalists should have the first choice of jobs.

What Spence did not understand in the 1960s was that Catholics were asking for the same civil rights accorded to other citizens of the United Kingdom: one

man one vote in council elections, a commission to
examine electoral boundaries and ensure electoral fair-
ness, laws against discrimination in local-government
employment, a points system for housing selection to
ensure a just allocation, the repeal of the Special Powers
Act, which was aimed at the Catholic population, and
the disbanding of the B Specials, seen by Catholics as
the paramilitary arm of Unionism. The Special Powers
Act was a noxious piece of legislation that banned
meetings, processions or writings which confronted the
State. The judiciary at every level was dominated by
Protestants, many with close ties to the Unionist Party.

But working-class Protestants, too, were exploited,
for the benefit of the ruling Unionist party: for example,
almost forty per cent of council housing needed to be
replaced. In the mid 1960s, Gusty Spence, as he would
agree, was a bigot shaped for sectarian conflict. He was
an ideal candidate: he had served in the colonial
emergency in Cyprus and had a detailed knowledge of
weapons. But he finally decided to enter the UVF after a
meeting with a Unionist politician. He and three others
attended a swearing-in ceremony for membership of the
UVF, which took place in Pomeroy in Co. Tyrone.

Those present at the Pomeroy ceremony were not of
the working class like Spence and, for security reasons,
there was little dialogue between the new volunteers
and the strategists. To this day Spence insists that the
UVF was reconstituted in 1965 by the ultra right of the
Unionist Party to overthrow Captain Terence O'Neill.

The UVF was formed to whip up sectarian hatred, to
create fear and violence by drawing republicans into the
fray and to make Northern Irish society ungovernable.
His leaders believed that the violence would be attributed to O'Neill's liberalising policies and that he would

be forced to resign. The successor they had in mind was Brian Faulkner, then a right-wing bigot who plotted O'Neill's overthrow.

In 1966, the fiftieth anniversary celebrations of the Easter Rising passed off peacefully but were followed by the fire-bombing of Catholic premises. In one incident, a seventy-seven-year-old Protestant woman was badly burned and died later in hospital. Spence is correct in his assertion that the UVF had not been formed to combat the IRA but to rid the Unionist Party of O'Neill and his reform package: in one of its first statements, written by Spence and a Unionist politician, issued from the Shankill unit, the UVF warned that it would not tolerate interference from any source and warned the authorities against appeasement. The statement claimed that the organisation was composed of heavily armed Protestants – not heavily armed volunteers, loyalists or Unionists, but Protestants defending God and Ulster from reform.

Spence and his unit met regularly and their first innocent victim was Patrick Scullion, a twenty-eight-year-old Catholic from the Clonard area of the Falls. He was not their intended victim but for bigots any Catholic was a 'legitimate target'. He was, his killers alleged, staggering along a pavement singing a republican song when he was shot. It was hardly a reason to kill him, even if it was true, but it was allied to the belief that anyone singing a republican song was a member of the IRA.

Under the banner of the UVF, William McGrath alleged that Scullion had been a communist and a necessary target. O'Neill responded by declaring that he had no intention of using the Special Powers Act or of outlawing any Protestant organisations. The events that

convinced O'Neill that a dangerous organisation existed
in his community and threatened his premiership were
the killing of a Catholic and, several years later, the
emergence of a UVF plot to kill him. The first should
have been enough to warn him of the UVF's intentions
to unsettle his leadership by creating instability. It was a
serious error on his part that he did not understand this
until the first event took place on 26 June 1966. Four
Catholic barmen decided to have late-night drinks in the
Malvern Arms in the Shankill. They did not know that
it was the meeting place for Spence and his unit.

As they left the bar they were gunned down in the
street and one, eighteen-year-old Peter Ward, died at the
scene. Spence has always denied firing the fatal bullets
at Ward but testimony at his trial pinpointed him as the
prime mover that night. It was he who had joined the
four young barmen, bought them a drink, identified
them as Catholics and allegedly told his associates,
'They're IRA men. They'll have to go.' One of the
survivors, who was shot six times, identified Spence as
the man who had chased him and pumped bullets into
him.

Arnold McClean, one of the men charged with
Ward's murder, described Spence as his immediate boss
and said that he believed Spence took orders from
someone else. He revealed that on joining the UVF he
had been asked if he agreed with Ian Paisley and was
willing to follow him. After he was charged, McClean
told police, 'I am terribly sorry I ever heard of that man
Paisley or decided to follow him.'

There is not a shred of evidence to link Paisley to the
UVF and he was one of the first to condemn the
Malvern Street murder.

On his arrest, Spence asked, 'Is this what you get for being a Protestant?'

His interrogators kept asking him about ——, a prominent figure whom they believed was plotting with the UVF to overthrow O'Neill. According to Spence, they were more interested in —— than in the Malvern Street atrocity. At Spence's trial, one of the survivors, Liam Doyle, described how he had pleaded with Spence not to shoot him and all he received was six bullets. The shooting of Doyle seems to confirm Spence's oft-repeated claim that he was not the member of the UVF unit who had killed Peter Ward.

Under pressure of public opinion, O'Neill outlawed the UVF and the minister responsible for implementing the ban was William Craig, and from 1966 until 1973 no one was charged with membership of the UVF – despite several hundred murdered Catholics.

While Spence was in prison, the UVF was working to bring down O'Neill and finally achieved it with a series of explosions at reservoirs and electricity stations, attributed to the IRA. The involvement of the B Specials in the UVF and powerful political forces behind the conspiracy made it easy to conceal the organisation's activities: it is now known that McGrath was behind a campaign to convince the public through statements to the media that the IRA was in business.

From his prison cell, Spence maintained contact with his unit. Tea-towels were sold with his image emblazoned on them and the words 'His only crime was loyalty.' Every loyalist who entered prison wanted to meet him, and he became their commander and political lecturer. He organised prisoners into military groupings and prided himself on their cells being spotless, that they drilled and washed regularly. Like the republicans of the 1950s, Spence spent the late 1960s and early 1970s reading sociology, Irish history and socialism, and the uneducated loyalists who entered his prison circle were impressed with his wisdom. He could exercise control over them.

After his murder conviction, the Orange Order of which Spence was a member expelled him but Spence's affection for Orangeism remained central to his life in prison from 1966 to 1971. In his first year in the Crumlin Road prison in Belfast, the Orange Lodge of which he had been a member stopped briefly during a march outside the prison as a mark of respect to him. The Lodge was told by the Grand Lodge that such gestures were unseemly and should not be repeated. By 1971, though, Spence was beginning to question the role of the Order and whether it really was acting in defence of Protestantism. He criticised it for making rousing speeches while sitting on the sidelines.

One factor that encouraged Spence to re-evaluate his commitment to 'God and Ulster' and terror was his presence in the prison of a State he had believed he was defending. How could his State imprison him? What kind of State did he want? Was violence justifiable in defence of such a State?

Dialogue with republican prisoners, especially Marxists, had encouraged Spence to read history. It also led to discussions with the IRA about what separated them politically and culturally and what they shared. The Marxist dimension of the Official IRA impressed Spence, and through his contacts with its members he developed a mild socialist analysis of the impoverished conditions of the Protestant working class and began to understand the social factors that made his community susceptible to the narrow party politics of Unionism. It is worth noting that he regarded the Provisionals and members of the Official IRA as political prisoners and fought alongside them against the prison criminalisation policies of the British government, which enabled him to examine more broadly the ways in which people in both communities were drawn into conflict. He gradually realised that dialogue was an important element in finding a solution although the idea did not find favour with many UVF men, who were trapped in bigotry and the culture of the gun.

In the early 1970s he was startled to discover that others within the UVF now shared his socialist views, which in the 1960s would have been regarded as treasonable. This reinforced within him the conviction that nationalists and republicans should always have been free to voice their political opinions within the Northern Ireland State. In the early 1970s at his instigation, the UVF, particularly within the prisons, began to question the two pillars of established belief: the Unionist Party and the British government. Commitment to those institutions had been previously unchallenged but that changed when Spence opened up the prison population to political debate. The result was that loyalist prisoners reserved their strongest criticisms for the British government and the Unionist Party. It was a radical departure within the loyalist paramilitary psyche and coincided with God disappearing from the agenda. Spence held seminars within the compound he controlled in the Long Kesh internment camp and encouraged all loyalist inmates to question their role in society. Most agreed that reconstruction of politics was possible within a Unionist framework.

The socialist drift of the UVF and UDA worried

British intelligence, who employed a dirty-tricks campaign to halt it, issuing bogus statements which implied that loyalist paramilitaries were at war with the British and were being manipulated by Marxists. Talk of godless socialism among the Protestant population sent people rushing back towards violence and also prevented a fracturing of the traditionalism of Unionism or the coming together within both communities of Marxists. The inevitable consequence was the elevation of those who favoured bigotry and extermination. The enemy was not just the Catholic population but members of the UDA who were engaged in a secret dialogue with the Official IRA. British intelligence ultras feared that a coming together of socialists in both violent traditions would create a more dangerous enemy within Cold War politics. They preferred the clearly defined enemy to be the IRA and had no wish to see a forging of links between paramilitaries on both sides. They set out to scupper them. With the help of men like McGrath, they identified loyalists sympathetic to the views of the Marxists in the Official IRA, and had them assassinated by their own organisations.

Spence said that nothing focuses the mind quite like a hanging or a prison sentence, and the changing character of loyalist politics derived from the prison experience: 'Self-questioning is one of the most hurtful processes that man can undergo ... truthful self-questioning. We began to articulate a philosophy, an ideology which was of course Unionist in that it identified our determination to maintain the Union with Britain but not the Unionism of old. We had come to the conclusion that in the past Unionist manipulation created something which was not truly representative and we should do something about that.'

Spence, and those close to him, concentrated on changing the politics of detainees rather than long-term prisoners. 'We pumped them,' he admits, 'knowing, of course, that they would soon be out and would take with them a new form of thinking.'

The detainees were particularly vulnerable to unorthodox thinking because they were aggrieved that the State was imprisoning them on suspicion of terrorism, as it did with republicans to take them out of circulation. Problems arose when the detainees were released back into terrorist ranks and advocated a rudimentary form of socialism that had no place within the Protestant terrorist outlook: 'Socialism was legitimate everywhere else but Northern Ireland as far as our people were concerned. It was good enough for the British Labour Party but not for those in our community who wanted to maintain the link with Britain. Before '73 those of us who were in prison were engaged in a big debate. We made our questions known to people on the outside and we wanted to know if the UVF was simply taking its political leadership from the Unionist leadership because, the way they saw it, their job was to fight a war like the British Army, their job was not to involve themselves in politics. We said: "How can you say that? If you're prepared to fight a war, you need to know what kind of war you're fighting, what for and how best to fight that war once you're released." '

In prison Spence detected a deep cynicism that derived from awareness that people were manipulated, and about gunmen who became born-again Christians. He saw many return to the fundamentalism they had learned in childhood through Bible classes and became determined to break the God and Ulster principle that created bigots and gunmen. On the outside Spence's

supporters formed the Volunteer Political Party, one of
the first within the community to exclude 'Unionist'
from its title. In the eyes of many Unionists the new
party's name implied a severing of the traditional British
link enshrined even in the Tory Party's full name,
'Conservative and Unionist Party'. However, Spence's
attempts to explain his concept of socialism as similar to
the democratic socialism of the British Labour Party
failed to impress the right-wing hard men in the UVF,
and the Volunteer Political Party's entry into politics
was a failure. The hard men took over the leadership of
the UVF, ejecting those who favoured Spence's socialist
re-evaluation. They pointed to a statement by the
erstwhile UVF leadership that proposed a debating
forum in Ulster representing all shades of opinion,
including republicans. The prospect of talks with the
IRA was the last straw.

Spence's political experiment had been a call to
political and social reconciliation but the gunmen in the
UVF detected a quasi-ecumenical flavour. They could
not deal with words like love and peace in the text of a
1974 statement by those UVF leaders who supported
Spence.

Members of the United Ulster Unionist Council were
horrified by talk of reconciliation. They represented Ian
Paisley's Democratic Unionist Party and members of
organisations such as Vanguard, the Orange Order and
the Unionist Party, and made it clear that no deal could
be done with Catholics and that a solution might only
be found through violence. The present Unionist leader,
David Trimble, was a leading member of the Vanguard
organisation, which had been founded by William
Craig. McGrath, too, was keen to rid the UVF of 'the

communists'. His favourite tactic was to issue statements through either known or obscure or non-existent
organisations, a strategy familiar to the intelligence
community. He made it clear that the war was a holy
one, to defend the evangelical Protestant faith against
an enemy, the Catholics, with whom there was no basis
for negotiation or compromise. He was also involved
with those who were formulating the anti-UVF campaign within the United Ulster Unionist Council.

Disillusioned, Spence resigned from the UVF in 1977,
saying that he could no longer support violence as a
means of changing the society.

Leaving aside the ultras in British intelligence, other
groupings, too, helped to wreck the early 1970s
political changes within the UVF: Tara, run by
McGrath and senior figures within the Unionist Party,
and the Orange Order. The Unionist Party saw the
socialist trend in the UVF as a departure from orthodoxy that might have threatened the party's domination
in working-class areas. Its view of working-class Protestants was privately expressed at that time in the slogan:
'Keep them lean, keep them keen.'

In times of crisis, Unionist politicians often relied on
the UVF as the cutting edge of Unionism and were
happy as long as the paramilitaries toed the traditional
Unionist Party line, although some felt humiliated at
having to hand over power to men with guns. The
critical point came when they realised that, if the
socialist trend continued, they might be powerless to
stop its spread, which in turn might threaten the Union
in bringing equal rights to Catholics. But the introduction in the autumn of 1974 by the British and Irish
governments of the power-sharing executive under
Brian Faulkner was the last straw. The proposed role

for the Irish government in the affairs of Northern
Ireland cut deep into the Protestant siege mentality. It
brought together all Unionists: the paramilitaries with
the muscle to bring the Province to a standstill, and the
politicians who sought what benefit they could from
what seemed a populist cause. The gunmen in the UVF
and UDA were manipulated into bitter public
exchanges after statements appeared in the media,
placed there by McGrath and shadowy figures in British
intelligence, aimed at destroying socialism within the
two main loyalist groupings and questioning the determination of loyalist paramilitaries to confront the
threats from socialism and communism. The implication was that this trend within loyalism was emanating
from the enemy, the Marxist IRA. After the humiliating
election defeat of the UPP, UVF leaders made clear their
intention to ally with the Unionist parties. They said the
major threat to Ulster was from the Marxist-Leninist
IRA. But at that time the Official IRA had ended its
campaign and the real threat was from the Provisionals.
The UVF returned to violence, spawning groups like the
Shankill Butchers.

Roy Garland, a one-time member of Tara, has
written a scholarly thesis on the negotiating history of
the UVF. In it he blames Unionist politicians and British
intelligence for wrecking the Spence initiatives of the
early 1970s. He refers to a contemporary restricted
Army document that defined operations in Ireland as
counter-revolutionary, aimed at rooting out the communist menace.

In the 1970s bigots were not always loyalist paramilitaries. Some Unionist politicians lied about their contact
with terrorists yet the record shows that they met the
UVF leadership on numerous occasions. Their purpose

was not to negotiate a ceasefire or to persuade the UVF or UDA that dialogue was the way forward.

Members of the Unionist Party and the Democratic Unionist Party actively encouraged violence, used loyalist paramilitaries to further their political ambitions and, in some instances, set up their own private armies and benefited from the division of arms shipments. The UDA also flirted with members of the two Unionist parties, and the late John McMichael, a leader of the UDA's political and terrorist wings, told me about a meeting with a member of the Democratic Unionist Party. He said that ——— [name withheld for legal reasons] 'arrived at a particular location with a shopping list for weapons'. McMichael rejected the request.

It was notable that, after a long absence, Gusty Spence publicly returned to the political arena when the UVF declared its ceasefire in 1995. (I believe he wrote the ceasefire document.) As one of the strategists in the UVF's political party of the 1990s, the Progressive Unionist Party (note the word Unionist in the name), he was back politically where he would have liked to have been in 1974. During peace talks in the summer of 1996 he indicated the UVF's determination to find a solution exclusively through peaceful and democratic means. He had not forgotten the experience of 1974, or that hard men still lurked in the shadows, that the old smear of Marxism and socialism remained a potent weapon for them, and that until all violence ended, peace could not be guaranteed. Always a realist, he was reluctant to make predictions after watching the events at Drumcree in 1996. 'Here was an Orange parade in a backwater road that brought this Province to the brink of civil war. It would be a very brave person who would make predictions. It was that serious at Drumcree. There was

heavy, heavy pressure on the loyalists to break their
ceasefire in order to come to the aid of their besieged
brothers and so forth. Certain politicians were whip-
ping it up and saying there was no getting out of the
trenches after Drumcree.'

He defined the real threat to peace in the future as
'the respectable classes'. 'Respectability you always
have to watch. We always have to be conscious of the
respectable people with calls of "shoot to kill", "we'll
run the guns in". These are all bastions of morality,
pillars of virtue. I am always deeply suspicious of these
people. Never underestimate elements of constitutional
Unionism who are tempted to manipulate loyalist
paramilitaries as they did with paramilitaries in the
Portadown area at the time of Drumcree.'

If you accept the truth of that statement, it illustrates
the inherent dangers in the coming together of constitutional politics and paramilitaries under the 'For God
and Ulster' banner, and Spence was still listening for the
return of the old rallying cries. The future still poses
serious questions for him and his community. 'Unionism says, "We want Northern Ireland to remain an
integral part of the United Kingdom because the greater
number of people say so." That begs the question:
"What in the future will you do if a greater number of
people say they don't want to remain part of the UK?
Will Unionists remain law-abiding or return to type?" '

His dream, he told me, was to see the zealots
marginalised and religion taken out of politics. That, he
recognised, would be difficult to achieve in this decade.
'I believe that the Unionist Party and the SDLP are
attempting to take the religious tribal thing out of
politics and that will become more important when
dialogue really begins. We want Sinn Fein in there, in

the same clothes as ourselves and we will drown them in democracy.'

Before 1995 the concept of the UVF drowning the Provisionals in democracy would have been unthinkable and, for me, was a hopeful sign that bigots and gunmen might be eventually removed from politics – but no one should make predictions because many bigots and gunmen are not prepared to be converted. It was a curious phenomenon in the history of the conflict that it was in prison that gunmen from both sides were able to engage in dialogue and reach an understanding of the necessity for peaceful co-existence. Implacable enemies discussed issues over which they were killing each other in the world outside. Spence never doubted that prison had a significant influence on the changes that occurred: 'What we had to do was to ensure there was an understanding that that patch, that territory, would not be used as a battleground. There was a no-conflict policy. It was a recognised thing. This is where I started to get my teeth into the issues. Long Kesh was a microcosm of the society outside. The commanders of the paramilitaries came together for the mutual benefit and to create a more humane prison regime for their people. We agreed to leave the constitutional situation to one side. We agreed that whatever happened on the outside, it couldn't be allowed to pertain inside. With all the atrocities on both sides, we kept it out of there and that was the first glimmer of hope that we could do business. We wanted to export that tranquillity to the outside and to create the system which Merlyn Rees as secretary of state put into place whereby the organisa- tions had their own offices where people could come to talk about social or political issues. Unfortunately, Roy Mason became the new secretary of state and knocked

everything on the head. The policy was to stop the Long
Kesh Camp Council idea, and to keep us all separated.
The leading Provos of the present were in there at the
time in the seventies. There was an enlightened com-
manding officer, David Morley, who took over the
Provisionals from Billy McKee.'

If only the agreement reached at the Long Kesh Camp
Council, that divisive issues should be put aside to
permit dialogue and peaceful co-existence, could be
applied outside before the end of the 1990s to facilitate
a search for agreed political structures.

BIGOTS AND GUNMEN II: REPUBLICANS

In the 1980s I met a man, in his mid thirties, who provided me with information for a book I was writing. He was an experienced terrorist within the Provisional IRA and, though I knew something of his role within the organisation, I knew little of his history. I contacted him again while I was researching this book and discovered that he had voluntarily detached himself from terrorism to lead a normal family life. He was nervous when I met him in the autumn of 1996, and asked for time to consider whether he would talk to me. 'What guarantees do I have,' he asked, 'that you won't reveal details which will get me shot?'

I reminded him that in the previous book I had made every effort to conceal his identity.

'The last time, I had permission to talk to you,' he said. 'This time, if anybody thinks that I'm shootin' off my mouth, somebody's liable to stick the muzzle of a gun in it. I have a wife and kids.'

I assured him that over many years as a journalist and broadcaster I had never compromised any of my sources, whether they were within terrorism, the police or the intelligence community.

* * *

It is not always easy to protect the identity of a source because information I acquire may relate to a particular episode, and within the world of conflict all the combatants know that, by restricting the flow of information to specified individuals, it is easier to expose the source of a leak. One has to be aware of the motivation of the person who supplies information about the organisation to which he or she belongs. In the 1980s, I was working for the BBC when a journalist in the electronic media presented me with documents that contained devastating information about aspects of the British intelligence undercover war. I asked why he was prepared to give me the material, and he replied that it was of no use to him. It seemed a generous gesture, and I knew that journalists sometimes had information which they knew their editors would be unwilling to use. In my experience, as a producer/editor with BBC Northern Ireland over eighteen years, the editorial reasons for blocking or dumping material relate either to the editorial policy of a newspaper or broadcast network, or to reluctance to deal with controversial matters. Sometimes the significance of a story has not been recognised and therefore it has not been followed up. In the BBC, the constraints in the 1980s were such that sensitive issues were referred to London, to people who were not on the ground and did not fully understand the complexities of the situation. Also the BBC might occasionally be driven by a determination to walk a correct political line, which was not always possible.

There were other problems within the Corporation, which were not shared with the journalistic staff. I became aware that the organisation had been pene-trated by several people who were conduits or actual agents for the intelligence community. It was, perhaps, inevitable that, in an organisation which handled so much airtime and had journalists on the streets, the intelligence apparatus wanted some of its people in there. As a senior editor, I learned of one journalist who was quickly packed off to London after he blew his cover. I also saw two falsified personnel files of news people whom I knew had worked for the Ministry of Defence. In another episode, I became aware that Special Branch had been given access to BBC staff files. For example, they wanted to know who had appointed a member of staff who was having a romantic liaison with a member of Sinn Fein.

There were many fine journalists in the BBC but there were also people who deliberately shaped editorial policy to suit their political allegiances. Both Northern Irish communities suffered from the failure of the Corporation to reflect, without prejudice, the truth of a given situation. At times, I found myself in serious conflict with senior figures because I refused to bend to a policy detrimental to both sides. At the time of the Anglo-Irish Agreement, I was told that I should know where I was on the issue. The implication was that I should toe the government line and not reflect Unionist and loyalist opposition to it. I refused. I was castigated for permitting a leading Unionist politician to criticise the Corporation's policy of not permitting a proper analysis of Unionist disenchantment with British policy-making.

There are also instances when journalists and broadcasters face the moral dilemma of publishing material which, by its very nature, may compromise a source and place someone in jeopardy. What I call the conflict of conscience versus social obligation was highlighted for me when I unearthed material that exposed the role of a leading Catholic lawyer in the handling of a secret Irish government bank account in the early days of the present conflict. P. J. McGrory became an international figure during the Gibraltar inquest into the 1988 killing of three IRA activists by the SAS. To help the reader fully understand the background to the P. J. McGrory story, I must now return to matters I wrote about in an earlier book, *The Dirty War*. In 1969–70, at the outset of the present Troubles, the Irish government, much to the dismay of its British counterpart, conspired to supply weapons and funds to Catholic defence organisations in Northern Ireland. Within those organisations were nationalist politicians genuinely concerned about the failure of the indigenous security forces to protect the Catholic population, particularly in Belfast where hundreds of Catholic homes were burned and looted by loyalist mobs, often aided by the B Specials. Within the defence structure there were also respectable Catholic lawyers, businessmen and priests. However, the most powerful elements were republicans who would eventually use the defence structure to form the Provisional IRA. The Irish government and many others who gave themselves to what became the defence committees were in no doubt that the republican coterie, men with a long-term agenda, had their own views on how monies and weapons should be channelled. Part of the financing of the defence groups came from a £24,000 payment to Cardinal Conway, which was later ignored when the Irish Parliament set up a committee to investigate its government's willingness to supply guns and money to organisations that included the IRA. Several secret bank accounts were set up for the 'relief' of Northern Ireland Catholics, one of which was lodged in a bank in Clones.

P. J. McGrory was one of three signatories empowered to draw money from it. After two withdrawals had been made, the names of the account holders were changed to pseudonyms – John White, John Loughran and Roger White. Two factors led to the change: a desire to obscure McGrory's involvement, and to permit other unnamed people to withdraw money.

When I was writing *The Dirty War*, I was unable to name McGrory: if I had, he would have known the identity of my source. Several years later, when I was making a three-part documentary series for BBC2 on the history of the conflict, I decided to unmask McGrory as one of the account holders. In the course of making the series, I encountered BBC internal censorship of my work. In a five-month period I was engaged in a protracted series of communications with BBC management executives. It occurred at a time when I had published a controversial book that led to threats against my family, of which the BBC was made aware. My contractual role for the series was as its producer, writer and interviewer but the BBC attempted to redesignate me as a consultant, to diminish my ability to determine the nature of the information I was collating. When a decision was taken to abandon the series, after over forty hours of filmed interviews, I resigned, knowing that much of the material would be consigned to the BBC archives. An editorial decision was reached to make one programme, and I asked for my name to be removed from the credits. The Corporation paid me a five-figure sum, on the condition that I did not reveal details of the assembled material or of my dispute with them. They were concerned that my correspondence would be damaging to the BBC's reputation, both then and in the future. I withheld the material relating to P. J.

McGrory because I did not trust the BBC. I was later amazed when the Corporation claimed that its single programme contained new and controversial material on the funding of the defence committees and the IRA. No one in senior management understood that the majority of the content of the programme was already in the public domain as a result of what I had written in *The Dirty War*.

After I left the BBC, I was approached by a representative of the *Sunday Times*, which was being sued by P. J. McGrory, who alleged that the newspaper had portrayed him as a republican solicitor at the time he represented the families of the three IRA activists killed in Gibraltar. The *Sunday Times* representative was convinced that I had information about the Clones bank account. He was concerned about the newspaper's legal position because McGrory had successfully sued the *Today* newspaper, alleging a similar defamation. I faced a moral dilemma whereby my involvement in a libel action would require me to present documentation that would lead to exposure of my sources. It was something I could not morally undertake. Some may criticise me because I am revealing this, after the death of P. J. McGrory. However, I have lodged with lawyers documents containing conclusive proof of McGrory's involvement with the Clones account. There is no shred of evidence that the three account holders acted improperly or unlawfully. One of the other signatories was Paddy Devlin, a highly respected politician and a man of considerable courage. This is his account as published in *The Dirty War*:

'I accept that the money was to be used for relief work, though I also admit that at that time I was also asking for guns. I only asked for guns because I believed that the

police failed to protect the Catholic population in Belfast
on 13–14 August 1969, and even when the British Army
arrived I was still asking for guns because there was no
guarantee that they would act as protectors if violence
flared again. After the second withdrawal of monies, I was
approached by people within the defence committees and
it was suggested that the signatories to the Clones account
should not be actual names but pseudonyms.

Devlin believed that the use of signatories was a ruse
to remove him from the account and to obscure the
passage of monies, allowing others not connected with
it to make withdrawals. At that time he was a Labour
politician, who had rejected nationalism and his role in
the IRA in his teens. He was convinced that the Irish
government of Charles Haughey disapproved of his role
in the Clones account. After the pseudonyms were
introduced, he had no further dealings with the account.

On another occasion I was interviewed for a television documentary about material I had written regard-
ing a controversial shooting by members of a secret
military grouping. I insisted that the interview be
conducted in my home and not within the BBC. I was
subsequently contacted by the producer of the programme who said he was under editorial pressure from
Belfast and London. He allowed me privately to view
the programme, which was not broadcast on the day
scheduled. Under pressure, the BBC eventually transmit-
ted the programme. To the producer's dismay he had
been ordered to omit the material I had given him which
contained original source material. He regarded the
editorial interference with his project as an example of
censorship. It was one of many episodes which I have
privately documented.

I have always tended to be cautious about those

around my professional life, and when I received the classified documents from a journalist, whom I cannot name, I decided to check him out. Ninety-nine per cent of the information he gave me was of a highly sensitive nature, and was of little relevance to a book I was writing. I was fascinated to know how he had come by the material but he was unwilling to reveal his source. When I examined it, I thought, My God, this is dynamite. It was not the type of subject matter I would have given to anyone, and I wondered how his source would react if I published it. The journalist told me: 'Don't worry. It was given to me, so it doesn't matter if you use it.' But I was still puzzled that a journalist, knowing what I was writing about at the time, should present me with documents that had no place within my book. Had his source told him to give the material to me?

Closer examination of aspects of the documents revealed a crucial piece of data about someone I was investigating. I talked to a person I trusted, and whose assistance and knowledge had proved invaluable and accurate over a decade. He looked at the documents and breathed deeply. 'If you use this stuff, I will have to walk away from you,' he said. 'And it will destroy many of your contacts for the next twenty years.'

To say I was astounded would be to minimise the shock I felt. I guided him to three paragraphs unrelated to the main body of the material.

'What about that?' I asked.

He could not understand why it had been included, and assured me that he would check it. Two weeks later he arranged a meeting with me outside Belfast. 'The stuff you're interested in is probably accurate,' he told me, 'but there's a problem as I see it. Firstly, you can't prove it's true. My instinct is to accept it because the rest of the material is straight down the line. If you ask me, I would say that somebody wants you to put something into the public domain. Your reputation will guarantee that it is believed.'

It was apparent to him that I did not understand what he was trying to convey.

'Somebody has fed you a ton of dynamite but they only want you to use one stick. They know that most of the material they've handed you is of no value to what you're writing. To convince you of the truth of the material they want you to use, they're giving you a lot of information which they know you can probably check. Knowing you can verify ninety-nine per cent of the information through your own contacts, they're expecting you to run with the one story they know you want. You have to decide whether you believe the one per cent because ninety-nine per cent is accurate, or that somebody's pulling your tail. It's bloody clever. My instinct is that somebody knows you will not hand the rest of the dynamite to another writer or to the media. It's not your style.'

Later I discovered that the journalist in question was working for MI5. After further investigation, I verified the material and published it in a subsequent book. It almost got me killed. MI5 wanted the story in the public domain because it was damaging to the IRA. And someone in MI5 knew that most journalists would not have the contacts to verify it and that their editors would have dismissed it as an unsubstantiated allegation.

The lessons I learned from that experience remained with me: when I spoke to the former IRA operative, I was aware that any guarantees I gave him would have to be realised. In the shadowy undercover war, there are very clever people in the intelligence groupings of all the protagonists, and in writing this chapter I have tried to inform the reader as best I can without compromising informants.

Paramilitary sources are always frightened that a journalist or writer will unwittingly include details that will identify them and they know that betrayal carries a death sentence. Their stories are important to an understanding of how people are conditioned and shaped for terrorism, and whether they can leave behind the attitudes that made them kill. In following this story of a former terrorist I was aware that he was never charged with the crimes he committed and I did not wish to know exact details of individual crimes. For a writer, there is a fine dividing line between knowing what has happened in the past and what is about to happen. I would never have placed myself in a position where I would have wished to know about something being planned by terrorists. In those circumstances I would have been morally obliged to expose those concerned. However, to learn about terrorism, about how terrorists think, it is necessary to 'get down there'. One has to put aside indignation to provide knowledge about why people kill and the environment that makes it possible. Governments talk to terrorists when it is politically expedient and I talk to them because the public needs to understand the nature of the people who represent the threat in their midst. The argument about the 'oxygen of publicity' was a Thatcherite slogan in a propaganda war but any British prime minister should know that the history of conflict demonstrates that solutions are frequently found by talking to the enemy. Margaret Thatcher's administration and those before her were prepared to talk to the IRA secretly while they publicly condemned the media for reflecting what was happening in paramilitary ranks.

'Sean' is in his mid-forties, lives in Belfast and is married with children. He grew up in West Belfast with parents who were devout Catholic nationalists. In the 1940s one of his maternal uncles was in the IRA but later left the organisation and emigrated. Sean's early years were spent in a Catholic ghetto, isolated from the rest of the world and with little awareness of the nature of his society. It was on his grandmother's knee that he learned about Protestants, the hated B Specials and the brave IRA men who had defended Catholic districts in the 1920s. Policemen in his district were nicknamed 'the Pigs' and anyone talking to them was regarded with suspicion. At primary school he was in the hands of the Christian Brothers: tough, uncompromising men who used leather straps to enforce discipline. They augmented his small knowledge of history with accounts of British atrocities over hundreds of years, the 1916 Rising, and the execution of its leaders. The Brothers identified Padraig Pearse as the hero of the Rising and Sean was taught to recite poems by him. At the age of ten, he could quote relevant passages from Pearse's pronouncements: 'I remember the lines from Pearse: "The fools, the fools, they have left us our Fenian dead and Ireland unfree shall never be at peace." It was powerful stuff, and so were the opening lines from the Declaration of the Republic written by Pearse and Connolly and read by Pearse outside the post office in Dublin on that Easter Sunday morning in 1916: "Irishmen and Irishwomen: In the name of God and of the dead generations from which she receives her old tradition of nationhood, Ireland, through us, summons her children to her flag and strikes for her freedom." When I learned those lines I identified with them. In a childish kind of way they told me where I came from. It wasn't that I was anti-British or any of that. In fact I was probably more anti the B Specials even though I'd not seen a B Special. Protestants were the Specials and the RUC.'

One of the memorable events of his youth, to which he attributed great significance, was a screening of the film *Mise Eire*, which through music, commentary and poetry, presented him for the first time with the story of the 1916 Rising. He was one among thousands of Catholic schoolchildren who were taken to cinemas throughout Northern Ireland to see it. Archive footage of the British bombardment of the post office in O'Connell Street in Dublin, and other parts of the city, impressed upon him that the British were the oppressors. In 1964 he was aware of the Divis Street riots, which had been, to some degree, inspired by threats from Ian Paisley and other loyalists. Trouble began when the RUC, responding to loyalist pressure, removed a tricolour from the Sinn Fein electoral offices in the Catholic Lower Falls. Under the law at that time it was illegal to fly the Irish flag. 'Even as a teenager that was an important event. It showed me that we were not entitled to fly our own flag in our districts and that Protestants called the tune.'

On Easter Sunday 1966 a republican march took place along the Falls Road and, for the first time in more than a decade, ordinary people turned out to watch it, many of whom had no connection with the IRA. Flag bearers wore the IRA's customary dress of black berets, black jackets and black gloves. 'I walked off the

pavement and joined a lot of other young people who
swelled the ranks of the marchers. I felt really proud of
myself. There was something about it which gave me a
thrill. Now I think it was about identifying with my
own people. Mind you, I hoped that none of my
relatives would spot me and tell my parents. My mother
and father would have been angry. They were nationalists and regarded the republicans as a bunch of nutters.
My mother knew the history of some of the older IRA
men and said they weren't worth a damn. As far as my
mother was concerned, it was not about what you had
... everybody was poor ... it was about the way you
behaved.'

Between 1966 and 1969 girls, rather than civil rights,
were Sean's principal preoccupation. He had a job and,
like most young men of his generation, paid his mother
for his upkeep and spent most of the remainder on
drink. Even when the killings occurred in the Falls area
in August 1969, his interest in politics remained
minimal: 'There was nobody in Catholic districts who
was not frightened and angered by the burnings.
Everybody knew that the B Specials and the RUC had
helped the loyalists burn whole Catholic streets. I saw
people with their belongings on handcarts, on the backs
of lorries. When the British Army arrived, everybody
was happy. I got on with my life. Everywhere had
barricades and a lot of lads I knew from school were
running around as vigilantes. What happened to me is
that on the night of the Lower Falls Curfew [July 1970]
I was on my way to meet a girl when I got caught up in
a riot. I was minding my own business when two
soldiers grabbed me, threw me against a wall and one of
them hit me across the side of the head with a baton. I
was hauled into the back of a "pig" [armoured

personnel carrier] and taken to Springfield Road police station. Nobody bothered to look at the bruise on my head. They took details of my family and address and one policeman must have thought I sounded okay, and he let me go.'

He believed that his arrest led to his name appearing on lists of suspects because afterwards he was frequently stopped and questioned. It was a period when the Army was engaged in 'squeezing' the Catholic population and young men were a constant target for Army foot patrols. The stop and search technique was physical, humiliating and often brutal: 'It's like the drip, drip effect. After a while you build up an anger. I kept it under control but when internment came and the loyalists were ignored, a lot of things began to occur to me. That thing about the British that I had learned as a child came back with a vengeance. I suppose I felt hatred and it was not only about the Army but the State. In 1972 when the loyalists were butchering our people and the Brits were doing nothing about it – just interning our people – that was it for me. I thought, What the fuck are you doin'? I went to see an old schoolfriend I knew was in the Provos and said I would like to do something.'

His choice of the Provos had been dictated by the then belief of many young men that the IRA, by then known as the Officials, had failed to defend Catholics in August 1969 and that the Provisionals were the only people prepared to take on the British. Sean's hatred of the British now extended to bigoted resentment of the Protestant community, whom he saw as part of the oppression. 'You could say I was politically naïve when I joined the Provos but it didn't take long to be around other people in the republican movement to learn about

politics. The way I saw it was that our people were
being killed by the Brits and by the loyalists with the
connivance of the State. I hated the loyalists, though it's
fair to say that in hating the loyalists I was hating
Protestants. It was difficult to separate the loyalists
from everything that was Protestant and anti-Catholic.
Not that I was a devout Catholic. A lot of guys in the
IRA were Catholic in name only, although I did go to
church occasionally.'

Sean was initially in an active service unit, involved in
bombings and shootings, but after several years he was
transferred to IRA intelligence. 'I did things I regret and
you know what I'm talking about. I have to live with
that. At the time none of us questioned the struggle. The
enemy were the Brits and the loyalists. There were guys
I knew who would have killed any Protestant in
retaliation, but I had this sneaking moral thing that the
enemy had to be defined as the enemy ... in other
words, the RUC, UDR, British Army, UVF, UDA and
loyalist politicians who were stirring it. There were
other guys who thought we should teach the Prods a
lesson and give them some of their own medicine. We
knew the UVF and the UDA were happy to kill any
Catholic. We could have done the same but the
leadership wouldn't approve it. Some volunteers took it
upon themselves to hit Prods and that was bad.'

Sean knew which IRA members were keen on
committing sectarian outrages and he believed they
should never have been allowed into the organisation.
'The ranks were filled with fellas you wouldn't have
given the time of day to in a normal situation. The real
hotheads lived in small areas like Ardoyne and Oldpark
where they were surrounded by loyalists. It was as if
they were under so much pressure they were going to

explode. One of my close friends told me about somebody who was loosely connected to the movement, who was running a freelance squad. That guy was happy to torture anyone who fell into his clutches. I was told he used a cigarette on two innocent Protestants and then shot them. Things like that made me feel guilty.'

He felt that internment was a failure because the most effective people escaped the net, and some of the people with whom he operated were never on police or military files. By the late 1970s, some IRA leaders knew that a large organisation was difficult to control and easily penetrated. They also learned that to be drawn into a sectarian war was counterproductive. 'We knew the Brits liked the idea of our people whacking Prods because that made us look like the loyalists ... like thugs and criminals. By the late seventies a lot of the super bigots were out of the ranks. Everything was more streamlined.'

His role in intelligence was two-fold, to build information on potential targets and, occasionally, to help others root out informers: 'There is so much paranoia in the intelligence war and you will find it hard to believe but the people in that end of it are much more ruthless than people in active service units. A friend of mine was spotted talking to this girl and it was purely innocent business. He didn't know that she was under surveillance by some of our people. They were going to nut him and I stopped it. The Brits were clever. They used every tactic in the book to recruit our people. They used blackmail, money, violence and anything else that suited them. That made it easy for people like me to feel justified in what I was doing. When the State has no morals then violence is justified.'

In the early 1980s Sean met a girl who came to mean

a lot to him. The more intimate they became, the more he worried about his future. When a baby was born, he began to think about changing his life. 'She knew not to ask me about what I did. There was a kind of unspoken agreement that we could talk about politics but not about my thing. Married life made me realise a lot of things. I suppose it was easy to be what I was when I had no real commitments. I began to see that I had lost so many years of my life. I really began to feel the stress when the baby was born. I remembered how I used to go drinking and chasing girls and how all that changed when I joined the "RA". I couldn't really explain to myself where the years had gone. It's funny that ... in a peculiar sort of way. It's hard to explain that in a way I didn't know myself ... Maybe I didn't even know what was happening ... in politics I mean.'

He vividly remembers an evening when his wife was at her mother's and he was with the baby. A member of the IRA arrived at the door and told him, 'We need you.' Sean explained that he could not accompany him because he was baby-sitting. 'Leave it next door,' he was told, and that was what he did. 'It was days later when my wife exploded about me leaving the baby with two elderly neighbours. I had to ask myself what the hell I was about. It was also the "it". The baby meant nothing to that guy, and to my wife it seemed like I was the same. There was no Road to Damascus stuff but it was like a slowly burning fuse ... sorry for the pun.'

His disillusionment was heightened by the 1981 hunger strike in which ten prisoners died. He felt that the IRA could have called it off earlier, that the men had lost their lives in vain. In his view, the organisation had exploited the hunger strike for political gain: 'What began to worry me was that there were a lot of guys

running the organisation who had two hats. They had
an eye to politics and to the armed struggle and they
played the card that suited their political ambitions
when it mattered. A lot of guys like me began to
question the wisdom of having an organisation which
was run by politicians. That's why the IRA now has
turned the tables. The days of people promising things
they can't deliver is over. The whole thing should be
over.'

He discovered that it was not easy to leave the IRA
because his colleagues were suspicious of his motives,
but gradually he detached himself and began a process
of re-evaluation, beginning with a hard look at his own
life. He found a job and began to mix with Protestants:
'It was only then that I saw that this blanket hatred I'd
had for the other community was unadulterated bigotry. I don't have any regrets about what I felt for the
Brits ... they deserve all they get and I mean the British
Army. They trampled on people whereas the loyalists
were only doing what the Brits allowed and encouraged.
Meeting ordinary Protestants was quite a shock to my
system. Once or twice I said to myself: "What the fuck
were you doin'? These people are no different than
you." I know that's probably too simplistic but it was
that kinda gut feeling that I didn't know what it was all
about.'

During his terrorist career, Sean felt guilty. He went
to church but never to confession. He believed it
hypocritical to confess in the knowledge that he would
walk out of the church straight back into the same
world of terror.

I said that that had been an indication that he knew
he was acting immorally. He replied, 'Not quite. The
Church plays its own games. I knew priests who knew

exactly what was going on and would hear your confession no matter what you told them. I felt – maybe it was my upbringing – that you either go in and tell the lot and admit that is what you're goin' to do in the future or you don't do it at all. I know that sounds weird but it's like being in the IRA – you either give yourself to something totally or you don't. In my own conscience I felt justified, which is why I went to Mass.'

I asked him if he had received communion knowing that in terms of Church doctrine he was not in a state of grace.

'Once or twice. I used to feel that ... maybe it was something in the back of my brain ... I wasn't fit to receive it. It's all tied into those dilemmas about being in a state of grace. I didn't always feel I was.'

After he left the IRA he questioned the morality of his life as a terrorist and was overwhelmed with guilt. He attributes this to the fact that he was no longer in the company of others who could sustain his commitment to violence. He went to a priest in Clonard Monastery hoping to find an answer to his problems. 'I told him everything. I came out with all the bad stuff. It was like opening the tin and everything just spilled out. I told him it was over for me. I will never forget that priest. He really helped me to open up my soul and seek God's forgiveness. I walked out of there a free man. I remember walking down Clonard Street feeling like a free man.'

I asked Sean if he really believed it was possible to leave behind his history. His reply reminded me of the words of many loyalists to whom I had spoken.

'When Drumcree happened, I had that old gut feeling, that anti-Prod, anti-Brit thing. Here were the Prods pushing it, that old Stormont thing of thinking they are the people and they're gonna march wherever they want and that means over us. And the Brits, the RUC, they backed down. It was the old Unionist thing, "If you don't let us do what we want, we'll have a civil war and kill a lot of Taigs." '

Like others on both sides of the conflict, he had left the terrorism but his gut reaction to political events was unchanged. When he talked about Drumcree, there was a bitterness in his voice and a narrowing of his eyes and mouth.

I asked Sean if he could envisage a situation in which he would go back to violence. His answer was swift and decisive.

'Yes! If something like Drumcree led to a civil war, I would be there for my people.'

But did he now believe that violence was justifiable in pursuit of the republican ideal of a United Ireland?

'No! It will happen one day because of the population balance. We will never be back where we were ... at least you can put that down to the IRA. If they hadn't existed, there would have been no political change and the Brits would have handed Stormont back to the Prods. That's over. I don't want my kids to grow up like I did and so I'm happy to leave things as they are.'

His use of language, in particular his reference to 'Prods', reeked of the sectarianism characteristic of most paramilitaries. They often try to hide or disguise it with a rhetoric that speaks of ideals and traditions. However, it is firmly rooted in the psyche of the society. The unholy war of the mind is just as powerful as the one being fought with the gun and the bomb: they are interconnected, the mind providing reasons for the cause.

Sean suggested I talk to one of his contemporaries

who in the 1970s had left the Provisionals for the INLA.
Later he took the road of non-violence. His friend told
me that he believed the Provisionals were duplicitous
about reactive violence. He pointed to the IRA killing of
leading loyalists and defined it as sectarian. 'At least the
INLA was clear about its policy to target loyalist
paramilitaries. We knew we were in a sectarian war and
we didn't walk away from it. Like the Israelis, we were
prepared to fight fire with fire. The Provos pretended
that they were not involved in a sectarian war so they
stuck a bomb in a shop on the Shankill Road.'

He was referring to an IRA atrocity carried out on the
Shankill Road in October 1993. Ten people died in the
attack including the bomber Thomas Begley. Gerry
Adams helped to carry Begley's coffin at the funeral,
and was condemned by moderate Protestants for
appearing to condone sectarianism. The attack occurred
at a time when loyalist paramilitaries were killing a
Catholic every day.

The former INLA terrorist had none of Sean's guilt
about his past and I concluded that he had left terrorism
because the organisation was in a constant state of
chaos and he was worried that he might be targeted in
one of the many internal disputes, which led to
numerous assassinations. It was often said, within the
security forces, that the INLA was skilled in killing its
own.

My interviewee threatened me when I asked him
what kind of violence he had undertaken for the INLA,
dismissing my questions about religion with the remark:
'I don't give a fuck about the Catholic Church. It and
the Provos have always been bedfellows. Fianna Fail and
the Catholic Church put the Provos in place because
they're all wee green Catholic nationalists.'

He was alluding to a political conspiracy in the Irish Republic during 1969/1970 in which the government of Charles Haughey, elements within the Catholic Church and the SDLP conspired in the procurement of weapons for a defence organisation in Northern Ireland, which later became the Provisionals.

My former INLA interviewee did not believe in God although it was apparent that he identified with a Catholic community. He used the term 'my people', a description used by paramilitaries on both sides, but when I asked him to define it his reply was predictable: 'The oppressed people.'

I tried unsuccessfully to point out that the social injustice was not exclusively directed at Catholics, and that the Protestant working class suffered political exploitation, poverty, unemployment and bad housing conditions.

'You'd make a good socialist,' he said, laughing.

Unlike Sean, I detected within him a bitterness which, when allied with violence, must have been explosive. He was not Billy Wright, worried about losing his soul, or the former Provisional who sought out the confessional. He was a terrorist who enjoyed terror. I have met many people like that. They have always been in Northern Irish society and will always be there, like time bombs ticking away, ready to explode when the next historical melodrama imposes itself on the Province's tapestry of life.

REFLECTIONS

Much has been written about individual clergymen on both sides who have tried to encourage the paramilitaries to pursue dialogue rather than violence. A fine example was *The Troubles* by the respected writer and commentator Tim Pat Coogan. Nonetheless, I feel it necessary to deal briefly with the subject, particularly as it relates to men such as Father Alec Reid from Clonard and the Rev. Roy Magee, a Presbyterian clergyman, who was an intermediary between the Irish and British governments and the loyalist paramilitaries.

Alec Reid was unable to talk to me when I was researching this book, and from other sources I understood his reluctance related to his health. From the early 1980s he was at the forefront of a dialogue with the Provisionals, and the strain on him was such that, on the advice of his superiors within the Redemptorist Order, he spent recuperative periods out of Northern Ireland. He was central to a theological debate between Sinn Fein and the Catholic Church, which began in the 1980s when in seeking a resolution to the conflict Gerry Adams drafted a basis for the Church's involvement. Adams made the point that the Church could be central to persuading the IRA to end the conflict, provided it recognised injustice and the failure of politicians to alleviate the conditions that generated violence. Adams was determined to create a pan-nationalist coalition, a merging of republican and nationalist political organisations, with the Church at its centre.

As I pointed out, the Provisionals resented Bishop – later Cardinal – Cahal Daly's political pronouncements and condemnations of IRA violence. They believed that he was prejudiced in favour of a Unionist position that defended the use of violence against an armed IRA uprising aimed at overthrowing the State. Adams pointed out that the State had been founded on Unionist threats, and defended by force. To imply that it could ever have been changed by peaceful means was to ignore reality. The Provisionals said that it was not enough for the Catholic Church to condemn violence: it was morally obliged to demonstrate that there was an alternative means by which Irish freedom could be achieved.

Into the frame of that debate came the Redemptorist theologian Father Sean O'Riordan, who recognised that if conflict was to be avoided, the Church had a duty to help in finding a solution. That view was not shared by many conservative Catholic clergymen, who had no wish to be tainted by involvement with the Provisionals or to be seen to be part of a political process of pan-nationalist opinion that would be perceived by the British and the Unionists as a republican bandwagon.

Cahal Daly was a thorn in the side of the republican movement from the outset of the conflict. As Bishop of Ardagh and Conmacnoise in 1972, he said it was sinful for Catholics to be members of the IRA, an illegal body that acted in contravention of the democratic institutions of the State.

The IRA preferred Tomas O'Fiaich, an historian from Maynooth who was Cardinal from 1977 to 1990. He was unapologetically nationalist, and his roots were in the Border town of Crossmaglen. The British and the Unionists regarded him as a republican. When he met Margaret Thatcher during the 1981 hunger strike he was appalled at her demand to know if the IRA hunger strikers were dying to 'prove their virility'. In May 1990 there was considerable controversy when Gerry Adams and Martin McGuinness attended the televised funeral Mass for Cardinal O'Fiaich.

During his time as Cardinal, O'Fiaich was unable to hold sway over Bishop Daly, and some sources have said that he felt Daly was too hard on republicans and not tough enough on the British. It was Cardinal O'Fiaich who encouraged the Redemptorists, like Alec Reid, to pursue a dialogue with Provisional Sinn Fein.

Father Desmond Wilson, a Belfast priest regarded by many as a radical, was also instrumental in developing discussions with Sinn Fein. For years, he organised seminars in the Ballymurphy area of West Belfast, and in the early 1970s brought Mother Teresa and several of her sisters to Belfast. His view, which found favour with Adams, was that the Catholic Church had a duty to resist injustice, a principle that emanated from Vatican Council II and authorised bishops to confront injustice even if their action placed them at loggerheads with Church authorities.

Des Wilson was an outspoken critic of the British Army and once arrived late for a BBC broadcast because he was caught up in a British Army arrest programme when the Army were using this as a means of screening the whole Catholic population in areas such as West Belfast.

By the end of the 1980s the efforts of Redemptorists
such as Reid, O'Riordan and Father Gerry Reynolds,
and the discussions organised by Father Wilson led to
increasing demands from some of the more radical
clergy for Church involvement in finding a solution. It
was under the auspices of the Church, and with the
direct involvement of Alec Reid, that the SDLP leader,
John Hume, began a dialogue with Adams in 1988. It
was a courageous departure for Hume, who had had
unsuccessful meetings with IRA representatives in the
early and mid 1980s. In 1988, the presence of a Church
imprimatur, through the active involvement of Cardinal
O'Fiaich, made it easier for Hume to agree to initiate a
dialogue aimed at peace. Like Alec Reid, he was
depicted as a pariah in conservative circles in both
Britain and Northern Ireland. Hume offered the potential for a pan-nationalist agenda, and a broadening of
the debate to the United States where his reputation was
high. Cardinal O'Fiaich was pleased with the Hume–
Adams discussions and wanted them extended to
involve leading political figures in the Republic. It is
thought that if he had not died in 1990, he would have
given great impetus to the Hume–Adams process: he
would have placed himself at the forefront of the
strategy by meeting the two men. One can only
speculate on what effect that would have had on
Unionist and British opinion but it is likely that the
public presence of the Cardinal in the company of
Adams would have incensed Protestant opinion and led
to deteriorating relations between the Churches in
Ireland. At the time John Hume put his political career
on the line and faced the wrath of newspaper columnists and politicians in Britain and Northern Ireland.

Looking back on that period, it is clear that the

Hume–Adams process was of critical importance in the inter-governmental talks that led to the Downing Street Declaration, to an IRA ceasefire which lasted eighteen months and to the arrival of the loyalist paramilitaries in the peace process. The hand of the Catholic Church had been prominent in much of the secret dialogue and helped to move the IRA towards recognition that an alternative strategy to violence was indeed possible. It begs the question, 'What was the Church doing for much of the conflict?'

The same question could be asked of the Protestant Churches, who spent the fifty years of Stormont–Unionist rule ignoring the injustice and bigotry that underpinned Northern Irish life. Those Protestant clergymen who confronted sectarianism or supported ecumenism were forced out of their parishes, and some sought sanctuary in England. What little condemnation of violence existed was never enough to persuade right-minded people that the Protestant Churches were opposed to injustice or prepared to confront the State when it acted discriminately towards any section of the population. It was left to individuals like the Rev. Roy Magee and Archbishop Robin Eames, Anglican Primate of All-Ireland, to plough lonely furrows in an effort to move loyalist paramilitaries towards a peaceful resolution of the conflict.

From the early 1960s, the Protestant Churches failed to address the explosion of religious fundamentalism characterised by Ian Paisley and his Free Presbyterian Church. They backed away from their duty to point out to the Protestant population that Paisley's political and religious rhetoric had been instrumental in creating an atmosphere of hatred and violence. They ignored the yearly round of Orange marches, the anti-Catholic slogans and the Orangemen's determination to march through areas where they were unwelcome. They did not oppose the Unionist tendency to depict all Catholics as insurgents, and Irish nationalism as an extension of 'Popery and Rome Rule'.

It is reasonable to conclude that the Churches on both sides failed their community and society at large. It was left to individuals to make courageous efforts to address the causes of violence and encourage meaningful dialogue.

When the British government, through the British Army, the B Specials, RUC and UDR, acted beyond the bounds of what was expected of a democratic institution, the Protestant Churches were silent. They were frozen in the prejudice that Catholics were by nature republicans, fifth columnists intent on destroying the Protestant Unionist heritage. Ian Paisley's swift rise to prominence occurred because fertile ground awaited the seeds of his bigotry. Within Protestantism and Unionism in the 1960s, few were prepared to denounce him.

The principle of God and the Gun is endemic in both communities, and not only among paramilitaries. In Unionism, the prospect of change has often been met with the threat of righteous violence. Unionist politicians walked hand in hand with paramilitaries when the use of force suited their political objectives. Paisley appeared on a hillside with men waving firearms certificates to indicate the threat to British policy-making if the government stepped outside the boundaries of what was expected by the Protestant population. In hard-line loyalist circles, it earned him the title 'the Grand Old Duke of York', a clear reference to the line in the old nursery rhyme: 'He marched them up to the top of the hill and he marched them down again'. It was a typical Paisley stunt, but its significance was not lost on the Catholic population in a society where there were more than a hundred thousand legally held firearms in Protestant hands.

Paisley also attended the launch of Ulster Resistance, at a secret paramilitary display in November 1986 after the signing of the Anglo-Irish Agreement. Several days beforehand, Paisley informed me that he could not undertake a broadcast at a scheduled time because he was due to attend a prayer meeting. The 'prayer meeting', in the Ulster Hall in Belfast, was in fact a paramilitary rally to launch Ulster Resistance with Paisley on the platform wearing a red beret. Ulster Resistance was later involved with the UFF/UVF in arms procurement when Paisley was no longer associated with it.

When I was writing *Stone Cold*, I discovered that Michael Stone, a UFF hitman, had been involved in training members of Ulster Resistance. In March 1988, he entered Milltown Cemetery to kill IRA leaders who were attending the funerals of three Provisionals killed by the SAS in Gibraltar. In Milltown, Stone killed three mourners and wounded fifty others. Evidence showed that British intelligence knew of him and of his plan to kill people at the funerals.

Stone defined his actions in terms of fundamental righteousness, though he never succumbed to conversion. Today Ulster Resistance remains an armed grouping, waiting in the wings for the call to violence. It shares views expressed by men like Billy Wright that a time may come when the only alternative is civil war to defend the rights of Ulster Protestants. Among its leaders, like those who re-formed the UVF in the mid 1960s, are influential businessmen, members of the

RUC and former members of the UDR. A significant number are Free Presbyterians, who subscribe to the view that there can be no deal with the Catholic community, that until Unionism returns to a majority-rule position Ulster remains under threat.

I spoke briefly to a man who joined Paisley's flock in the 1960s and was involved with Ulster Resistance. When he became disillusioned with it he joined the UVF. In the autumn of 1986, he had left Paisley's Church and was committed to loyalist involvement in the peace process. Of Ulster Resistance he said, 'The idea was to smash the Anglo-Irish accord which was undemocratic. Big Ian was just a figurehead. Other people moved the thing towards creating an organisation which would always be there for the defence of Ulster. Everybody knows Paisley has a big mouth – the Grand Old Duke – but there were people who wanted Ulster Resistance to be more than just a stunt. Deals were done with the UVF and UFF to share a large consignment of weapons ... the idea was to swap Shorts' missile plans for the weapons. The UVF and some of the people in Ulster Resistance had maintained contacts with the old South African regime. There are plenty of good Ulstermen in South Africa and this was in the eighties when the whites were in power. The South Africans couldn't get past the embargo on missiles and some of our people working at Shorts outside Belfast had access to the designs for new missiles so contact was made with high rankers in the South African military. The deal was Shorts' missile designs for weapons. It was a good deal. The whole thing didn't succeed but we got our share of a big consignment. People don't realise that Ulster Resistance is there for a doomsday situation. There are plenty of people who would answer the call … people with legal weapons as well. I got fed up with all talk and no action and left. I packed up the Free Presbyterian thing as well. Now I'm just a normal Prod if you like!'

When I asked him about the connection between religious fundamentalism and violence, he replied, 'Roman Catholics just don't understand that for us God, our faith and our land are one and the same thing. As Protestants we have our roots here and we're not goin' to give them up for a republican Ireland. You just can't say that we're Unionists. We're Protestants, Ulstermen, we're British. Our heritage is in our faith as much as it is in our Britishness. One without the other makes us nobodies. If there was a united Ireland tomorrow we would just be Protestants like the ones who live south of the Border and have no identity.'

Religion in Northern Ireland needs to be detached from politics so that the two communities may address together the political and social issues, which might bring them closer to peaceful co-existence. Perhaps they should try to remember that in making a good confession to each other the basis for reasoned dialogue will present itself through a reconciling of the two traditions. Some people understand reconciliation to mean ecumenism, others peaceful dialogue. I understand it to mean putting aside hostility and resentment and recognising the importance of compromise. It means bringing people together in friendship.

APPENDIX:
SIGNIFICANT INFLUENCES

Irish Republican Army [Provisionals]
In the wake of the attacks on Catholic areas of Belfast in 1969, there was growing disillusionment with the IRA leadership based in Dublin. In August, when Protestant mobs, aided by B Specials and members of the Royal Ulster Constabulary, attacked Catholic districts in Belfast, there were few guns in IRA hands in Belfast. The violence resulted in a massive displacement of Catholic families and the destruction of hundreds of homes. After British troops arrived to restore order, the letters IRA appeared on gable walls as 'I Ran Away'.

Traditionalists within the IRA, already disillusioned with its new trend towards socialism, were dismayed in December when its Army Council voted to recognise the three parliaments in London, Dublin and Belfast – a major departure for an organisation that had always advocated abstentionism and physical-force politics. They left to form their own IRA, known as the Provisional IRA.

The split was mirrored in the IRA's political wing, Sinn Fein, and the result was a Provisional Sinn Fein. After January 1970, two IRA organisations and two

Sinn Feins were in place: the Officials and the Provisionals.

It was the Provisional IRA that quickly captured the
hearts and minds of young men, who were ready to join
a body whose basic *raison d'être* was defence of the
Catholic population. The Catholic Church in Ireland,
and important elements in the Irish government, favoured the Provisionals, seeing them as a traditional
Catholic/republican organisation. The Provisionals also
attracted veterans of earlier IRA campaigns, which
accorded the organisation a high degree of acceptance
among republicans. The Official IRA was regarded as a
Marxist, ungodly grouping, whose rhetoric, rooted in
contemporary socialist doctrine, did not neatly fit the
tribal politics of Ireland.

The Provisionals duplicated the historical structure of
the IRA with brigades, battalions, companies and units.
They quickly acquired weapons from the United States
and Europe, and through the mediation of politicians in
the Irish Republic.

After the British Army operation known as the Lower
Falls Curfew in July 1970, the strength of the Provisionals greatly increased. It was clear to Catholics that the
British Army had identified them as the enemy even
though they had arrived in Northern Ireland to defend
them. The majority Unionist government at Stormont
was still in place and influenced not only British
government policy but also the strategy of the British
Army. Crude operations, like the curfew of a civilian
district, provided the Provisionals with recruiting propaganda. By the autumn of 1970, the Provisionals were
no longer simply concerned with defence: they were
developing a long-term strategy that would eventually
be known as the Long Way. Unlike the Officials, they

were the archetypal long-term men with the declared
objective of a united Ireland.

Throughout the 1970s and 1980s the Provisionals
became the dominant force in the conflict, developing a
bomb-and-ballot-box strategy. They realised that the
dual thrust of violence and politics enabled them to fight
the British on two fronts. Far from being the mindless
thugs portrayed by the British tabloid media, they were
clever tacticians, militarily and politically. They used
their political strength to exploit British weaknesses,
always with a view to being part of any political process
that might be put in place. They took their bombing
campaign to the British mainland, convinced that the
British government could deal with an 'acceptable level
of violence' in Northern Ireland but not in cities like
London. History will show that it was the sustained
bombing of London, and particularly the City, the
financial heart of the capital, that led to secret negotiations with the IRA in the late 1980s and early 1990s.

Unlike the IRA before 1969, the Provisionals placed
much of the control of their organisation in the hands of
Ulstermen who were shaping strategy. In the past, the
IRA leadership had been mostly composed of men from
the Irish Republic, who regarded northerners as hotheads. In the 1960s, as the IRA embraced socialism, the
northern element had upheld the traditional values of
romantic nationalism, of blood sacrifice, and still
believed the gun more powerful than politics. The
Provisionals eventually refined that concept, adopting
the duality of Armalite and the ballot box. In maintaining control in the hands of northerners, who shared a
similar political and cultural history, the Provisionals
prevented serious splits occurring in their military and
political wing. Over the years, commentators have

speculated that the Provisionals would divide, and have failed to recognise that those who controlled the organisation were those who formed it.

They also established contacts with Middle East terrorists, and with Colonel Gadaffy in Libya, and through those sources acquired large supplies of weapons and explosives.

In the 1980s and 1990s, they initiated secret discussions with the Catholic Social Democratic and Labour Party led by John Hume. The objective was to find common political ground within the Catholic nationalist population so that Catholics could present a coherent political objective. This concerned the British government and Protestants, who described the dialogue between the two groupings as the beginning of a pan-nationalist front. The Catholic nationalist community was always divided between traditional democratic nationalism and republicanism. The prospect of change was worrying as it might lead to the development of a simple republican demand for a united Ireland.

If the Provisionals had remained a merely military organisation, it is unlikely that they would have flourished, but their development of Sinn Fein has enabled them to claim a political mandate.

The exact nature of the relationship between Provisional Sinn Fein and the Provisional IRA has constantly frustrated commentators. The simple answer is that they are two parts of a republican struggle sometimes defined as the republican movement, and that essentially the IRA is the controlling body in terms of overall strategy. The conflict cannot be ended without the consent of the IRA. In the 1970s and 1980s Sinn Fein was often run by men who had served prison sentences and were no longer suitable for IRA active service: they

were known to the authorities and could not be faceless
terrorists. By the mid 1980s and into the 1990s, Sinn
Fein worked hard to attract members who were
republican by conviction but had no desire to enter
directly into the armed struggle. However, Sinn Fein
and the IRA are inseparable in that some of the leading
members of the former are part of the IRA's decision-
making structures. Both organisations have the same
agenda and the freedom to pursue different methods.
Only the IRA, though, can decide to end its campaign.

Irish Republican Army (Official)

The Officials were so-called after the split in 1970 that
led to the emergence of the Provisionals, when they
insisted that they were the official IRA organisation.
They were also termed 'Stickies' because at republican
anniversary celebrations they stuck labels to coat lapels.
Their chief of staff, Cahal Goulding, who was Dublin-
based, moved the IRA towards a socialist agenda from
the early 1960s.

After the failure of the 1956–62 campaign, the IRA,
led by Goulding, examined its past in the light of a
modern world in which political protest was more
effective than the politics of the gun. Goulding had
come to socialism through his reading in prison, and
within the organisation he found many other ex-prison-
ers who shared his beliefs and were looking for a new
way to develop republicanism. They formed social
action groups in the Irish Republic, only to be
denounced as communists by the State and the Catholic
Church, and were instrumental in forming the civil-
rights movement in Northern Ireland. Goulding and
other Dublin-based leaders were opposed to sectarianism in Northern Ireland and, during periods of tension

in early 1969, refused requests for guns. When violence erupted on a massive scale in Belfast, Goulding's decision not to arm the city's IRA units was the first and most significant element that led to the split in the IRA.

However, after the Provisionals broke away from the organisation, the Officials also put themselves on a war footing, often trying to outdo the Provisionals in attacks on the British Army. It was they who engaged the Army in a massive gun battle during the Lower Falls Curfew in July 1970, and who bombed the Parachute Regiment Headquarters at Aldershot in revenge for Bloody Sunday.

By May 1972, the Officials were disillusioned with the nature of the conflict and declared a ceasefire, saying that this was in response to the wishes of the people. In fact, they had been upstaged by the Provisionals who were now the dominant force. There was also a feeling within the organisation that they had drifted away from the socialist principles they had adopted in the 1960s and were being drawn into a traditional republican conflict. The Officials' Army Council stipulated that the organisation would keep its weapons purely for defence. Goulding said that they would develop class politics.

In 1975, the Officials' ranks split with the formation of the Irish Republican Socialist Party (see p. 280), which later became the Irish National Liberation Army (see pp. 280–1), and a bitter feud ensued between those who wanted to remain within the Official IRA and those who wanted to leave. Nonetheless, the ceasefire continued and as the military wing of the Official IRA faded into the background, Official Sinn Fein became the Workers' Party, fighting elections in both parts of Ireland. This pleased the British government, who

believed that support for the Workers' Party would
diminish the influence of the Provisionals. That did not
happen: in Northern Ireland, the Workers' Party was
eclipsed by Provisional Sinn Fein.

Saor Uladh (Free Ulster)
A small organisation, which broke away from the IRA
in the mid 1950s and carried out its own operations,
but which quickly faded into obscurity. Its members
were adherents of the orthodox republican tradition.

Irish Republican Socialist Party
The IRSP was formed in 1974 as a breakaway grouping
from the Official IRA, also including members of the
Provisionals unhappy with a Provisional IRA ceasefire
in that year. Like most republican organisations, it soon
formed a military wing which became the INLA.

Irish National Liberation Army
The INLA came into being in 1975 as the military wing
of the Irish Republican Socialist Party, and fast acquired
a reputation for ruthlessness. During another Provisional IRA ceasefire in 1975, hard-line members eager
for action joined the INLA. One of its first killings was
that of the Belfast Official IRA commander, Billy
McMillen and the group reached prominence when it
killed Airey Neave, Margaret Thatcher's Northern
Ireland adviser, with a mercury tilt switch bomb
attached to the underside of his car. It was the first time
such a device had been used and it exploded as Neave
left an underground car park at the House of Commons. The INLA declared that its objective had been to
force a British military and economic withdrawal from
Northern Ireland. It acquired arms from terrorist

organisations in the Middle East, and throughout the 1970s and 1980s it was responsible for killings and bombings of security-forces personnel. It was also involved in sectarian murders.

Like many republican groupings, the INLA experienced internal differences over tactics, and with so many hotheads in its ranks it was inevitable that the gun would settle them. In a series of feuds in the mid 1980s, INLA members murdered each other. Between December 1986 and January 1987, twelve were killed and others injured. By the mid 1990s it was a tiny organisation, yet still with the capability to kill, and regarded as unstable and highly sectarian.

Ulster Defence Association (UDA)/Ulster Freedom Fighters (UFF)

The UDA/UFF was formed in 1971 to act as a co-ordinating body for the many Protestant vigilante organisations that emerged after the violence across the community in August 1969.

The use of 'defence' in its title was hardly expressive of the real nature of the organisation: from the outset, it was run by extreme anti-Catholics, and in the early 1970s its members were guilty of some of the most horrific murders of the conflict. Any Catholic straying into a Protestant area was seen as a target and many innocent people were tortured in front of UDA revellers in illegal drinking clubs, then shot or stabbed to death. It was also involved in extortion and racketeering.

At one point it claimed forty thousand recruits, displaying its strength in mass rallies of masked men dressed in combat jackets. It saw itself as the defender of Protestant values and the constitutional link with Britain, and its membership included ex-servicemen and

former members of the B Specials, the State's paramilitary arm (see pp. 286–7). The sheer size of the UDA
deterred the British Army from engaging with them, and
very often the organisation's acts of violence were
ignored: it was a legal body which gave it a high level of
immunity from prosecution.

In order to maintain this status, and to prevent itself
being declared illegal, in 1973 it established the Ulster
Freedom Fighters. The UFF was soon declared illegal,
like the IRA. However, the UDA, still legal, was able to
organise violence and claim responsibility while using
the name of the UFF. The UDA and UFF were
effectively the same organisation, but the British government did not ban the UDA for another twenty years.

In the loyalist strike of 1974 the UDA was the major
threat to the British government and the Army. UDA
members controlled the streets and many were prominent in restricting power and petrol supplies. The
organisation was easily penetrated by British intelligence, who used UDA units to carry out actions that
were then attributed to the IRA. British intelligence also
placed within the UDA agents who were able to select
republican targets. Intelligence on individual targets was
supplied to the agents who, in turn, handed to UDA
units the necessary details for planned assassinations.

Unionist politicians regarded the UDA as an ideal
vehicle with which to threaten the British government: it
was not an organisation that would accept a surrender
of Protestant/Unionist values. However, politicians did
not wish to see the UDA enter the political arena: the
Unionist Party liked having the hard men at their
disposal but not on election platforms. There were two
sides to that, though: it could lead to a division of votes

that might let a Catholic claim a seat, and the working class were there to vote, not to run Ulster.

The late John McMichael, the UDA leader, recognised those elements within the political life of his community and decided to give the UDA a political dimension. He was impressed by the Armalite/ballot-box strategy of the Provisionals. McMichael did not achieve great success because he was murdered by the Provisionals. Part of his legacy was the UDA's development of a political agenda which took it into the peace talks of 1996–7.

Ulster Volunteer Force

The UVF was originally set up to fight Irish Home Rule in 1912, and faded into obscurity in the 1930s. It was secretly reactivated in 1965 by prominent Unionists opposed to the perceived liberalising policies of the then Unionist prime minister, Captain Terence O'Neill. Its first major act was the killing of a Catholic, Patrick Scullion, as he walked in the Clonard area of West Belfast in May 1966. A month later the same unit of the UVF, based in the Shankill area, murdered a young Catholic barman, Peter Ward, and wounded three of his friends. The unit was led by Gusty Spence, who was subsequently sentenced to life imprisonment and became a folk hero. That the killings were carried out from the Shankill area was significant: it had always been the heartland of extreme Protestantism sitting parallel with the Catholic Falls, a republican stronghold. For almost a hundred years the two communities had confronted each other in that part of the city. O'Neill made the UVF illegal, and accused Ian Paisley of having links with it, which Paisley strenuously denied.

Like many ex-soldiers who joined the UVF between

1965 and 1972, Gusty Spence believed the extreme politicians within his community who claimed that Ulster was under threat from the IRA. At that time, he did not know that some were conspiring to overthrow O'Neill, whose talk of reform was anathema to them. The UVF was used to carry out acts of violence, such as bombings, which were attributed to the IRA and which heightened the fear in the Protestant community that an IRA plot was afoot to destabilise the State. The UVF's most active units were centred in the Shankill area of West Belfast, East Antrim and Co. Armagh. In 1974 the Labour secretary of state, Merlyn Rees, lifted the ban on the UVF in an effort to encourage it to enter the political arena, and at the next general election the organisation's political arm, the Volunteer Political Party, fought the West Belfast seat – with humiliatingly poor results. The organisation returned to violence, forcing Rees to reinstate the ban.

Throughout its contemporary history the UVF, like the UDA, has tried to develop a political wing much in the mould of the Provisional IRA. Many of its efforts have been thwarted by hard men, who preferred the gun to dialogue and did not like the socialist policies adopted by some of the organisation's leaders, such as Gusty Spence. During his imprisonment he, like others who went through the prison system, espoused social policies at variance with the orthodox conservatism of Unionism to which they had previously given unquestioning allegiance. Throughout the conflict the UVF has been known as a ruthless organisation. In the 1970s, particularly, many of its members, including the famous Shankill Butchers, carried out grisly killings of innocent Catholics.

Like the IRA, the UVF was structured on military

lines and was regarded as a more efficient organisation than the UDA. It had a criminal element, involved in racketeering, but not on the same scale as that of the UDA. After a ceasefire in 1995, it entered the peace talks with the UDA.

Ulster Resistance

This group was launched in 1986 at a private rally in the Ulster Hall in Belfast. Ian Paisley was on the platform, wearing a red beret which became the group's symbol. Its apparent objective was to campaign against the Anglo-Irish Agreement. Relations between Paisley, his Democratic Unionist Party and Ulster Resistance were said to have deteriorated after Paisley opted for dialogue rather than confrontation.

Ulster Resistance acquired weapons from a consignment smuggled into Northern Ireland by the UDA and UVF. During the 1980s several members also tried to sell missile plans to the South African government, when a ban on arms sales to South Africa was in place, in return for guns. The missile plans were from the Shorts factory outside Belfast, which had a predominantly loyalist workforce. The deal did not go through.

There is no evidence that Ulster Resistance has been directly involved in violence, although it seems that they may have been acquiring guns for a Doomsday-style situation.

Young Citizens Volunteers

Active mainly in 1974–5 and regarded as the youth wing of the UVF, it mirrored Fianna Eireann, the youth wing of the IRA. Its members were involved in petrol-bombing Catholic homes and the security forces believed it had been formed to train young men to kill

Catholics. According to a police officer, giving evidence
in court in February 1975, that was its sole purpose.

Ulster Vanguard

Formed by William Craig, the former home affairs
minister sacked in 1968 by Unionist prime minister
Terence O'Neill. Craig was a controversial figure, prone
to make inflammatory statements. He also appeared at
a rally in Belfast, flanked by motorcycle outriders –
provided by the Vanguard Service Corps, the group's
paramilitary arm – and told his audience of target lists.

In the autumn of 1981 he and Ian Paisley (see pp.
290–7) demanded the creation of a 'Third Force' to
defend Ulster.

At a meeting of the Monday Club in the House of
Commons on 19 October 1972 Craig said that he could
mobilise eighty thousand men to oppose the British
government. He said he was prepared to shoot and kill
to defend Ulster: 'Let us put the bluff aside.' At an
outdoor rally in the Ormeau Park in Belfast he said that
'It will be our duty to liquidate the enemy if the
politicians fail.'

Essentially Vanguard was a political pressure group
that counted among its members David Trimble, a
lawyer and now leader of the Ulster Unionist Party. In
1978 Trimble was Craig's deputy in Vanguard. The
group did not make a major contribution to the
political life of the Province and faded into obscurity
during the 1980s and 1990s.

Ulster Special Constabulary (B Specials)

The B Specials were established in 1920 to counter the
IRA, and quickly became a symbol for the defence of
the State. For Protestants the group was the front line of

defence – in essence, a Protestant army. Catholics feared the force and regarded it as the military arm of Unionism. A paramilitary force of ten thousand, it had only a hundred full-time members. During 1968–9, members of the B Specials acted in collusion with Protestants in attacking Catholic civil-rights marches and were involved in the violence that led to the burning of hundreds of Catholic homes in the Falls district in August 1969. In October that year an inquiry into the role of the RUC and the B Specials led to the disbanding of the Specials and the creation of the Ulster Defence Regiment (*q.v.*) as part of the British Army.

An interesting note about the Specials is that when they were being disbanded, British Army officers inspected their armouries and were astounded at the amount of weapons they held, including heavy-calibre machine-guns.

Ulster Defence Regiment

The UDR replaced the B Specials in 1969, and was joined, unfortunately, by many former B Specials as well as members of the UVF and UDA, who regarded it as a suitable organisation in which to train paramilitaries, one of its most dangerous aspects. The UDA was a legal organisation, and therefore free to encourage its members to join the regiment for training in the use of guns. When a British Army brigadier was asked why the regiment allowed UDA men in its ranks, he replied that there was nothing incompatible about joint membership of both organisations – and members of the UVF's Shankill Butcher gang were in the UDR.

Files on UDR membership of that early period are not available for scrutiny, and details of paramilitaries who spent six months or less in the regiment are no longer kept.

Membership of the UDR also provided loyalist paramilitaries with British Army and police intelligence on the Catholic population and the republicans in its midst. Throughout the 1970s and 1980s members of the regiment were found guilty of crimes ranging from murder to attempted murder and causing explosions. Both the Catholic population and the Irish government frequently pointed to the UDR as a regiment in the mould of the old B Specials, but many of those who joined the UDR did so for genuine reasons and the majority did not transgress. On 9 July 1991, after an inquiry into collusion between members of the security forces and loyalist paramilitaries within the UDA/UVF, the British government decided to merge the UDR with another army regiment, the Royal Irish Rangers, so that greater control could be exercised in areas such as vetting and in the use of weapons. It enabled the government to ensure that, in the event of civil war in Northern Ireland, the UDR would be firmly under the control of the British Army. This move satisfied the Irish government, which had earlier demanded the disbandment of the UDR.

Tara
Led by William McGrath, an MI6 agent, it was a sinister anti-Catholic organisation, bitterly opposed to communism. By its own description, Tara was the hard core of Protestant resistance. The group also claimed that Ulster Protestants were descended from the lost tribes of Israel. McGrath, a known paedophile who had his own Orange Lodge, was a British intelligence agent in Northern Ireland from the mid-1950s. His task was to monitor the activities of the IRA and in the Cold War

period of the 1960s he regularly filed reports on the developing socialist policies of the IRA.

In 1969 Tara encouraged Protestants to arm themselves and create a military structure to defend Ulster. McGrath said constantly that Tara was not involved with the UVF or the UDA, even though membership of the three organisations overlapped. He sought to exercise control over other loyalist paramilitary organisations with the strategy of joint membership. When the UVF or UDA articulated views deemed to contain socialist rhetoric or anti-British sentiments, McGrath used black propaganda to discredit those involved. At the behest of shadowy elements within British intelligence, he circulated documents discrediting senior Unionist figures and those within the UVF who were considering the creation of a new political agenda rooted in social issues. McGrath believed that the Catholic Church should be declared illegal and its schools closed.

McGrath recruited young men into his organisation and abused many of them. He was also the house father at the Kincora Boys' Home, close to his own home, where he sexually assaulted the young men in his care and took some to paedophile parties in London and Brighton.

McGrath was an associate of the MI6 agent Sir Anthony Blunt, later Keeper of the Queen's Pictures. Shortly before his death, Blunt was unmasked as a spy, recruited by the Russians while he was a student at Cambridge.

In 1981, McGrath and two of his associates were jailed for their paedophile activities at the Kincora Boys' Home. McGrath was given a two-year sentence, which fuelled rumours that he had been shown leniency because he had information damaging to British intelligence. On his release from prison, he settled quietly in the Co. Down seaside town of Millisle and refused to talk to anyone about his past.

One of his close associates was John McKeague, another paedophile, who ran a small terrorist group, the Red Hand Commandos. Like McGrath, McKeague abused the young men he brought into the organisation. The Red Hand Commandos were savage and their crimes included branding victims with red-hot pokers then shooting them. McKeague was shot dead by the INLA in January 1982.

McGrath and McKeague were members of Ian Paisley's Free Presbyterian Church, although there is no evidence that they were regular churchgoers.

N.B. Colin Wallace, who worked for the British Army's Policy Information Unit, involved in black propaganda during the early 1970s, told the journalist Paul Foot (*Who Framed Colin Wallace?* 1989) that by then McGrath was working for MI5, which had taken control of intelligence operations in Northern Ireland, leaving the Republic to MI6. Wallace said that he reported McGrath's activities at the Kincora Boys' Home to a member of the intelligence staff at Army Headquarters in Lisburn, Northern Ireland, and that no action was taken because Kincora was part of an MI5 Operation. I understand Wallace to have meant that McGrath was being protected because he was working for MI5.

Paisleyism

The Rev. Ian Kyle Paisley was born in 1926, the son of a Baptist minister. The story goes that he began preaching as a teenager on a soapbox, and in 1951, he established the Free Presbyterian Church on a site that later became his Martyrs' Memorial Church.

His rise to prominence came in the early 1960s with the appointment of Captain Terence O'Neill as Unionist prime minister. Paisley detected within the Protestant psyche a fear of reform and a reluctance to tolerate a Unionist leader who departed from orthodoxy: any concessions to Catholics symbolised betrayal, a capitulation, in Paisley's view, to the Church of Rome, to the IRA and a dangerous trend that would undermine Protestant Ulster. Paisley's gospel merged the two elements of Unionism: politics and religion.

His first major action was to organise a rally at Belfast City Hall in 1963 to protest at the lowering of the Union flag to mark the death of Pope John XXIII. Then, many people in the media and politics underestimated Paisley, failing to recognise that he was touching an important nerve in the historical structure of Unionism: the fear of Protestants that one day they would be swallowed up in a Catholic Ireland. Paisley understood the exact nature of the Protestant siege mentality; their insecurity over their place on an island where the majority population was Catholic nationalist and wanted a united Ireland. Protestants feared Catholics, seeing them as IRA supporters and representing the enemy within.

In 1964 when violence broke out in West Belfast, Paisley's photograph was prominent in media coverage of the events. He had complained about the flying of an Irish tricolour in the headquarters of a republican election office on the Falls Road in Catholic West Belfast. Under political pressure, members of the Royal Ulster Constabulary broke into the premises and removed the flag. Rioting followed on a scale not seen since the 1920s.

When Terence O'Neill invited his Irish counterpart to visit him in Belfast, someone within O'Neill's cabinet told Paisley. He branded O'Neill treacherous, and organised an 'O'Neill Must Go' campaign. Unionist figures such as Brian Faulkner, who had been denied the job of prime minister in favour of Terence O'Neill, were secretly pleased with the pressure Paisley was exerting on him and plotted his downfall.

Faulkner was then a hard-liner, who in the 1950s had led an Orange march, with the assistance of the B Specials, through the Catholic Longstone Road area of Co. Down to symbolise Protestant triumphalism. He craved power and in 1974 was willing to ignore the majority wishes of his own community to lead the power-sharing executive that collapsed under loyalist pressure. By then Faulkner was regarded as a moderate, yet many people did not see that he was someone who wanted power at any cost.

While Faulkner plotted against O'Neill, Paisley's large presence and sectarian oratory captured the headlines. In the *Protestant Telegraph*, a news-sheet that regularly carried his views – and anti-Catholic articles that resembled in style the propaganda of 1930s Nazi Germany – he railed against Rome. In 1966, after the UVF shootings in the Shankill, in which Gusty Spence had been a ringleader (see pp. 230–1), O'Neill accused Paisley of an association with the UVF, which Paisley denied. But as the Catholic civil-rights movement took to the streets, Paisley formed two retaliatory organisations, the Ulster Constitution Defence Committee and Ulster Protestant Volunteers, whose members were prominently involved in counter-demonstrations

against the marchers. On 30 November 1968, Paisley
and his ex-British Army associate Major Ronald Bunting sealed off the town of Armagh to prevent a civil-
rights march. They later served six weeks in prison for
organising an illegal assembly. Ironically, Bunting's son
became a leading figure in the INLA (*q.v.*) and was
assassinated by loyalists.

Events such as the civil-rights marches, sectarian
violence, and the batoning of marchers in Derry in
October 1968 by the RUC contributed to the fall of
Terence O'Neill in the spring of 1969. However, one of
the most important factors in his failure as a potentially
reforming prime minister was Paisley.

Paisley was no longer a solitary preacher on a
soapbox but the leader of a political movement that
attracted extremists within the Protestant community
and was known as Paisleyism. His claim to have
brought down O'Neill showed other Unionist politicians that a power figure in their midst commanded
considerable support.

Paisley's dual role of pastor and firebrand politician
made him a potent political force. People listened to him
because he seemed to get things right. For example,
towards the end of 1971, he predicted that the British
government would impose direct rule and deprive
Protestants of their own parliament. Four months later,
in March 1972, he was proved correct. What everyone
failed to realise was that the British government had
recognised in Paisley a useful microphone to test public
opinion and to prepare people for the implementation
of unwelcome policies. In the years that followed they
used Paisley to predict other policies.

After Paisley and two of his henchmen had secured
parliamentary seats at Westminster, he set up the

Democratic Unionist Party (DUP), which confirmed the
pivotal role of Paisleyism in the Unionist structure. If
anything was responsible for the fracturing of the
Unionist monolith, it was Paisleyism: it created two
power bases, and several times frustrated attempts by
the British government to find a settlement with the
community. From the 1970s and into the 1990s, Paisley
and his DUP made it impossible for official Unionism to
seek accommodation with nationalism or with British
government initiatives: he was always there to thwart
any measure he deemed a sell-out. The shadow of
Paisleyism was so powerful that one former Conservative minister told me in 1995 that the British government needed to marginalise Paisley to create any
reasonable opportunity for a peace settlement. I
reminded him that such a task was both risky and
difficult to achieve: while many Protestants might not
vote for Paisley, most would agree privately that his
finger was always on the political pulse. There was even
a sneaking regard for him in political circles in Dublin,
which I have interpreted as Dubliners trying to appear
overly moderate.

Without doubt, though, Paisley's views mirrored the
nature of the sectarian divide. The Scarman Report into
disturbances in Northern Ireland in 1969 recognised
that Paisley's rhetoric had been a seminal influence on
events, although he had not plotted or organised the
disorders that had taken place. Some within the loyalist
paramilitary groups resented Paisley and branded him
'the Grand Old Duke of York'. The nickname derived
from an event in February 1991 when he appeared on a
hillside in Co. Antrim with five hundred men who
waved firearms certificates. Some quoted the line in the
nursery rhyme: 'He marched them up to the top of the

hill and he marched them down again.' The gesture was reminiscent of the activities of the founder of the Northern Ireland State, Sir Edward Carson, who went on a 'trail' of eleven rallies to protest against Irish home rule.

Paisley had also demanded, with William Craig (see p. 286), the creation of a 'Third Force', which culminated in a parade of five thousand men before him at a rally in Newtownards on 21 November 1981. Paisley declared that the organisation's objective was to protect loyalists and demand tougher security measures. Like many of Paisley's creations, it faded into obscurity after it had achieved the goal of striking fear into the British government and Northern Ireland Catholics, who regarded Paisley as a dangerous extremist.

'Irresponsible' is a word that can be validly applied to Paisley's political rhetoric and some of his actions throughout the conflict, but in his own community, he has been seen as a saviour, a hero, a man of God who pursues a moral crusade, the defender of the Protestant faith and basic Unionist values. There can be no doubt that he developed the skills of a clever politician, always looking for the opportunity to strike at those whom he believed were undermining his heritage. He was relentless in condemning British governments who used political expediency to undermine the Unionist position, and rightly detected within the Anglo-Irish Agreement an undemocratic process. The Agreement, hatched by Margaret Thatcher and the Dublin government, had been put in place without proper consultation with the majority Protestant community in Northern Ireland.

In 1988, Paisley was forcibly ejected from the European Parliament, of which he was a member, when

he interrupted a speech by Pope John Paul II. It was
vintage Paisley anti-Catholic railing, reminiscent of his
speeches throughout the conflict about the perverse
influence of the Church of Rome in Northern Ireland
politics. He saw the hand of the Jesuit order in every
political agenda within nationalism both in Northern
Ireland and in the Republic.

In 1997 while loyalist paramilitary organisations
were engaged in the talks for peace, Paisley opposed
their involvement. Some might have interpreted that as
a rejection of loyalism but it was something much more
fundamental. He recognised that the presence of loyalists in the negotiations made it imperative to include
Provisional Sinn Fein. A prominent figure in the UVF
leadership alleged: 'Paisley doesn't want the UDA or
UVF to have a political voice in the search for a political
solution. He knows if we are in there, his power base
could be weakened, and it might lead to the entry of
Sinn Fein at some stage. We will talk to Sinn Fein, if like
us they are serious about an end to violence. But Paisley
has hung himself on so many political hooks over the
years that he knows he can't sit down with Sinn Fein. So
what does he do? He snipes at us because he doesn't
want us in there. His cohorts would like to see loyalism
return to the bad old days with people like Wright
controlling it.' The British government worked hard to
keep the loyalist paramilitaries in the talks, even though
terrorist acts continued to be carried out by the UVF
and UDA despite a ceasefire, which generated Sinn
Fein's demand that its own entry into the talks did not
require major concessions by the IRA.

Paisley's place in the history of the conflict is well
documented, and most commentators have permitted

him little praise or sympathy. Lord Scarman, who was one of Britain's finest judges, delivered perhaps the most reasonable assessment of Paisley in April 1972: 'Those who live in a free country must accept as legitimate the powerful expression of views opposed to their own, even if, as often happens, it is accompanied by exaggeration, scurrility and abuse. Dr Paisley's spoken words were always powerful and must have frequently appeared to some as provocative: his news-sheet, the *Protestant Telegraph*, was such that its style and content were likely to rouse the enthusiasm of his supporters and the fury of his opponents. We are satisfied that Dr Paisley's role in the events under review [the disturbances of August 1969] was fundamentally similar to that of the political leaders on the other side of the sectarian divide. While his speeches and writings must have been one of the many factors increasing tension in 1969, he neither plotted nor organised the disorders under review, and there is no evidence that he was party to any of the acts of violence investigated by us.'

It should be pointed out that Lord Scarman did not live in Northern Ireland and one wonders how he would assess Paisley twenty-five years later in the light of the 'Third Force', men on hillsides with firearms certificates, and Paisley in his red beret at the formation of Ulster Resistance. In his own community Paisley will always be the defender of the culture of 'For God and Ulster', and at times, he has been adept at identifying British policy-making that was not always to the benefit of the people he was elected to serve. As a politician he has proved a formidable opponent to anyone who has sought to confront him.

Northern Ireland Civil Rights Association

This was established in 1967, and part of the dynamic for its appearance was the developing socialism of the IRA, led by Cahal Goulding, the existence of social-action groups, and the Campaign for Social Justice which, during the early 1960s, documented civil-rights abuses against Catholics, referring them to the British Labour government. Also, an atmosphere of protest prevailed within the Catholic community, partly fuelled by the civil-rights movement in the United States and the London-based National Council for Civil Liberties. The original committee of NICRA was a broadly based group, representing republicans, nationalists, the Northern Ireland Labour Party, and some trade unions. Its aims were basic: the ending of gerrymandering (the deliberate manipulation of electoral boundaries to ensure Unionist control), one man one vote in council elections, mechanisms to be put in place to end discrimination in public authorities and to process complaints, the repeal of the Special Powers Act, which was aimed solely at the Catholic population, the disbanding of the B Specials and fair allocation in housing. The slogan of the campaign was 'We shall overcome' and its strategy was the protest demonstration, which, however, was regarded as a provocative and dangerous activity.

The risks were clearly demonstrated on 5 October 1968, in Duke Street in Derry, when marchers, among them prominent members of the British Parliament such as Gerry Fitt, were driven off the streets by the RUC wielding batons, at the behest of the Unionist home affairs minister William Craig. The police were out of control and their actions were captured on television, and circulated worldwide. As Bernadette Devlin, then a

student activist, and later MP for Mid-Ulster, com-
mented at the time: 'After Duke Street we all said
wherever we have been we're not going back.'

Unionists saw NICRA as an IRA front and, though
the IRA was involved as one of a number of Catholic
nationalist bodies, it was not the defining element. As
time passed, though, the IRA used its people to steward
marches and was prominent in the organisation's
decision-making process.

The unfortunate aspect of the civil-rights campaign is
that it was not a cross-community organisation seeking
better conditions for both communities. The Protestant
population also suffered from unemployment and poor
housing in areas like the Shankill and the Newtownards
Road. But Protestants feared that Catholics, with larger
families, would 'breed them out of power', if they were
granted equal rights, and therefore clung to the status
quo. Unionists fought hard to control their own people
with the tactics of fear, the threat of the enemy within
and cries of 'no surrender'. Its manipulation of working-class Protestant politics is one of the terrible
consequences of a State rooted in a siege mentality.

Nowadays some commentators in the academic and
political life of Northern Ireland claim that the Catholic
legacy of injustice was not as bad as it was portrayed.
That is simply not true and the historical data is there
for anyone to examine. The original civil-rights
demands were not unreasonable and should have been
in place anyway in a democratic country. The early
civil-rights leaders were demanding only the rights of
other British citizens. It was protest and counter-pro-
test, the failure of the State to reform, and the enmity
between both communities that made Northern Ireland
ungovernable. Civil rights should never have been an

exclusively Catholic demand: enlightened Protestants, some now within the UVF, recognise that reality. The imposition of the Anglo-Irish Agreement was a denial of civil rights, and the campaign against it was justified, if only on that basis.

also available from
THE ORION PUBLISHING GROUP

☐ **The Discovery of the Titanic** £7.99
DR ROBERT D BALLARD
1 85797 660 6

☐ **On Foot Through Africa** £6.99
FFYONA CAMPBELL
1 85797 813 7

☐ **The Whole Story** £6.99
FFYONA CAMPBELL
0 75280 988 1

☐ **The Lost Fortune of the Tsars** £6.99
WILLIAM CLARKE
1 85797 405 0

☐ **River out of Eden** £6.99
RICHARD DAWKINS
1 85799 405 1

☐ **The Quick and the Dead: Under Siege in Sarajevo** £5.99
JANINE DI GIOVANNI
1 85799 333 0

☐ **The Bible Code** £6.99
MICHAEL DROSNIN
0 75280 932 6

☐ **The Octopus** £7.99
BRIAN FREEMANTLE
0 75280 351 4

☐ **The Riddle of the Titanic** £5.99
ROBIN GARDINER & DAN VAN DER VAT
0 75280 167 8

☐ **The Romanov Conspiracies** £5.99
MICHAEL OCCLESHAW
1 85797 428 X

☐ **Do Robins Cough?** £6.99
BEVERLY PEBERDY
0 75280 880 X

☐ **For God, Country & Coca-Cola** £12.99
MARK PENDERGRAST
1 85799 180 X

☐ **Eminent Churchillians** £7.99
ANDREW ROBERTS
1 85799 213 X

☐ **Romans** £6.99
MICHAEL SHERIDAN
1 85799 243 1

☐ **The Man in the Ice** £7.99
KONRAD SPINDLER
1 85799 155 9

☐ **The Jesus Papyrus** £6.99
CARSTEN PETER THIEDE & MATTHEW d'ANCONA
1 85799 958 4

☐ **Life on the Screen** £7.99
SHERRY TURKLE
1 85799 888 X

☐ **Eccentrics** £6.99
DAVID WEEKS & JAMIE JAMES
1 85799 396 9

All Orion/Phoenix titles are available at your local bookshop or from the following address:

Littlehampton Book Services
Cash Sales Department L
14 Eldon Way, Lineside Industrial Estate
Littlehampton
West Sussex BN17 7HE

telephone 01903 721596, *facsimile* 01903 730914

Payment can either be made by credit card (Visa and Mastercard accepted) or by sending a cheque or postal order made payable to *Littlehampton Book Services.*
DO NOT SEND CASH OR CURRENCY.

Please add the following to cover postage and packing

UK and BFPO:
£1.50 for the first book, and 50p for each additional book to a maximum of £3.50

Overseas and Eire:
£2.50 for the first book plus £1.00 for the second book and 50p for each additional book ordered

----

BLOCK CAPITALS PLEASE

name of cardholder ....

address of cardholder ....

....

....

....

postcode ....

delivery address
(if different from cardholder)

....

....

....

....

postcode ....

☐ I enclose my remittance for £.............................

☐ please debit my Mastercard/Visa (delete as appropriate)

card number ☐☐☐☐☐☐☐☐☐☐☐☐☐☐☐☐☐☐

expiry date ☐☐☐☐

signature ....

prices and availability are subject to change without notice